Language, Culture, and Teaching
Critical Perspectives for a New Century

Language, Culture, and Teaching

Sonia Nieto, Series Editor

Language, Culture, and Teaching
Critical Perspectives for a New Century

Sonia Nieto
University of Massachusetts

 LAWRENCE ERLBAUM ASSOCIATES, PUBLISHERS
2002   Mahwah, New Jersey   London

Cover design by Patty Bode

Copyright © 2002 by Lawrence Erlbaum Associates, Inc.

Lawrence Erlbaum Associates, Inc., Publishers
10 Industrial Avenue
Mahwah, NJ 07430

Library of Congress Cataloging-in-Publication Data

Nieto, Sonia.
Language, culture, and teaching. Critical perspectives for a new century / Sonia Nieto.
    p. cm.
    Includes bibliographical references and index.
    ISBN 0-8058-3738-8 (alk. paper)
    1. Multicultural education—United States. 2. Minorities—Education—United States.   I. Language, culture, and teaching.
    LC1099.3 .N543   2001
    370.117 —dc21

                    2001041795
                    CIP

Printed in the United States of America
10   9   8   7   6   5

ITEM ON HOLD

Title: Language, culture, and teaching : critical perspectives for a new century / Sonia Nieto.

Author: Nieto, Sonia.
Call Number: 370.117 N677
Enumeration:
Chronology:
Copy:
Item Barcode: 1

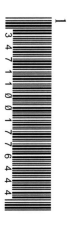

3 4 7 1 1 0 0 1 7 7 6 4 4 4

Item Being Held For:

Patron: Ferreira Moreno, Jenny P
Patron Barcode:

2 4 2 1 1 H 0 0 7 2 0 4 4 4

Patron Phone:
Hold Expires: 8/14/2017
Pickup At: CON CIRCULATION

Contents

113163

Acknowledgments

We are grateful to the following publishers for permission to reprint the journal articles and book chapters that appear in this book: "Language, Literacy, and Culture: Intersections and Implications" in *Yearbook of the National Reading Conference*, 2000. "Multicultural Education and School Reform" (chap. 9, pp. 303–322). *Affirming Diversity: The Sociopolitical Context of Multicultural Education* by Sonia Nieto. (New York: © Longman Publishers, 3rd. ed., 2000). Reprinted by permission of Addison Wesley Educational Publishers, Inc. "Cultural Difference and Educational Change in a Sociopolitical Context" in *International Handbook of Educational Change*, edited by Andy Hargreaves, Ann Lieberman, Michael Fullan, and David Hopkins, © Kluwer Academic Publishers, 1998, pp. 418–439. Reprinted with kind permission from Kluwer Academic Publishers, The Netherlands. "We Speak in Many Tongues: Language Diversity and Multicultural Education" in *Multicultural Education for the Twenty-first Century* edited by Carlos P. Díaz, 2nd rev. ed. (New York: © Longman Publishers, 2nd ed., 2001). Reprinted by permission of Addison Wesley Educational Publishers, Inc. "On Becoming American: An Exploratory Essay." Reprinted by permission of the publisher from Ayers, W. C. & Miller, J. L., *A Light in Dark Times: Maxine Greene and the Unfinished Conversation* (New York: Teachers College Press, 1998 © by Teachers College, Columbia University. All rights reserved), pp. 45–57. "Lessons from Students on Creating a Chance to Dream." *Harvard Educational Review*, v. 64, n. 4 (Winter, 1994) pp. 392–426. Copyright © 1994 by the President and Fellows of Harvard College. All rights reserved. "Writing for Real: Exploring and Affirming Students' Words and Worlds," parts 1 & 2, *MABE Newsletter*, v. 18, n. 2

(February, 1997) and v. 18, n. 3 (June, 1997). Reprinted with permission of the Massachusetts Association for Bilingual Education. "Diversity: What do Teachers Need to Know?" From *Foundations of Special Education: Basic Knowledge Informing Research and Practice in Special Education, 1st ed.*, by J. L. Paul, M. Churton, H. Rosselli-Kostoryz, W. C. Morse, K. Marfo, C. Lavely, & D. Thomas © 1997. Reprinted with permission of Wadsworth Publishing, a division of Thomson Learning. "Bringing Bilingual Education Out of the Basement, and Other Imperatives for Teacher Education" in *Lifting Every Voice: Pedagogy and Politics of Bilingualism*, edited by Zeynep F. Beykont (pp. 187–208). Cambridge, MA: Harvard Education Publishing Group, 2000. Copyright © 2000 by the President and Fellows of Harvard College. All rights reserved. "Conflict and Tension, Growth and Change: The Politics of Teaching Multicultural Education Courses" in *Tongue-Tying Multiculturalism: The Politics of Race and Culture in the Ivy League*, edited by Donaldo Macedo (forthcoming). Copyright © by Rowman and Littlefield. Reprinted with permission of the publishers. "Affirmation, Solidarity, and Critique: Moving Beyond Tolerance in Multicultural Education." *Multicultural Education*, v. 1, n. 4 (Spring, 1994), pp. 9–12, 35–38. Reprinted with permission of the National Association for Multicultural Education. "What Does it Mean to Affirm Diversity in Our Nation's Schools?" Reprinted with permission from the May 1999 issue of *The School Administrator* magazine, pp. 32–34.

Series Editor's Foreword

The United States is becoming more ethnically, racially, and linguistically diverse than it ever has been before. Between 1970 and 1990, a period of intense immigration, more newcomers came to our country than at almost any other time in our history. From 1981 to 1990 alone, more than 7.3 million people entered the United States legally, increasing immigration by 63% over the previous decade (U.S. Bureau of the Census, 1994). Unlike previous immigrants who were principally from Europe, approximately one third of the newest immigrants are now from Asia and another third from Latin America (U.S. Immigration and Naturalization Service, 1995), changing both the complexion and the complexity of our society. Moreover, approximately 32 million people speak a language other than English at home, with almost half of those people speaking Spanish. Put another way, the percentage of those who speak languages other than English as their native language increased in just 10 years from 11% to 14% of our total population (Portes & Rumbaut, 1996).

The impact of this growing cultural and linguistic diversity is nowhere more visible than in our schools. For instance, by 1992, 50 of the largest 99 school districts in the United States had more than 50% enrollment of what were classified as "minority" students, that is, students of African American, Native American, Latino/a, and Asian backgrounds (National Center for Education Statistics [NCES], 1994). In addition, at present almost 20% of elementary and high school students have at least one foreign-born parent, and nearly 5% of students are themselves foreign born (U.S. Bureau of the Census, 1999). Related to the increase in immigration, more than 3 million or 7.4% of students in all public and private schools in the United States are limited in their English proficiency (Macías, 1998).

But diversity is not limited to urban centers; many suburban and rural schools are also experiencing tremendous changes in student diversity and, in the not-too-distant future, every school in the nation will be characterized by similar cultural, racial, and language diversity. The percentage of students of African American, Latino, Native American, and Asian backgrounds has reached about 35% in the nation's schools as a whole, and it is expected to grow steadily (U.S. Bureau of the Census, 1999).

Despite the growing diversity in schools around the country, racial and ethnic segregation in schools has been on the rise. As improbable as it may have sounded just a couple of decades ago, the largest backward movement toward segregation for Blacks since the *Brown v. Board of Education* decision occurred between 1991 and 1995 (Orfield, Bachmeier, James, & Eitle, 1997). Currently, Latinos are the most segregated of all ethnic groups in our schools: Three quarters of all Latinos attend predominately "minority" schools, schools that are also among the most high-poverty schools in the nation (Orfield et al., 1997).

Poverty in the United States as a whole increased from 1970 through the mid-1990s: The percentage of persons living below the poverty level was 12.6% in 1970, 13% in 1980, 13.5% in 1990, and 14.5% in 1994 (U.S. Bureau of the Census, 1995). Poverty has been especially grim among people of color: 33.1% of all African Americans, 30.6% of Latinos, and 18.8% of other people of color lived in poverty in 1996, as compared to 9.9% of White residents (Taeuber, 1996). Although the situation has improved somewhat since the mid-1990s because of the booming U.S. economy, African Americans, Latinos, and American Indians are still over-represented among the poor. The connection between poverty and poor academic achievement is seriously high, for reasons ranging from ill-equipped schools, to poorly prepared teachers, to the mismatch between how families prepare their children for school and the expectations that schools have of families.

Along with the changing complexion of U.S. schools, notions of how best to educate students of different backgrounds have also changed over the years. Joel Spring (1997), for example, made a compelling case that even the common school movement of the 1830s and 1840s, rather than a noble effort to provide all students with an equal education, was primarily "an attempt to halt the drift towards a multicultural society" (p. 4). Indeed, United States educational history is replete with examples of racist and exclusionary policies that served to segregate or remove from school students of Native, African American, Asian, and Latino backgrounds, and that discriminated against children of Southern and Eastern European immigrants (Kaestle, 1983; Spring, 1997; Takaki, 1993; Weinberg, 1977).

It is clear that assumptions about cultural and racial superiority and inferiority have a long and deep-seated history in our educational history. For much of that history, the conventional wisdom was that students whose cultures and languages differ from the majority were functioning with a deficiency rooted in their very identities. Consequently, the sooner students assimilated to become more like the majority—in culture, language, appearance, experience, and values—the easier would be their transition to the mainstream and middle class. In the latter part of the 20th century, these ideas began to be repudiated, largely by people from the very cultural backgrounds being pressured to change. It is no accident that educational movements in favor of ethnic studies, bilingual and multicultural education, and affirmative action all emerged at around the same time. These movements represented a denouncement of ideologies that had heretofore excluded large segments of the population from achieving educational success. Continuing in that tradition, the books in the Language, Culture, and Teaching series challenge traditional biases about cultural and linguistic diversity and about students who embody those differences.

The Language, Culture, and Teaching series attempts to fill the gap that currently exists in preparing teachers for the schools and classrooms of the 21st century. The books, aimed primarily at teachers and prospective teachers, focus on the intersections of language, culture, and teaching—specifically, on how language and culture inform classroom practice. At the same time, the series reframes the conventional idea of the textbook by envisioning classroom practice as critical, creative, and liberatory. Rather than viewing the textbook as unquestioned authority, the Language, Culture, and Teaching series asks readers to reflect, question, critique, and respond to what they read. Using the problem-posing approach proposed by Paulo Freire (1970), the books in this series ask prospective and practicing teachers to think imaginatively and critically about teaching and learning, especially as they refer to cultural and linguistic diversity.

The books in this series also support the Freirian idea that education is never neutral or objective. The role of teachers is likewise never neutral, but a *political project* on behalf of, or against, the interests of those they teach. The books in this series do not claim to have all the answers, but they engage readers to question their beliefs and attitudes about their students and to consider why and how they teach. By taking the intelligence of teachers seriously, these books remind teachers, in the words of Paulo Freire (1985), that "to study is not to consume ideas, but to create and recreate them" (p. 4).

—Sonia Nieto

REFERENCES

Freire, P. (1970). *Pedagogy of the oppressed*. New York: Seabury Press.

Freire, P. (1985). *The politics of education: Culture, power, and liberation*. South Hadley, MA: Bergin & Garvey.

Kaestle, C. F. (1983). *Pillars of the republic: Common schools and American society, 1780–1860*. New York: Hill & Wang.

Macías, R. F., & Kelly, C. (1996). *Summary report of the Survey of the States' Limited English Proficient Students and Available Educational Programs and Services 1994–1995*. Washington, DC: United States Department of Education, Office of Grants and Contracts Services, The George Washington University.

National Center for Education Statistics (NCES) (1994). *Characteristics of the 100 largest public elementary and secondary school districts in the United States: 1991–1992*. Washington, DC: Author.

Orfield, G., Bachmeier, M. D., James, D. R., & Eitle, T. (1997). *Deepening segregation in America's public schools*. Cambridge, MA: Harvard University.

Portes, A. & Rumbaut, R. G. (1996). *Immigrant America: A portrait* (2nd ed.). Berkeley: University of California.

Spring, J. (1997). *Deculturalization and the struggle for equality: A brief history of the education of dominated cultures in the United States* (2nd ed.). New York: McGraw-Hill.

Taeuber, C. (Editor & Compiler). (1996). *The statistical handbook on women in America*, 2nd ed. Phoenix, AZ: Oryx Press.

Takaki, R. (1993). *A different mirror: A history of multicultural America*. Boston: Little, Brown & Company.

U.S. Bureau of the Census (1994). *Statistical abstract of the United States* (114th ed). Washington, DC: U.S. Government Printing Office.

U.S. Bureau of the Census (1995). *Current population reports, Series P-60, No. 188*. Washington, DC: U.S. Government Printing Office.

U.S. Bureau of the Census (1999). School enrollment social and economic characteristics of students. *Current population reports*. Washington, DC: U.S. Government Printing Office.

U.S. Immigration and Naturalization Service (1995). *Statistical yearbook of the immigration and naturalization service*. Washington, DC: U.S. Government Printing Office.

Weinberg, M. (1977). *A chance to learn: A history of race and education in the U.S.* Cambridge, UK: Cambridge University.

Preface

Whether teaching in a large urban public school system, a small rural schoolhouse, or an affluent private academy in the suburbs, all teachers today face students who are more diverse than ever before in terms of race, culture and ethnicity, language background, social class, and other differences. Our schools are becoming more diverse every day, a diversity evident in the faces we see and the languages we hear in school hallways and playgrounds. Demographic changes in the United States are making it evident that our society is enormously different from what it was just a generation ago. This situation has serious implications for teaching and learning and for the way that teachers are prepared to meet the challenges of diversity.

As a result of the changing demographics of our country and world, language and culture are increasingly vital concerns in contemporary classrooms across the United States. Yet few educators besides specialists in bilingual education, English as a second language (ESL), or urban education have been adequately prepared through their course work and other prepracticum experiences to teach students who embody these differences. As a result, many educators are at a loss as to what to do when faced with differences in their students' race, ethnicity, social class, and language. For many teachers, their first practicum or teaching experience represents their introduction to diversity.

Many textbooks designed for current and future teachers devote little attention to issues of difference, and even less to critical perspectives in teaching. I became concerned with this issue when looking over the kinds of textbooks available for future and current teachers. I found many of them to be little more than dry and boring treatments of "best practices" or thoughtless techniques that leave teachers' creativity and analysis on the sidelines. That is the motivation behind the series *Language, Culture, and Teaching*, and for this, the first textbook in the series.

ABOUT THIS BOOK

In this book I attempt to present examples of real-life dilemmas about diversity that you will face in your own classrooms; ideas about how language, culture, and teaching are linked; and ways to engage with these ideas through reflection and collaborative inquiry. There are no easy answers, no "programs in place" that can fix the uncertainties that teachers encounter every day. But there are more thoughtful ways to address these problems than is currently the case in many textbooks, ways that honor both teachers' professionalism and students' abilities. It is my hope that *Language, Culture, and Teaching: Critical Perspectives for a New Century* will accomplish these goals.

Specifically, this textbook will:

- explore how language and culture are connected to teaching and learning in educational contexts;
- examine the sociocultural and sociopolitical contexts of language and culture to understand how these contexts may affect student learning and achievement;
- analyze the implications of linguistic and cultural diversity for school reform and educational equity; and
- encourage practicing and preservice teachers to reflect critically on classroom practices related to linguistic and cultural diversity based on the above understandings.

Language, Culture, and Teaching: Critical Perspectives for a New Century is a compilation of previously published journal articles and book chapters I have written over the past decade that focus on diversity in language and culture. It is organized in five sections, each beginning with a brief description of the themes considered in that part of the text. Following the chapters are critical questions, ideas for classroom and community activities, and suggested resources for further reflection and study. *Critical Questions* are based on the ideas presented in the chapter and they ask you to build on the knowledge you have learned by analyzing the concepts further. *Classroom Activities* are suggestions for applying what you have learned to your own teaching context. Often, these activities recommend that you work with colleagues in developing curriculum or other classroom-based projects. *Community Activities* are projects outside of your particular classroom setting, but they may take place in the school or the school district as well as in the city or town in which you teach, or even at the state or national level.

Beginnings consists of a preliminary chapter, "Language, Literacy, and Culture: Intersections and Implications," which provides an overall background for the text and the series by describing historic paradigmatic shifts concerning language and culture that are occurring in our schools and society. It also suggests some implications for teaching and learning.

Part I, *Setting the Groundwork* consists of three chapters that set the conceptual framework for links among language, culture, and teaching. The first chapter, "Multicultural Education and School Reform," proposes a sociopolitical definition of multicultural education and introduces you to major concepts and significant literature in the field. Chapter 2, "Cultural Difference and Educational Change in a Sociopolitical Context," explores how taking into account cultural and linguistic differences can make a positive difference in student learning. The chapter provides an international perspective so that issues are addressed from more than simply a United States context. The final chapter in this section, chapter 3, "We Speak in Many Tongues: Language Diversity and Multicultural Education," expands the conventional framework of multicultural education by incorporating language and language differences as central to diversity.

Questions of identity are related to student learning because it is through their identities as competent learners that students can succeed academically. Young people of all backgrounds struggle with issues of identity and belonging, and for those who are culturally marginalized, the stress is even greater. Hence, questions of identity are central to an appreciation of linguistic and cultural diversity. In Part II, *Identity and Belonging*, the links among selfhood, learning, and community are explored more deeply. Chapter 4, "On Becoming American: An Exploratory Essay," investigates what it means to be an American and why this question needs to be carefully thought about by teachers. Chapter 5, "Lessons From Students on Creating a Chance to Dream" analyzes research based on the perceptions of students of diverse backgrounds about their education. Chapter 6, "Writing for Real: Exploring and Affirming Students' Words and Worlds," examines how students' identities and knowledge can serve as a meaningful foundation for school learning, in this case, writing.

The three chapters in Part III, *Implications for the Preparation of Critical Teachers*, concern the kind of information teachers need about diversity to be effective with a wide range of students. In chapter 7, "Diversity: What Do Teachers Need to Know?," a series of questions about difference are posed for teacher educators and future teachers to consider. Chapter 8,

"Bringing Bilingual Education Out of the Basement and Other Impera-tives for Teacher Education" uses the motif of the *basement* to describe the physical and metaphorical space that many bilingual programs, and other programs for linguistically and culturally diverse students, inhabit. The chapter concludes with practical suggestions that teachers and teacher ed-ucators can use to bring bilingual education out of that space and make it a more central concern for all educators. Chapter 9, "Conflict and Ten-sion, Growth and Change: The Politics of Teaching Multicultural Educa-tion Courses," describes the joys and dilemmas I have experienced in teaching multicultural education courses, and it presents a rationale for the need, purpose, and design of preservice and inservice courses con-cerning diversity.

The final section of the text, *Praxis in the Classroom*, is a critical analysis of multicultural education in practice. Chapter 10, "Affirmation, Solidar-ity, and Critique: Moving Beyond Tolerance in Multicultural Education," explicitly describes five scenarios that illustrate different levels of support for multicultural education and suggests concrete practices for classroom instruction. The last chapter, chapter 11, "What Does It Mean to Affirm Diversity in Our Nation's Schools?," is a short chapter that proposes a number of guidelines for affirming diversity. This final chapter also serves to recapitulate many of the points addressed throughout the book.

NEW TEXTS FOR A NEW CENTURY

Educational inequality is repugnant in a society that has pledged to pro-vide an equal education for all students regardless of circumstance. Yet educational inequality is commonplace in schools all over our country. It continues to be the case that far too many students are shortchanged be-cause educational policies and practices favor students from backgrounds that are more privileged in social class, race, language, or other differ-ences. Schools also remain grossly unequal in terms of the resources they are given, and it is undeniably true that students' addresses have more to do with the quality of the education they receive than most of us would care to admit. In addition, students' linguistic and cultural differences are often dismissed or ignored by teachers who have been trained to be "color-blind" and refuse to see differences.

These realities make it apparent that educational change needs to take place in a number of domains, including at the ideological, societal, and national levels. In the meantime, students who differ culturally and lin-guistically from the "mainstream" are particularly vulnerable in a society that has deemed differences to be deficiencies, and poverty to be a moral transgression. Change, however, can begin at any level, and this text is based on the assumption that teachers can and, in fact, *must* make a difference in the lives of the children they teach. Teachers alone cannot do it all, but when they work together with other educators and concerned citizens, they can do a great deal to change not only their own practices but also to help schools and districts change their policies to become more equitable for all students. When district-wide policies as well as classroom practices change to promote the learning of all students, and when our society, teachers, and schools view students' differences in a more hopeful and critical way, then the result can be that all students soar to the heights they deserve.

We are living in a new century, a century different from any other in many ways, not the least of which is the tremendous cultural and linguistic diversity evident in our schools. Yet the ways in which new teachers are prepared to face these differences, and the books used to help them, have not changed enough. New times deserve new textbooks, textbooks that respect the professionalism of teachers and other educators, that honor the identities of students and their families, and that validate the nation's claim to educate all students of all backgrounds. That is the premise of this book.

ACKNOWLEDGMENTS

Finally, a word of thanks to friends and colleagues who had a hand in this book. When I originally wrote the journal articles and book chapters reprinted in this text, many people helped me think more clearly and carefully about my ideas. These friends and colleagues are too numerous to mention here, but I acknowledged them in the original works. I also want to reiterate that my work has been enormously enriched by the wise counsel of the many colleagues, students, and young people I have worked with over the years. Many years ago when we first met, my editor and friend, Naomi Silverman, helped me think differently and creatively about textbooks for teachers. She continues to do so, and for that, I am grateful. Denise Gaskin and Lori Mestre provided editorial assistance with resources. I also want to thank the publishing companies that allowed me to reprint the articles and book chapters included in the text.

The reader should note that because the volume is a compilation of previously published journal articles and book chapters, there may be inconsistencies of style in some reference citations.

—Sonia Nieto

BEGINNINGS

Language, Literacy, and Culture: Intersections and Implications

It has only been in the past several years that scholars have begun to connect the issues of language, literacy, and culture in any substantive way. Prior to this time, they were considered to exist largely separate from one another. As a result, educators usually thought about culture, for example, as distinct from language and from reading and writing except in the most superficial of ways; or as English as a Second Language (ESL) divorced from the influence of native culture on learning; or as the contentious debate about phonics and whole language as somehow separate from students' identities. These dichotomies have largely disappeared in the past 20 years. It is now evident that language, literacy, and culture are linked in numerous ways and that all teachers—whether they teach preschool art or high school math—need to become knowledgeable in how they affect students' schooling.

Even more crucial to our purposes in this textbook, until recently, critical perspectives were almost entirely missing from treatments of reading, writing, language acquisition and use, and an in-depth understanding of race, culture, and ethnicity. If broached at all, differences were "celebrated," typically in shallow ways such as diversity dinners and the commemoration of a select few African American and other heroes and through "ethnic" holiday fairs. But discussions of stratification and inequality were largely absent until recently in most teacher education courses. Despite their invisibility, questions about equity and social justice are at the core of education. As such, education is always a political undertaking.

The fact that education is not a neutral endeavor scares many people because it challenges cherished notions that education is based solely on equality and fair play. Power and privilege, and how they are implicated in language, culture, and learning, also typically have been invisible in school discourse. This situation is changing as the connections among language, literacy, and culture are becoming more firmly established, and as

1

inequality and the lack of access to an equal education faced by many students is becoming more evident.

In this chapter, I describe the links among language, literacy, and culture beginning with my own story and concluding with some central tenets of sociocultural theory: agency, experience, identity/hybridity, context, and community. As you read this chapter, think about how your own understanding of language, literacy, and culture has shifted over the years, and how you have changed your ideas about teaching as a result.

INTRODUCTION: LANGUAGE, LITERACY, AND CULTURE: INTERSECTIONS AND IMPLICATIONS*

Given my background and early life experiences, I should not be here today talking with you about literacy and learning. According to the traditional educational literature, my home and family situation could not prepare me adequately for academic success. My mother did not graduate from high school, and my father never made it past fourth grade. They came to the United States as immigrants from Puerto Rico and they quietly took their place in the lower paid and lower status of society. In my family, we never had bedtime stories, much less books. At home, we didn't have a permanent place to study, nor did we have a desk with sufficient light and adequate ventilation, as teachers suggested. We didn't have many toys and I never got the piano lessons I wanted desperately from the age of five. As a family, we didn't go to museums or other places that would give us the cultural capital (Bourdieu, 1986) it was thought we needed to succeed in school. We spoke Spanish at home, even though teachers pleaded with my parents to stop doing so. And when we learned English, my sister and I spoke a nonstandard, urban Black and Puerto Rican version of English: we said *ain't* instead of *isn't* and *mines* instead of *mine*, and no matter how often our teachers corrected us, we persisted in saying these things. In a word, because of our social class, ethnicity, native language, and discourse practices, we were the epitome of what are now described as "children at risk," young people who were described when we were coming up as "disadvantaged," "culturally deprived," and even "problem" students.

I was fortunate that I had a family that, although unable to help me with homework, would make sure that it got done; a family who used "Education, Sonia, education!" as a mantra. But they kept right on speaking Spanish (even when my sister and I switched to English), they still didn't buy books for our home, and they never read us bedtime stories. My parents, just like all parents, were brimming with skills and talents: They were becoming bilingual, they told us many stories, riddles, tongue-twisters,

---

*This material is based on a keynote address given at the National Reading Conference in December, 2000.

and jokes; when my father, 20 years after coming to this country, bought a *bodega*, a small Caribbean grocery store, I was awed by the sight of him adding up a column of figures in seconds, without a calculator or even a pencil. My mother embroidered beautiful and intricate patterns on handkerchiefs, blouses, and tablecloths, a trade practiced by many poor women in Puerto Rico to stock the shelves of Lord and Taylor's and Saks' Fifth Avenue in New York. These skills, however, were never called on by my teachers; my parents were thought of as culturally deprived and disadvantaged, another segment of the urban poor with no discernible competencies.

Sometime in my early adolescence, we bought a small house in a lower middle-class neighborhood and I was able to attend a good junior high and an excellent high school. I didn't particularly like that high school—it was too competitive and impersonal and I felt invisible there—but in retrospect I realize that my sister and I got the education we needed to prepare us for college, a dream beyond the wildest imagination of my parents, most of my cousins, and the friends from our previous neighborhood. My new address made a profound difference in the education that I was able to get. I eventually dropped the *ain't* and the *mines*, and I hid the fact that I spoke Spanish.

I begin with my own story, not because I believe that autobiography is sacrosanct, or that it holds the answer to all educational problems. My story is not unique and I don't want to single myself out as an exception, in the way that Richard Rodriguez (1982) ended up doing, intentionally or not, in his painful autobiography *Hunger of Memory*. I use my story because it underscores the fact that young people of all backgrounds can learn and that they need not be compelled, as Rodriguez was, to abandon their family and home language in the process for the benefits of an education and a higher status in society. In many ways, I am like any of the millions of young people in our classrooms and schools who come to school eager (although perhaps not, in the current jargon, "ready") to learn, but who end up as the waste products of an educational system that does not understand the gifts they bring to their education. They are the reason that I speak with you today about language, literacy, and culture, and the implications that new ways of thinking about them have for these children.

Language, literacy, and culture have not always been linked, either conceptually or programmatically. But this is changing, as numerous schools and colleges of education around the country are beginning to reflect a growing awareness of their intersections, and of the promise they hold for rethinking teaching and learning. My own reconceptualized program at the University of Massachusetts, now called Language, Literacy, and Culture, mirrors this trend.[1] I believe the tendency to link these issues is giving us a richer picture of learning, especially for students whose identi-

---

[1]I wish to acknowledge my colleagues in the Language, Literacy, and Culture Doctoral Research Area, School of Education at the University of Massachusetts, Amherst: Jerri

ties—particularly those related to language, race, ethnicity, and immigrant status—have traditionally had a low status in our society. One result of this reconceptualization is that more education programs are reflecting and promoting a sociocultural perspective in language and literacy, that is, a perspective firmly rooted in an anthropological understanding of culture; a view of learning as socially constructed and mutually negotiated; an understanding of how students from diverse segments of society—due to differential access, and cultural and linguistic differences—experience schooling; and a commitment to social justice. I know that multiple and conflicting ideas exist about these theoretical perspectives, but I believe some basic tenets of sociocultural theory can serve as a platform for discussion. I explore a number of these tenets, illustrating them with examples from my research and using the stories and experiences of young people in U.S. schools.

The language of sociocultural theory includes terms such as *discourse, hegemony, power, social practice, identity, hybridity,* and even the very word *literacy.* Today, these terms have become commonplace, but if we were to do a review of the literature of some 20 years ago or less, we would probably be hard pressed to find them, at least as currently used. What does this mean? How has our awareness and internalization of these terms and everything they imply changed how we look at teaching and learning? Let's look at literacy itself. It is generally accepted that certain family and home conditions promote literacy, including an abundant supply of books and other reading material, consistent conversations between adults and children about the books they read, and other such conditions (Snow, Barnes, Chandler, Goodman, & Hemphill, 1991). I have no doubt that this is true in many cases, and I made certain that my husband and I did these things with our own children. I am sure we made their lives easier as a result. But what of the children for whom these conditions are not present, but who nevertheless grow up literate (Taylor & Dorsey-Gaines, 1988)? Should children be doomed to educational failure because their parents did not live in the right neighborhood, were not privileged enough to be formally educated, or did not take their children to museums or plays? Should they be disqualified from learning because they did not have books at home?

TENETS OF SOCIOCULTURAL THEORY

I began with my story to situate myself not just personally, but socially and politically, a primary premise of sociocultural theory. Given traditional theories, the only way to understand my educational success was to use tra-

Willett, Judith Solsken, Masha Rudman, Catherine Luna, and Theresa Austin. Working with them to conceptualize and develop our program over the past 3 years has had a profound influence on my thinking about these issues.

ditional metaphors: I had "pulled myself up by my bootstraps;" I had "melted;" I had joined the "mainstream." But I want to suggest that these traditional metaphors are as unsatisfactory as they are incomplete because they place individuals at the center, isolated from the social, cultural, historical, and political context in which they live. Traditional theories explain my experience, and those of others who do not fit the conventional pattern, as springing primarily if not solely from our personal psychological processes. Sociocultural theory, on the other hand, gives us different lenses with which to view learning, and different metaphors for describing it. This is significant because how one views learning leads to dramatically different curricular decisions, pedagogical approaches, expectations of learning, relationships among students, teachers and families, and indeed, educational outcomes.

Sociocultural and sociopolitical perspectives are first and foremost based on the assumption that social relationships and political realities are at the heart of teaching and learning. That is, learning emerges from the social, cultural, and political spaces in which it takes place, and through the interactions and relationships that occur between learners and teachers. In what follows, I propose five interrelated concepts that undergird sociocultural and sociopolitical perspectives. These concepts are the basis of my own work, and they help me make sense of my experience and the experiences of countless youngsters that challenge traditional deficit views of learning. The concepts are also highly consistent with a critical multicultural perspective, that is, one that is broader than superficial additions to content or "holidays and heroes" approaches.

I focus on five concepts: *agency/co-constructed learning*; *experience*; *identity/hybridity*; *context/situatedness/positionality*; and *community*. Needless to say, each of these words holds many meanings, but I use them here to locate some fundamental principles of sociocultural and sociopolitical theory. In addition, the terms are both deeply connected and overlapping. I separate them here for matters of convenience, not because I see them as fundamentally independent concepts.

Agency

In many classrooms and schools, learning continues to be thought of as transmission rather than as *agency*, or mutual discovery by students and teachers. At the crudest level, learning is thought to be the reproduction of socially sanctioned knowledge, or what Michael Apple (1991) has called "official knowledge." These are the dominant attitudes and behaviors that society deems basic to functioning. The most extreme manifestation of this theory of learning is what Paulo Freire (1970) called "banking education," that is, the simple depositing of knowledge into students who are thought to be empty receptacles. In an elegant rejection of the banking concept of education, Freire instead defined the act of study as constructed by active agents. According to Freire (1985), "To study is not to consume ideas, but to create and re-create them" (p. 4).

Although learning as the reproduction of socially sanctioned knowledge is repudiated by teachers and theorists alike, it continues to exist in many schools and classrooms. It is the very foundation of such ideas as "teacher-proof curriculum," the need to "cover the material" in a given subject, and the endless lists of skills and competencies "that every student should know" (Hirsch, 1987). This contradiction was evident even near the beginning of the 20th century when John Dewey (1916) asked:

> Why is it, in spite of the fact that teaching by pouring in, learning by a passive absorption, are universally condemned, that they are still so entrenched in practice? That education is not an affair of "telling" and being told but an active and constructive process, is a principle almost as generally violated in practice as conceded in theory. (p. 38)

Why does this continue to happen? One reason is probably the doubt among the public that teachers and students have the ability to construct meaningful and important knowledge. Likewise, in low-income schools with students from diverse cultural and linguistic backgrounds, very little agency exists on the part of either students or teachers. In such schools, teachers learn that their primary responsibility is to "teach the basics" because students are thought to have neither the innate ability nor the experiential background of more privileged students. In the case of students for whom English is a second language, the assumption that they must master English before they can think and reason may prevail.

Let me share some examples of agency, or lack of it, from the words of students of diverse backgrounds who a number of colleagues[2] and I interviewed for my first book (Nieto, 1992, 2000). We found that students' views largely echoed those of educational researchers who have found that teaching methods in most classrooms, especially those in secondary schools and even more so in secondary schools attended by poor students of all backgrounds, vary little from traditional "chalk and talk" methods; that textbooks are the dominant teaching materials used; that routine and rote learning are generally favored over creativity and critical thinking; and that teacher-centered transmission models still prevail (Cummins, 1994; Goodlad, 1984). Students in my study (Nieto, 2000) had more to say about pedagogy than about anything else, and they were especially critical of teachers who provided only passive learning environments for students. Linda Howard, who was just graduating as the valedictorian of her class in an urban high school, is a case in point. Although now at the top of her

---

[2] I am very grateful to those who assisted me with the interviews and gave me suggestions for crafting the case studies: Paula Elliott, Haydée Font, Maya Gillingham, Beatriz McConnie Zapater, Mac Lee Morante, Carol Shea, Diane Sweet, and Carlie Tartakov.

class, Linda had failed seventh and eighth grade twice, for a variety of reasons, both academic and medical. She had this to say about pedagogy:

> Because I know there were plenty of classes where I lost complete interest. But those were all because the teachers just, "Open the books to this page." They never made up problems out of their head. Everything came out of the book. You didn't ask questions. If you asked them questions, then the answer was "in the book." And if you asked the question and the answer *wasn't* in the book, then you shouldn't have asked that question! (pp. 55–56)

Rich Miller, a young man who planned to attend pharmacy school after graduation, described a "normal teacher" as one who "gets up, gives you a lecture, or there's teachers that just pass out the work, you do the work, pass it in, get a grade, good-bye!" (p. 66).

The students were especially critical of teachers who relied on textbooks and blackboards. Avi Abramson, a young man who had attended Jewish day schools and was now in a public high school, had some difficulty adjusting to the differences in pedagogy. He believed that some teachers did better because they taught from the point of view of the students: "They don't just come out and say, 'All right, do this, blah, blah, blah.' . . . They're not so *one-tone voice*" (p. 116). Yolanda Piedra, a Mexican student, said that her English teacher "just does the things and sits down" (p. 221). Another student mentioned that some teachers "just teach the stuff. 'Here,' write a couple of things on the board, 'see, that's how you do it. Go ahead, page 25' " (p. 166).

These students didn't just criticize, however; they also gave examples of teachers who promoted their active learning. Hoang Vinh, in his junior year of high school, spoke with feeling about teachers who allowed him to speak Vietnamese with other students in class. He also loved working in groups, contrary to conventional wisdom about Asian students' preference for individual work (demonstrating the dangers of generalizing about fixed cultural traits). Vinh particularly appreciated the teacher who asked students to discuss important issues, rather than focus only on learning what he called "the word's *meaning*" (p. 143) by writing and memorizing lists of words. Students also offered thoughtful suggestions to teachers to make their classrooms more engaging places. One student recommended that teachers involve more students actively: "More like making the whole class be involved, not making only the two smartest people up here do the whole work for the whole class" (p. 125).

Teaching becomes much more complex when learning is based on the idea that all students have the ability to think and reason. Sociocultural and sociopolitical theories emphasize that learning is not simply a question of transmitting knowledge, but rather of working with students so that they can reflect, theorize, and create knowledge. Given this theory of agency, "banking education" (Freire, 1970) makes little sense. Instead, the focus on

reflective questions invites students to consider different options, to question taken-for-granted truths, and to delve more deeply into problems.

Experience

That learning needs to build on experience is a taken-for-granted maxim,
based on the idea that it is an innately human endeavor accessible to all
people. But somehow this principle is often ignored when it comes to young
people who have not had the *kinds* of experiences that are thought to prepare them for academic success, particularly those students who have not
been raised within "the culture of power" (Delpit, 1988), or who have not
explicitly learned the rules of the game for academic success. The experiences of these students—usually young people of culturally and linguistically diverse backgrounds and those raised in poverty—tend to be quite different from the experiences of more economically and socially advantaged
students, and these differences become evident when they go to school.

Pierre Bourdieu (1986) described how different forms of cultural capital help maintain economic privilege, even if these forms of capital are not
themselves strictly related to economy. Cultural capital is evident in such intangibles as values, tastes, and behaviors and through cultural identities
such as language, dialect, and ethnicity. Some signs of cultural capital have
more social worth, although not necessarily more intrinsic worth, than others. If this is true, then youngsters from some communities are placed at a
disadvantage relative to their peers simply because of their experiences and
identities. Understanding this reality means that power relations are a fundamental, although largely unspoken, aspect of school life.

We also need to consider the impact of teachers' attitudes concerning
the cultural capital that their students *do* bring to school, and teachers'
subsequent behaviors relative to this cultural capital. Sociocultural theories help to foreground these concerns. For example, a 1971 article by Annie Stein cited a New York City study in which kindergarten teachers were
asked to list in order of their importance the things a child should learn in
order to prepare for first grade. In schools with large Puerto Rican and
Black student populations, socialization goals were predominant, but in
mostly White schools, educational goals were invariably first. "In fact," according to Stein, "in a list of six or seven goals, several teachers in the minority-group kindergartners forgot to mention any educational goals at
all" (p. 167). This is an insidious kind of tracking, where educational ends
for some students were sacrificed for social aims. The effects of this early
tracking were already evident in kindergarten.

All children come to school as thinkers and learners, aptitudes usually
recognized as important building blocks for further learning. But there
seems to be a curious refusal on the part of many educators to accept as
valid the *kinds* of knowledge and experiences with which some students
come to school. For instance, speaking languages other than English, es-

pecially those languages with low status, is often thought of by teachers as a potential detriment rather than a benefit to learning. Likewise, although traveling to Europe to ski is generally considered culturally enriching, the same is not true of traveling to North Carolina, Haiti, or the Dominican Republic to visit relatives. The reason that these kinds of experiences are evaluated differently by teachers, and in fact in the general society, has more to do with their cultural capital than with their educational potential or intrinsic worth.

The reluctance or inability to accept and build on students' experiences is poignantly described by Mary Ginley, a teacher in Massachusetts who taught in a small city with a large Puerto Rican student population. A gifted teacher, Mary also knew that "being nice is not enough," an idea she elaborated on in a journal she kept for a class she took with me:

> Every child needs to feel welcome, to feel comfortable. School is a foreign land to most kids (where else in the world would you spend time circling answers and filling in the blanks?), but the more distant a child's culture and language are from the culture and language of school, the more at risk that child is. A warm, friendly, helpful teacher is nice but it isn't enough. We have plenty of warm friendly teachers who tell the kids nicely to forget their Spanish and ask mommy and daddy to speak to them in English at home; who give them easier tasks so they won't feel badly when the work becomes difficult; who never learn about what life is like at home or what they eat or what music they like or what stories they have been told or what their history is. Instead, we smile and give them a hug and tell them to eat our food and listen to our stories and dance to our music. We teach them to read with our words and wonder why it's so hard for them. We ask them to sit quietly and we'll tell them what's important and what they must know to "get ready for the next grade." And we never ask them who they are and where they want to go. (Nieto, 1999, pp. 85–86)

A case in point is Hoang Vinh, the Vietnamese student I mentioned previously. Vinh was literate in Vietnamese and he made certain that his younger siblings spoke it exclusively at home and they all wrote to their parents in Vietnam weekly. He was a good student, but he was also struggling to learn English, something that his teachers didn't always understand. He described how some teachers described his native language as "funny," and even laughed at it. But as he explained, "[To keep reading and writing Vietnamese] is very important. . . . So, I like to learn English, but I like to learn my language too" (Nieto, 2000, p. 178). Even more fundamental for Vinh was that teachers try to understand their students' experiences and culture. He explained: "[My teachers] understand some things, just not all Vietnamese culture. Like they just understand some things *outside*. . . . But they cannot understand something inside our hearts" (p. 178). Vinh's words are a good reminder that when students' skills and knowledge are dismissed as inappropriate for the school setting, schools lose a golden opportunity to build on their students' lives in the service of their learning.

Identity/Hybridity

How students benefit from schooling or not is influenced by many things including the particular individual personalities of students and the values of the cultural context in which they have been raised. Traditional theories, however, privilege individual differences above all other circumstances. As a result, it is primarily through tests and other measures of students' individual abilities that their intelligence is determined. Sociocultural theory goes beyond this limited perspective to include other issues such as students' cultural identities. But culture should not be thought of in this context as unproblematic. Mary Kalantzis, Bill Cope, and Diana Slade (1989) remind us that

> we are not simply bearers of cultures, languages, and histories, with a duty to reproduce them. We are the products of linguistic-cultural circumstances, actors with a capacity to resynthesize what we have been socialized into and to solve new and emerging problems of existence. We are not duty-bound to conserve ancestral characteristics which are not structurally useful. We are both socially determined and creators of human futures. (p. 18)

Culture is complex and intricate; it cannot be reduced to holidays, foods, or dances, although these are of course elements of culture. Everyone has a culture because all people participate in the world through social and political relationships informed by history as well as by race, ethnicity, language, social class, sexual orientation, gender, and other circumstances related to identity and experience.

If culture is thought of in a sentimental way then it becomes little more than a yearning for a past that never existed, or an idealized, sanitized version of what exists in reality. The result may be an unadulterated, essentialized "culture on a pedestal" that bears little resemblance to the messy and contradictory culture of real life. The problem of viewing some aspects of culture as indispensable attributes that must be shared by all people within a particular group springs from a romanticized and uncritical understanding of culture.

Let me share an example of this with you: Last year, I received an e-mail message with the subject heading "You Know You're Puerto Rican When. . . ." The message was meant to be humorous, and it included a long list of experiences and characteristics that presumably describe what it means to be Puerto Rican in the United States (e.g., being chased by your mother with a *chancleta*, or slipper in hand; always having a dinner that consists of rice and beans and some kind of meat; having a grandmother who thinks Vick's Vapor Rub is the miracle cure for everything). I laughed at many of these things (and I shared a good number of these experiences when I was growing up in New York City), but it was also sobering to read the list because it felt like a litmus test for *puertorriqueñidad* (Puerto Ricanness). If you could prove that you had these particular experiences, you could claim to be authentic; otherwise, you could not. By putting them to paper, the author was making it clear that these experiences defined the very essence of being Puerto Rican.

Reading the list made me reflect on my own daughters, born and raised in the United States by highly educated middle-class parents. My daughters would likely not pass the Puerto Rican litmus test: Their dinner was just as likely to consist of take-out Chinese or pizza as of rice and beans; they barely knew what Vick's Vapor Rub was; and I don't remember ever chasing them with *chancleta* in hand. But both of them identify as Puerto Rican, and they speak Spanish to varying degrees and enjoy rice and beans as much as the next Puerto Rican. But they also eat salmon and frog's legs and pizza and Thai food. The e-mail message I received made it seem as if there was only one way to be Puerto Rican. The result of this kind of thinking is that we are left with just two alternatives: either complete adherence to one definition of identity, or total and unequivocal assimilation. We are, in the words of Anthony Appiah (1994), replacing "one kind of tyranny with another" (p. 163).

My daughters' identities are complicated. They live in a highly diverse society in terms of race, ethnicity, social class, and other differences, and they enjoy the privileges they have received as a result of their parents' social-class position in society. The point of this story is to emphasize that culture does not exist in a vacuum but rather is situated in particular historical, social, political, and economic conditions, another major tenet of sociocultural theory. That is, culture needs to be understood as dynamic; multifaceted; embedded in context; influenced by social, economic, and political factors; created and socially constructed; learned; and dialectical (Nieto, 1999). Steven Arvizu's (1994) wonderful description of culture as a *verb* rather than a *noun* captures the essence of culture beautifully. That is, culture is dynamic, active, changing, always on the move. Even within their native contexts, cultures are always changing as a result of political, social, and other modifications in the immediate environment. When people with different backgrounds come in contact with one another, such change is to be expected even more.

Let me once again use the example of Linda Howard, one of the young women we interviewed for *Affirming Diversity* (2000). As I mentioned, Linda was a talented young woman who was graduating as valedictorian of her class. But the issue of identity was a complicated one for her. Being biracial, she identified as "Black American and White American," and she said,

> I don't always fit in—unless I'm in a mixed group . . . because if I'm in a group of people who are all one race, then they seem to look at me as being the *other* race . . . whereas if I'm in a group full of [racially mixed] people, my race doesn't seem to matter to everybody else. . . . Then I don't feel like I'm standing out . . . It's hard. I look at history and I feel really bad for what

some of my ancestors did to some of my other ancestors. Unless you're mixed, you don't know what it's like to be mixed (pp. 51–52).

The tension of Linda's identity was not simply a personal problem, however. It was evident throughout her schooling, and especially when she reached secondary school. She found that teachers jumped to conclusions about her identity, assuming she was Latina or even Chinese, and identifying her as such on forms without even asking her.

Linda won a scholarship to a highly regarded university. When discussing her future, she exclaimed proudly, "I've got it all laid out. I've got a 4-year scholarship to one of the best schools in New England. All I've gotta do is go there and make the grade." Linda's future seemed hopeful, overflowing with possibilities, but she didn't quite "make the grade." When Paula Elliott, who interviewed Linda the first time, spoke with her again 10 years later, she found out that Linda dropped out of college after just a few months, and she never returned. Over dinner, Linda described her experience at the university in this way: "I felt like a pea on a big pile of rice." Using a sociocultural lens, we can see that identity is not simply a personal issue, but that it is deeply embedded in institutional life. Had there been a way to validate her hybridity, perhaps Linda might have graduated. She certainly had the intellectual training and resources; what she didn't have was the support for her identity to ease the way.

In some ways, we can think of culture as having both surface and deep structure, to borrow a concept from linguistics (Chomsky, 1965). For instance, in the interviews of students of diverse backgrounds that I mentioned previously (Nieto, 2000), we were initially surprised by the seeming homogeneity of the youth culture they manifested. Regardless of racial, ethnic, linguistic background, or time in the United States—but usually intimately connected to a shared urban culture and social class—the youths often expressed strikingly similar tastes in music, food, clothes, television viewing habits, and so on. When I probed more deeply, however, I also found evidence of deeply held values from their ethnic heritage. For instance, Marisol, a Puerto Rican high school student, loved hip hop and rap music, pizza, and lasagna. She never mentioned Puerto Rican food, and Puerto Rican music to her was just the "old-fashioned" and boring music her parents listened to. But in her everyday interactions with parents and siblings, and in the answers she gave to my interview questions, she reflected deep aspects of Puerto Rican culture such as respect for elders, a profound kinship with and devotion to family, and a desire to uphold important traditions such as staying with family rather than going out with friends on important holidays. Just as there is no such thing as a "pure race," there is likewise no "pure culture." That is, cultures influence one another, and even minority cultures and those with less status have an impact on majority cultures, sometimes in dramatic ways.

Power is deeply implicated in notions of culture and language (Fairclough, 1989). Indeed, what are often presented as cultural and linguistic differences are above all differences in power. Put another way, cultural conflict is sometimes little more than political conflict. Let me give you another example concerning the link between culture and context based on an experience I had that took me by surprise even as a young adult. As you probably know, rice is a primary Puerto Rican staple. There is a saying in Spanish that demonstrates how common it is: "*Puertorriqueños somos como el arroz blanco: estamos por todas partes*" (Puerto Ricans are like white rice: we are everywhere), an adage that says as much about rice as it does about the diaspora of the Puerto Rican people, almost half of whom live outside the island. As a rule, Puerto Ricans eat short-grained rice, but I have always preferred long-grained rice. Some Puerto Ricans have made me feel practically like a cultural traitor when I admitted it. I remember my surprise when a fellow academic, a renowned Puerto Rican historian, explained the real reason behind the preference for short-grained rice. This preference did not grow out of the blue, nor does any particular quality of the rice make it innately better. On the contrary, the predilection for short-grained rice was influenced by the historical context of Puerto Ricans as a colonized people.

It seems that, near the beginning of the 20th century when Puerto Rico was first taken over by the United States as spoils of the Spanish-American War, there was a surplus of short-grained rice in the United States. Colonies have frequently been the destination for unwanted or surplus goods from the metropolis, so Puerto Rico became the dumping ground for short-grained rice, which had lower status than long-grained rice in the United States. After this, of course, the preference for short-grained rice became part of the culture. As is true of all cultural values, however, this particular taste was influenced by history, economics, and power. This example was a good lesson to me that culture is not something inherent, but often arbitrary and negotiated.

Hybridity complicates the idea of cultural identity. It means that culture is always heterogeneous and complex; it also implies that assimilation or cultural preservation are not the only alternatives. Ariel Dorfman's (1998) autobiography *Heading South, Looking North: A Bilingual Journey* eloquently describes the turmoil he experienced as a child in developing his identity, first in New York City and later in Chile: "I instinctively chose to refuse the multiple, complex, in-between person I would someday become, this man who is shared by two equal languages and who has come to believe that to tolerate differences and indeed embody them personally and collectively might be our only salvation as a species" (p. 42). As an adult, he reflected on the demand to be "culturally pure" that he experienced in the United States as a graduate student:

> Sitting at my typewriter in Berkeley, California, that day, precariously balanced between Spanish and English, for the first time perhaps fully aware of how extraordinarily bicultural I was, I did not have the maturity—or the

emotional or ideological space, probably not even the vocabulary—to answer that I was a hybrid, part Yankee, part Chilean, a pinch of Jew, a mestizo in search of a center, I was unable to look directly in the face the divergent mystery of who I was, the abyss of being bilingual and binational, at a time when everything demanded that we be unequivocal and immaculate. (p. 22)

The idea of hybridity, and of culture as implicated with power and privilege, complicate culturally responsive pedagogy. Rather than simply an incorporation of the cultural practices of students' families in the curriculum, or a replication of stereotypical ideas about "learning styles," culturally responsive pedagogy in the broadest sense is a political project that is, according to Gloria Ladson-Billings (1994) about "questioning (and preparing students to question) the structural inequality, the racism, and the injustice that exist in society" (p. 128). Culturally responsive pedagogy is not simply about instilling pride in one's identity or boosting self-esteem. It is also about context and positionality, to which I now turn.

Context/Situatedness/Positionality

When culture is thought of as if it were context-free, we fragment people's lives, in the words of Frederick Erickson (1990), "as we freeze them outside time, outside a world of struggle in concrete history" (p. 34). Context is also about *situatedness* and *positionality*, reminding us that culture is not simply the rituals, foods, and holidays of specific groups of people, but also the social markers that differentiate that group from others. It is once again the recognition that questions of power are at the very heart of learning. This view of culture also implies that differences in ethnicity, language, social class, and gender need not, in and of themselves, be barriers to learning. Instead, it is how these differences are viewed in society that can make the difference in whether and to what extent young people learn.

Judith Solsken's (1993) definition of *literacy* as the "negotiation of one's orientation toward written language and thus one's position within multiple relations of power and status" (p. 6) brings up a number of questions that have traditionally been neglected in discussions of reading and writing, questions such as: How do students learn to use language in a way that both acknowledges the context in which they find themselves, and challenges the rules of that context? How do young people learn to negotiate the chasm that exists between their home languages and cultures and those of school? Let me share with you another example from Linda Howard. What helped Linda go from a struggling student in junior high to valedictorian of her class several years later? There are probably many answers to this question, but one ingredient that made a tremendous difference was Mr. Benson, her favorite teacher in high school. He too was biracial, and Linda talked about some of the things she had learned from Mr. Benson about positionality and context:

I've enjoyed all my English teachers at Jefferson. But Mr. Benson, my English Honors teacher, he just threw me for a whirl! 'Cause Mr. Benson, he says, I can go into Harvard and converse with those people, and I can go out in the street and rap with y'all. It's that type of thing, I love it. I try and be like that myself. I have my street talk. I get out in the street and I say "ain't" this and "ain't" that and "your momma" or "wha's up?" But I get somewhere where I know the people aren't familiar with that language or aren't accepting that language, and I will talk properly. . . . I walk into a place and I listen to how people are talking, and it just automatically comes to me. (Nieto, 2000, p. 56)

Linda's statement is an example of the tremendous intelligence needed by young people whose Discourses (Gee, 1990) are not endorsed by schools, and who need to negotiate these differences on their own. Linda's words are also a graphic illustration of James Baldwin's (1997) characterization of language as "a political instrument, means, and proof of power" (p. 16). In the case of African American discourse, Baldwin suggested—as Linda learned through her own experience—"It is not the Black child's language that is in question, it is not his language that is despised: It is his experience" (p. 16). As David Corson (1993) reminds us, ". . . education can routinely repress, dominate, and disempower language users whose practices differ from the norms that it establishes" (p. 7).

What does this mean for teachers? Situations such as Linda Howard's suggest that, in the words of Sharon Nelson-Barber and Elise Trumbull Estrin (1995), "We are faced with essential epistemological questions such as, what counts as important knowledge or knowing?" (p. 178). These questions are at the core of sociocultural theory, and they are neither neutral nor innocent. They are rarely addressed openly in school, although they should be. As Ira Shor (1992) said, "A curriculum that avoids questioning school and society is not, as is commonly supposed, politically neutral. It cuts off the students' development as critical thinkers about their world" (p. 12).

Sociocultural and sociopolitical perspectives have been especially consequential because they have shattered the perception that teaching and learning are neutral processes uncontaminated by the idiosyncrasies of particular contexts. Whether and to what extent teachers realize the influence social and political context have on learning can alter how they perceive their students and, consequently, what and how they teach them. A good example of positionality is the status of bilingual education. Bilingualism is only viewed as a problem and a deficit in a context where speakers of a particular language are held in low esteem or seen as a threat to national unity. This is the case of bilingual education in the United States, and especially for children who speak Spanish. That is, there is nothing inherently negative about the project of becoming bilingual (many wealthy parents pay dearly for the privilege), but rather it is the identities of the students, and the status of the language variety they speak, that make bilingual education problematic. This was clearly explained by Lizette Román, a bilingual teacher whose journal entry for one of my classes reads as follows:

> Unfortunately, most bilingual programs exist because they are mandated by law, not because they are perceived as a necessity by many school systems. The main problem that we bilingual teachers face every day is the misconception that mainstream teachers, principals, and even entire school systems have about bilingual education. . . . As a consequence, in many school districts bilingual education is doubly disadvantaged, first because it is seen as remedial and, second, because little attention is paid to it. Many mainstream teachers and administrators see bilingual education as a remediation program and do not validate what bilingual teachers do in their classrooms even when what they are teaching is part of the same curriculum. . . . The majority think that there must be something wrong with these children who cannot perform well in English. As soon as the children transfer out of the bilingual program, these teachers believe that *this* is the moment when the learning of these children starts. The perception of the majority distorts the importance and the purpose of bilingual education. It extends to bilingual children and their parents. Bilingual children and their parents sense that their language places them in a program where they are perceived to be inferior to the rest of the children. What isolates children in the bilingual program is not the way the program is conducted, but the perceptions the majority has about people who speak a language different from the mainstream. (Nieto, 1999, pp. 87–88)

Lizette's reflections suggest that if teachers believe that intelligence and learning are somehow divorced from context, then they will conclude that the political and economic realities of their students' lives—including their school environments—have nothing to do with learning. In short, teachers can delude themselves by believing that they and the schools in which they work inhabit an "ideology-free zone" in which dominant attitudes and values play no role in learning. When students are asked to give up their identities for an elusive goal that they may never reach because of the negative context in which they learn, students may be quite correct in rejecting the trade.

Community

How we define and describe *community* is of central significance in sociocultural theory. Lev Vygotsky's (1978) research in the first decades of the 20th century was a catalyst for the viewpoint that learning is above all a social practice. Vygotsky suggested that development and learning are firmly rooted in—and influenced by—society and culture. Accepting this idea means that it is no longer possible to separate learning from the context in which it takes place, nor from an understanding of how culture and society influence and are influenced by learning.

Vygotsky and others who have advanced the sociocultural foundation of cognition (Cole & Griffin, 1983; Scribner & Cole, 1981) have provided us with a framework for understanding how schools can either encourage or discourage the development of learning communities. Because schools organize themselves in specific ways, they are more or less comfortable and inviting for students of particular backgrounds. Most schools closely reflect the traditional image of the intelligent, academically prepared young person, and consequently, these are the young people who tend to feel most comfortable in school settings. But institutional environments are never neutral; they are always based on particular views of human development, of what is worth knowing, and of what it means to be educated. When young people enter schools, they are entering institutions that have already made some fundamental decisions about such matters, and in the process, some of these children may be left out through no fault of their own. The ability to create community, so important in sociocultural theory, is lost.

Maria Botelho, a doctoral student of mine and a former early childhood teacher and librarian, remembers very clearly what it was like to begin school as a young immigrant student in Cambridge, Massachusetts. After viewing a short video on bilingual education in one of my classes, she felt almost as if she had stepped back in time. The video highlights a number of students, one of them Carla, a young Portuguese student in a bilingual class in Cambridge. Maria reflected on her reactions to the video in the journal she kept for my class:

> I viewed the video "Quality Bilingual Education" twice. I wept both times. The Portuguese-speaking girl, Carla, attended kindergarten in a school that is less than a block from where my parents live in Cambridge; it was too close to home, so to speak. Like Carla, I entered the Cambridge Public Schools speaking only Portuguese. Unlike Carla, I was placed in a mainstream first-grade class. I still remember my teacher bringing over a piece of paper with some writing on it (a worksheet) and crayons. I fell asleep. There I learned quietly about her world, and my world was left with my coat, outside the classroom door. (Nieto, 1999, p. 110)

Sociocultural theories are a radical departure from conventional viewpoints that posit learning as largely unaffected by context. Traditional viewpoints often consider that children such as Maria who do not speak English have low intelligence. As a result, such children are automatically barred from entering a community of learners. A Vygotskian perspective provides a more hopeful framework for thinking about learning because if learning can be influenced by social mediation, then conditions can be created in schools that can help most students learn. These conditions can result in what Carmen Mercado (1998) described as the "fashioning of new texts—texts of our collective voices" (p. 92) that emerge as a result of organizing a learning environment in which literacy is for sharing and reflecting. Particularly significant in this regard is the idea of the *zone of prox-imal development* or ZPD (Vygotsky, 1978). But the ZPD is not simply an *individual* space, but a *social* one. Thus, according to Henry Trueba (1989), if we accept Vygotsky's theory of ZPD, then failure to learn cannot be defined as *individual* failure but rather as *systemic* failure, that is, as the failure of the social system to provide the learner with an opportunity for successful social interactions.

In order to change academic failure to success, appropriate social and instructional interventions need to occur. For teachers, this means that they need to first acknowledge students' differences and then act as a bridge between their students' differences and the culture of the dominant society. The metaphor of a bridge is an appropriate one for teachers who want to be effective with students of diverse backgrounds. This is a lesson I learned from Diane Sweet, a former student who had been an engineer until she fell in love with teaching ESL at the plant where she worked and decided to become a teacher. Diane was well aware of the benefits of bridges, and she applied the metaphor to teaching: A bridge provides access to a different shore without closing off the possibility of returning home; a bridge is built on solid ground but soars toward the heavens; a bridge connects two places that might otherwise never be able to meet. The best thing about bridges is that they do not need to be burned once they are used; on the contrary, they become more valuable with use because they help visitors from both sides become adjusted to different contexts. This is, however, a far cry from how diverse languages and cultures tend to be viewed in schools: the conventional wisdom is that, if native languages and cultures are used at all, it should be only until one learns the *important* language and culture, and then they should be discarded or burned. It is definitely a one-way street with no turning back.

The metaphor of the bridge suggests a different stance: You can have two homes, and the bridge can help you cross the difficult and conflict-laden spaces between them. Teachers who take seriously their responsibility for working with students of diverse backgrounds become bridges, or what Estéban Díaz and his colleagues (1992) called *sociocultural mediators.* That is, they accept and validate the cultural symbols used by all their students, not just by those from majority backgrounds. In sociocultural theory, learning and achievement are not merely cognitive processes, but complex issues that need to be understood in the development of community.

Three of my colleagues provide a hopeful example of using students' experiences and identities as a basis for creating community. Jo-Anne Wilson Keenan, a teacher researcher, working with Judith Solsken and Jerri Willett, professors at the University of Massachusetts, developed a collaborative action research project in a school in Springfield, Massachusetts, with a very diverse student body. The project—based on the premise that parents and other family members of children from widely diverse backgrounds have a lot to offer schools to enhance their children's learning—

was distinct from others in which parents are simply invited to speak about their culture and to share food. Instead, their research focused on demonstrating how parents, through visits that highlight their daily lives, talents, and skills, can promote student learning by transforming the curriculum. But engaging in this kind of project is not always easy. The researchers pointed out that collaborating with families "requires that we confront our own fears of difference and open our classrooms to discussions of topics that may raise tensions among the values of different individuals, groups, and institutions" (p. 64). Through inspiring stories based on indepth analysis of the families' visits, Wilson Keenan, Solsken, and Willett (1999) described how they attempted to build reciprocal relationships with parents. They concluded:

> Both the extent and the quality of participation by the parents belies the common perception that low-income and minority parents are unable or unwilling to collaborate with the school. Even more important, our study documents the wide range of knowledge, skills, and teaching capabilities that parents are already sharing with their children at home and that are available to enrich the education of their own and other children in school. (p. 64)

The important work of Luis Moll, Norma Gónzalez, and their colleagues (1997) is another well-known example of research that builds on family knowledge.

CONCLUSION

No theory can provide all the answers to the persistent problems of education because these problems are not just about teaching and learning, but about a society's ideology. But sociocultural theories give us different insights into these problems. Although we need to accept the inconclusiveness of what we know, we also need to find new and more empowering ways of addressing these concerns. Maxine Greene (1994), in a discussion of postmodernism, poststructuralism, feminism, literary criticism, and other sociocultural theories, discussed both the possibilities and the limits they have. She wrote: "The point is to open a number of fresh perspectives on epistemology in its connection with educational research" (p. 426). But she added, "no universalized or totalized viewing, even of a revised sort . . ." (p. 426) is possible.

Nevertheless, despite this inconclusiveness, we know enough to know that teachers need to respect students' identities and they need to learn about their students if they are to be effective with them. This means understanding the students we teach, and building relationships with them. Ron Morris, a young man attending an alternative school in Boston, described the disappointing relationships he had with teachers before attending the alternative school where he now found himself, a school that finally allowed him to have the relationships he craved. He said:

When a teacher becomes a teacher, she acts like a teacher instead of a person. She takes her title as now she's mechanical, somebody just running it.
Teachers shouldn't deal with students like we're machines. You're a person.
I'm a person. We come to school and we all act like people. (Nieto, 2000, p.
265)

Ron reminds us that we do not have all the answers, and indeed, that some
of the answers we have are clearly wrong. Ray McDermott (1977), in an
early ethnography, described this fact beautifully: "We are all embedded
in our own procedures, which make us both very smart in one situation
and blind and stupid in the next" (p. 202). More recently, Herbert Kohl
(1995) suggested that students' failure to learn is not always caused by a
lack of intelligence, motivation, or self-esteem. On the contrary, he maintained that "to agree to learn from a stranger who does not respect your
integrity causes a major loss of self" (p. 6), or what Carol Locust (1988)
called "wounding the spirit" (p. 315).

Much has been written in the past few years about teachers' reluctance
to broach issues of difference, both among themselves and with their students (Fine, 1992; Jervis, 1996; McIntyre, 1997; Sleeter, 1994; Solomon,
1995; Tatum, 1997). This is especially true of racism, which is most often
addressed in schools as if it were a personality problem. But prejudice and
discrimination are not just personality traits or psychological phenomena;
they are also manifestations of economic, political, and social power. The
institutional definition of racism is not always easy for teachers to accept
because it goes against deeply held theories of equality and justice in our
nation. Bias as an institutional system implies that some people and
groups benefit and others lose. Whites, whether they want to or not, benefit in a racist society; males benefit in a sexist society. Discrimination always helps somebody—those with the most power—which explains why
racism, sexism, and other forms of discrimination continue to exist. Having a different language to speak about differences in privilege and power
is the first step in acquiring the courage to make changes.

Finally, sociocultural and sociopolitical concepts give us a way to confront what Henry Giroux (1992) called our nation's "retreat from democracy" (p. 4). Paulo Freire (1998), writing a series of letters to teachers, focused on this problem:

When inexperienced middle-class teachers take teaching positions in peripheral areas of the city, class-specific tastes, values, language, discourse,
syntax, semantics, everything about the students may seem contradictory to
the point of being shocking and frightening. It is necessary, however, that
teachers understand that the students' syntax; their manners, tastes, and
ways of addressing teachers and colleagues; and the rules governing their
fighting and playing among themselves are all part of their *cultural identity*,
which never lacks an element of class. All that has to be accepted. Only as
learners recognize themselves democratically and see that their right to say

"I be" is respected will they become able to learn the dominant grammatical reasons why they should say "I am." (p. 49)

All students are individuals as well as members of particular groups whose identities are either disdained or respected in society. When we understand this, then my own story and those of countless others, can be understood not simply as someone "pulling herself up by her bootstraps," or "melting," or joining "the mainstream," but as a story that the concepts I've spoken about today—*agency/co-constructed learning*; *experience*; *identity/hybridity*; *context/situatedness/positionality*; and *community*—can begin to explain. When language, literacy, and culture are approached in these ways, we have a more hopeful way of addressing teaching and learning for all students.

REFERENCES

Appiah, A. (1994). Identity, authenticity, survival: Multicultural societies and social reproduction. In A. Gutmann (Ed.), *Multiculturalism* (pp. 149–163). Princeton, NJ: Princeton University.

Apple, M. W. (1993). The politics of official knowledge: Does a national curriculum make sense? *Teachers College Record, 95*(2), 222–241.

Arvizu, S. F. (1994). Building bridges for the future: Anthropological contributions to diversity and classroom practice. In R. A. DeVillar, C. J. Faltis, & J. P. Cummins (Eds.), *Cultural diversity in schools: From rhetoric to reality* (pp. 75–97). Albany: State University of New York Press.

Baldwin, J. (1997). If Black English isn't a language, then tell me, what is? *Rethinking Schools, 12*(1), p. 16.

Bourdieu, P. (1986). The forms of capital. In Richardson, J. G. (Ed.), *Handbook of theory and research for the sociology of education* (pp. 241–248). Westport, CT: Greenwood Press.

Chomsky, N. (1965). *Aspects of the theory of syntax.* Cambridge, MA: MIT.

Cole, M. & Griffin, P. (1983). A socio-historical approach to re-mediation. *The Quarterly Newsletter of the Laboratory of Comparative Human Cognition, 5*(4), 69–74.

Corson, D. (1993). *Language, minority education and gender: Linking social justice and power.* Clevedon, UK: Multilingual Matters.

Cummins, J. (1994). Knowledge, power, and identity in teaching English as a second language. In F. Genesee (Ed.), *Educating second language children: The whole child, the whole curriculum, the whole community* (pp. 33–58). Cambridge, UK: Cambridge University.

Delpit, L. D. (1988). The silenced dialogue: Power and pedagogy in educating other people's children. *Harvard Educational Review, 58,* 280–298.

Dewey, J. (1916). *Democracy and education.* New York: The Free Press.

Díaz, E., Flores, B., Cousin, P. T., & Soo Hoo, S. (1992, April). *Teacher as sociocultural mediator.* Paper presented at the annual meeting of the American Educational Research Association, San Francisco, CA.

Dorfman, A. (1998). *Heading south, looking north: A bilingual journey.* New York: Penguin.

Erickson, F. (1990). Culture, politics, and educational practice. *Educational Foundations, 4*(2), 21–45.

Fairclough, N. (1989). *Language and power.* New York: Longman.

Fine, M. (1991). *Framing dropouts: Notes on the politics of an urban high school.* Albany, NY: SUNY.

Freire, P. (1970). *Pedagogy of the oppressed.* New York: Seabury.

Freire, P. (1985). *The politics of education: Culture, power, and liberation*. New York: Bergin & Garvey.

Freire, P. (1998). *Teachers as cultural workers: Letters to those who dare teach*. Boulder, CO: Westview.

Gee, J. P. (1990). *Social linguistics and literacies: Ideologies in discourse*. Bristol, PA: Falmer.

Giroux, H. (1992). Educational leadership and the crisis of democratic government. *Educational Researcher, 21*(4), 4–11.

Goodlad, J. I. (1984). *A place called school*. New York: McGraw-Hill.

Greene, M. (1994). Epistemology and educational research: The influence of recent approaches to knowledge. In L. Darling-Hammond (Ed.), *Review of research in education* (Vol. 20; pp. 423–464). Washington, DC: American Educational Research Association.

Hirsch, E. D. (1987). *Cultural literacy: What every American needs to know*. Boston: Houghton Mifflin.

Jervis, K. (1996). "How come there are no brothers on that list?": Hearing the hard questions all children ask. *Harvard Educational Review, 66*, 546–576.

Kalantzis, M., Cope, B., & Slade, D. (1989). *Minority languages*. London: The Falmer Press.

Kohl, H. (1994). *"I won't learn from you" and other thoughts on creative maladjustment*. New York: The New Press.

Ladson-Billings, G. (1994). *The dreamkeepers: Successful teachers of African American children*. San Francisco: Jossey-Bass.

Locust, C. (1988). Wounding the spirit: Discrimination and traditional American Indian belief systems. *Harvard Educational Review, 3*, 315–330.

Mercado, C. I. (1998). When young people from marginalized communities enter the world of ethnographic research: Scribing, planning, reflecting, and sharing. In A. Egan-Robertson & D. Bloome (Eds.), *Students as researchers of culture and language in their own communities* (pp. 69–92). Cresskill, NJ: Hampton.

McDermott, R. P. (1977). Social relations as contexts for learning in school. *Harvard Educational Review, 47*, 198–213.

McIntyre, A. (1997). Constructing an image of a white teacher. *Teachers College Press, 98*(4), 653–681.

Moll, L., & Gonzalez, N. (1997). Teachers as social scientists: Learning about culture from household research. In P. M. Hall (Ed.), *Race, ethnicity, and multiculturalism* (Vol. 1; pp. 89–114). New York: Garland.

Nelson-Barber, S., & Estrin, E. T. (1995). Bringing Native American perspectives to mathematics and science teaching. *Theory into Practice, 34*(3), 174–185.

Nieto, S. (1999). *The light in their eyes: Creating multicultural learning communities*. New York: Teachers College Press.

Nieto, S. (2000). *Affirming diversity: The sociopolitical context of multicultural education* (3rd ed.). New York: Longman.

Perry, T., & Delpit, L. (Eds.). (1998). *The real ebonics debate: Power, language, and the education of African-American children*. Boston: Beacon Press & Rethinking Schools.

Rodriguez, R. (1982). *Hunger of memory: The education of Richard Rodriguez*. Boston: David R. Godine.

Scribner, S., & Cole, M. (1981). *The psychology of literacy*. Cambridge, MA: Harvard University.

Shor, I. (1992). *Empowering education: Critical teaching for social change*. Chicago: University of Chicago.

Sleeter, C. E. (1994). White racism. *Multicultural Education, 1*(4), 5–8, 39.

Snow, C. E., Barnes, W. S., Chandler, J., Goodman, I. F., & Hemphill, L. (1991). *Unfulfilled expectations: Home and school influences on literacy*. Cambridge, MA: Harvard University.

Solomon, R. P. (1995). Beyond prescriptive pedagogy: Teacher inservice education for cultural diversity. *Journal of Teacher Education, 46*(4), 251–258.

Solsken, J. W. (1993). *Literacy, gender, and work in families and in school*. Norwood, NJ: Ablex.

Stein, A. (1971). Strategies for failure. *Harvard Educational Review, 41*, 133–179.

Taylor, D., & Dorsey-Gaines, C. (1988). *Growing up literate: Learning from inner-city families.* Portsmouth, NH: Heinemann.

Tatum, B. D. (1997). *"Why are all the Black kids sitting together in the cafeteria?" and other conversations about race.* New York: HarperCollins.

Trueba, H. T. (1989). *Raising silent voices: Educating the linguistic minorities for the 21st century.* Cambridge, MA: Newbury House.

Vygotsky, L. S. (1978). *Thought and language.* Cambridge, MA: MIT Press.

Wilson Keenan, J., Solsken, J., & Willett, J. (1999). "Only boys can jump high": Reconstructing gender relations in a first/second grade classroom. In B. Kamler (Ed.), *Constructing Gender and Difference: Critical Research Perspectives on Early Childhood* (pp. 33–70). Cresskill, NJ: Hampton Press.

CRITICAL QUESTIONS

1. How have language, literacy, and culture affected your life and your experiences as a student and teacher? Write another introduction to this chapter by beginning with your own story. How is it different from mine? What implications might there be for teaching and learning? Would they be different?

2. How do you think that language, literacy, and culture affect your students' lives? What if you wrote the beginning of the chapter from the perspective of one of your students? What might you learn about them in the process?

3. Have you usually accepted the traditional metaphors I mention in the chapter ("pulling yourself up by your bootstraps;" "melting;" "joining the mainstream")? Can you think of other metaphors that might be more appropriate to describe the situations of the students you teach?

4. Look back on the examples I've used when describing the five tenets of sociocultural and sociopolitical theory. As you can see, they all proceed from my own experience. What examples might you use to illustrate these concepts from your experience? from the experiences of your students? What is the danger of using just one's own reality to reach conclusions about teaching and learning?

5. Give some illustrations of *hybrid culture* from your experience as a teacher of students of diverse backgrounds. (My assumption in asking this question is that *all* teachers work with students of diverse backgrounds because diversity encompasses many things, including race/ethnicity, gender, social class, native language, sexual orientation, family configuration, and so on.)

ACTIVITIES FOR YOUR CLASSROOM

1. For a serious semester-long project, develop a classroom-based curriculum that includes in a central way the major tenets of sociocultural and sociopolitical theory as described in the chapter. Include the topic, goals, grade level/subject matter, several activities, resources, and evaluation. Clearly explain how each of the tenets is included in the curriculum.

2. Work with a colleague or group of colleagues (in this course or in your school). Think about ways to address students' experiences and backgrounds in your classroom. Be specific, referring to actual materials, family and community resources, and classroom projects.

COMMUNITY-BASED ACTIVITIES AND ADVOCACY

Are language, literacy, and culture significant issues in the community in which you teach? To find out, engage your students in research about their cultural and literacy practices. Depending on their age, experience, and grade level, you can ask them to:

- interview family members about their language use;
- do a survey of community language resources by finding out how many languages are used in everyday interactions;
- visit a community preschool to see how literacy is promoted; and
- do a study of the community's policies concerning language and culture (e.g., Is there an "English-Only" policy in place? Are cultural festivals encouraged? Does the public library promote multicultural literature? Literature in languages other than English? etc.).

SUPPLEMENTARY RESOURCES FOR FURTHER REFLECTION AND STUDY

Appiah, K. Anthony (1994). Multicultural societies and social reproduction. In Amy Gutmann (Ed.), *Multiculturalism* (pp. 149–163). Princeton, NJ: Princeton University Press.

The author highlights some major problems with multiculturalism, including a focus on large categories such as gender, race, ethnicity, that are far removed from the individual.

Egan-Robertson, Ann & Bloome, David (1998). *Students as researchers of culture and language in their own communities.* Cresskill, NJ: Hampton Press.

In this edited text, various educators write compelling accounts of how students' research of language and culture in their communities has empowered them not only in terms of their literacy, but also in terms of their understanding of the world. This is an excellent resource for teachers who want to do similar research with their students.

Nieto, Sonia (1999). *The light in their eyes: Creating multicultural learning communities.* New York: Teachers College Press.

Using excerpts from journals kept in graduate courses, this text explores how teachers' reflections on course content, reading, and activities provide the framework for a deeper understanding of the effect of culture and language on students' education.

Reyes, María de la Luz (1992). Challenging venerable assumptions: Literacy instruction for linguistically different students. *Harvard Educational Review, 62*(4), 427–446.

In this thought-provoking article, Reyes challenges widely accepted progressive notions about teaching students of limited English proficiency and she critiques current implementations of process instruction that may have the tendency to ignore culturally and linguistically supportive adaptations for these students.

Part I

SETTING THE GROUNDWORK

As you saw in the introductory chapter, a number of foundational elements are crucial to understanding the links among language, literacy, and culture. These include the learners' status and experience, the complex nature of identity, community as a necessary component of learning, and the context in which education takes place. Consequently, a sociocultural understanding of education means learning to look at literacy and other schooling matters in a broader way than has generally been the case.

The chapters that follow continue the same theme, and each defines in more detail some of the basic elements alluded to more generally in the previous chapter. In Chapter 1, there is a comprehensive definition of multicultural education that connects it with school reform and with the sociopolitical context of education. Chapter 2 focuses on a global context by providing examples of diversity and change throughout the world. Finally, in Chapter 3, language diversity is placed squarely within the broader framework of multicultural education, with implications for school and classroom policy and practice.

Multicultural Education and School Reform

INTRODUCTION

Although the idea of multicultural education has been a mainstay in educational circles for more than a decade (and in academic circles for much longer), it has not been widely understood or systematically put into practice. In many schools, to have multicultural education means to set aside a particular time of year for special units or assembly programs about specific people or topics, or to support extracurricular activities that center on ethnic diversity.

The following piece, "Multicultural Education and School Reform," is a chapter from the book *Affirming Diversity: The Sociopolitical Context of Multicultural Education*. Through an indepth definition of multicultural education, this chapter challenges the conventional wisdom that multicultural education is simply a "feel-good" additive to the curriculum or a program to boost self-esteem for "minority" students. Instead, multicultural education is framed within a context of social justice and critical pedagogy, and it encompasses antiracist and basic education for all students of all backgrounds. Throughout the chapter, examples of how this definition goes beyond the "heroes and holidays" approach to diversity are given, with various implications for our nation's schools.

"We don't need multicultural education here; most of our students are White."
"I want to include multicultural education in my curriculum, but there's just no time for it."
"Oh, yes, we have multicultural education here: We celebrate Black History Month and there's an annual Diversity Dinner."

"Multicultural education is just therapy for Black students."
"Multicultural education is divisive. We need to focus on our similarities and then everything will be fine."
"I don't see color. All my students are the same to me."
"We shouldn't talk about racism in school because it has nothing to do with learning. Besides, it'll just make the kids feel bad."
"Let's not focus on negative things. Can't we all just get along?"

In discussing multicultural education with teachers and other educators over many years, I have heard all these comments and more. Statements such as these reflect a profound misconception of multicultural education.

When multicultural education is mentioned, many people first think of lessons in human relations and sensitivity training, units about ethnic holidays, education in inner-city schools, or food festivals. If limited to these issues, the potential for substantive change in schools is severely diminished. On the other hand, when broadly conceptualized, multicultural education can have a great impact on redefining how the four areas of potential school conflict already discussed can be addressed. These are: racism and discrimination, structural conditions in schools that may limit learning, the impact of culture on learning, and language diversity. This chapter focuses on how multicultural education addresses each of these areas.

Schools are part of our communities and as such they reflect the stratification and social inequities of the larger society. As long as this is the case, no school program, no matter how broadly conceptualized, can change things completely and on its own. Moreover, in our complex and highly bureaucratic school systems, no single approach can yield instant and positive results for all students. Thus multicultural education is not a panacea for all educational ills. It will not cure underachievement, remove boring and irrelevant curriculum, or stop vandalism. It will not automatically motivate families to participate in schools, reinvigorate tired and dissatisfied teachers, or guarantee a lower dropout rate.

Despite these caveats, when multicultural education is conceptualized as broad-based school reform, it can offer hope for substantive change. By focusing on major conditions contributing to underachievement, a broadly conceptualized multicultural education permits educators to explore alternatives to a system that leads to failure for too many of its students. Such an exploration can lead to the creation of a richer and more productive school climate and a deeper awareness of the role of culture and language in learning. Multicultural education in a sociopolitical context is both richer and more complex than simple lessons on getting along or units on ethnic festivals. Seen in this comprehensive way, educational success for all students is a realistic goal rather than an impossible ideal.

This chapter proposes a definition of multicultural education based on the conceptual framework developed in the preceding chapters, and it analyzes the seven primary characteristics included in the definition. These characteristics underscore the role that multicultural education can play in reforming schools and providing an equal and excellent education for all students. They address the conditions that contribute to school achievement that have been discussed previously. My definition of multicultural education has emerged from the reality of persistent problems in our nation's schools, especially the lack of achievement among students of diverse backgrounds. A comprehensive definition emphasizes the context and process of education, rather than viewing multicultural education as an add-on or luxury disconnected from the everyday lives of students.

Despite some differences among major theorists, there has been remarkable consistency over the past quarter century in the field about the goals, purposes, and reasons for multicultural education.[1] But no definition can truly capture all the complexities of multicultural education. The definition I present here reflects my own way of conceptualizing the issues, and it is based on my many years of experience as a student and as an educator of children, youths, and adults. I hope that it will encourage further dialogue and reflection among readers.

Although I have developed seven qualities that I believe are important in multicultural education, you might come up with just three, or with fifteen. The point is not to develop a definitive way to understand multicultural education, but instead to start you thinking about the interplay of societal and school structures and contexts and how they influence learning.

What I believe *is* essential is an emphasis on the sociopolitical context of education and a rejection of multicultural education as either a superficial adding of content to the curriculum, or alternatively, as the magic pill that will do away with all educational problems. I hope that in the process of considering my definition, you will develop your own priorities and your own perspective of multicultural education.

A DEFINITION OF MULTICULTURAL EDUCATION

I define *multicultural education* in a sociopolitical context as follows:

> Multicultural education is a process of comprehensive school reform and basic education for all students. It challenges and rejects racism and other forms of discrimination in schools and society and accepts and affirms the pluralism (ethnic, racial, linguistic, religious, economic, and gender, among others) that students, their communities, and teachers reflect. Multicultural

---

[1]See James A. Banks, "Multicultural Education: Historical Development, Dimensions, and Practice." In *Handbook of Research on Multicultural Education*, edited by James A. Banks and Cherry A. McGee Banks (New York: Macmillan, 1995).

education permeates the schools' curriculum and instructional strategies, as well as the interactions among teachers, students, and families, and the very way that schools conceptualize the nature of teaching and learning. Because it uses critical pedagogy as its underlying philosophy and focuses on knowledge, reflection, and action (*praxis*) as the basis for social change, multicultural education promotes democratic principles of social justice.

The seven basic characteristics of multicultural education in this definition are:

Multicultural education is *antiracist education*.
Multicultural education is *basic education*.
Multicultural education is *important for **all** students*.
Multicultural education is *pervasive*.
Multicultural education is *education for social justice*.
Multicultural education is a *process*.
Multicultural education is *critical pedagogy*.

Multicultural Education Is Antiracist Education

Antiracism, indeed antidiscrimination in general, is at the very core of a multicultural perspective. It is essential to keep the antiracist nature of multicultural education in mind because in many schools, even some that espouse a multicultural philosophy, only superficial aspects of multicultural education are apparent. Celebrations of ethnic festivals are as far as it goes in some places. In others, sincere attempts to decorate bulletin boards or purchase materials with what is thought to be a multicultural perspective end up perpetuating the worst kind of stereotypes. And even where there are serious attempts to develop a truly pluralistic environment, it is not unusual to find incongruencies. In some schools, for instance, the highest academic tracks are overwhelmingly White and the lowest are populated primarily by students of color, or girls are invisible in calculus and physics classes. These are examples of multicultural education *without* an explicitly antiracist and antidiscrimination perspective.

I stress multicultural education as antiracist because many people believe that a multicultural program *automatically* takes care of racism. Unfortunately this is not always true. Writing about multicultural education almost two decades ago, Meyer Weinberg asserted,

Most multicultural materials deal wholly with the cultural distinctiveness of various groups and little more. Almost never is there any sustained attention to the ugly realities of systematic discrimination against the same group that also happens to utilize quaint clothing, fascinating toys, delightful fairy tales, and delicious food. Responding to racist attacks and defamation is *also* part of the culture of the group under study.[2]

Being antiracist and antidiscriminatory means paying attention to all areas in which some students are favored over others: the curriculum, choice of materials, sorting policies, and teachers' interactions and relationships with students and their families.

To be more inclusive and balanced, multicultural curriculum must by definition be antiracist. Teaching does not become more honest and critical simply by becoming more inclusive, but this is an important first step in ensuring that students have access to a wide variety of viewpoints. Although the beautiful and heroic aspects of our history should be taught, so must the ugly and exclusionary. Rather than viewing the world through rose-colored glasses, antiracist multicultural education forces teachers and students to take a long, hard look at everything as it was and is, instead of just how we wish it were.

Too many schools avoid confronting in an honest and direct way both the positive and the negative aspects of history, the arts, and science. Michelle Fine calls this the "fear of naming," and it is part of the system of silencing in public schools.[3] To name might become too messy, or so the thinking goes. Teachers often refuse to engage their students in discussions about racism because it might "demoralize" them. Too dangerous a topic, it is best left untouched.

Related to the fear of naming is the insistence of schools on sanitizing the curriculum, or what Jonathan Kozol many years ago called "tailoring" important men and women for school use. Kozol described how schools manage to take the most exciting and memorable heroes and bleed the life and spirit completely out of them. It is dangerous, he wrote, to teach a history "studded with so many bold, and revolutionary, and subversive, and exhilarating men and women." Instead, he described how schools drain these heroes of their passions, glaze them over with an implausible veneer, place them on lofty pedestals, and then tell "incredibly dull stories" about them.[4]

The process of "sanitizing" is nowhere more evident than in current depictions of Martin Luther King, Jr. In attempting to make him palatable to the mainstream, schools have made Martin Luther King a Milquetoast.

---

[2]Meyer Weinberg, "Notes from the Editor." *A Chronicle of Equal Education*, 4, 3 (November, 1982), 7.

[3]Michelle Fine, *Framing dropouts: Notes on the politics of an urban public high school* (Albany, NY: State University of New York Press, 1991).

[4]Jonathan Kozol, "Great Men and Women (Tailored for School Use)." *Learning Magazine* (December, 1975), 16–20.

The only thing most children know about him is that he kept having a dream. Bulletin boards are full of ethereal pictures of Dr. King surrounded by clouds. If children get to read or hear any of his speeches at all, it is his "I Have a Dream" speech. As inspirational as this speech is, it is only one of his notable accomplishments. Rare indeed are allusions to his early and consistent opposition to the Vietnam War; his strong criticism of unbridled capitalism; and the connections he made near the end of his life among racism, capitalism, and war. Martin Luther King, a man full of passion and life, becomes lifeless. He becomes a "safe hero."

Most of the heroes we present to our children are either those in the mainstream or those who have become safe by the process of "tailoring." Others who have fought for social justice are often downplayed, maligned, or ignored. For example, although John Brown's actions in defense of the liberation of enslaved people are considered noble by many, in our history books he is presented, if at all, as somewhat of a crazed idealist. Nat Turner is another example. The slave revolt that he led deserves a larger place in our history, if only to acknowledge that enslaved people fought against their own oppression and were not simply passive victims. Yet his name is usually overlooked, and Abraham Lincoln is presented as the "great emancipator," with little acknowledgment of his own inconsistent ideas about race and equality. Nat Turner is not safe; Abraham Lincoln is.

To be antiracist also means to work affirmatively to combat racism. It means making antiracism and antidiscrimination explicit parts of the curriculum and teaching young people skills in confronting racism. It also means that we must not isolate or punish students for naming racism when they see it, but instead respect them for doing so. If developing productive and critical citizens for a democratic society is one of the fundamental goals of public education, antiracist behaviors can help to meet that objective.

Racism is seldom mentioned in school (it is bad, a dirty word) and therefore is not dealt with. Unfortunately, many teachers think that simply having lessons in getting along or celebrating Human Relations Week will make students nonracist or nondiscriminatory in general. But it is impossible to be untouched by racism, sexism, linguicism, heterosexism, ageism, anti-Semitism, classism, and ethnocentrism in a society characterized by all of them. To expect schools to be an oasis of sensitivity and understanding in the midst of this stratification is unrealistic. Therefore, part of the mission of the school becomes creating the space and encouragement that legitimates talk about racism and discrimination and makes it a source of dialogue. This includes learning the missing or fragmented parts of our history.

The dilemma becomes how to challenge the silence about race and racism so that teachers and students can enter into meaningful and constructive dialogue. In the words of Marilyn Cochran-Smith,

How can we open up the unsettling discourse of race without making people afraid to speak for fear of being naive, offensive, or using the wrong language? Without making people of color do all the work, feeling called upon to expose themselves for the edification of others? Without eliminating conflict to the point of flatness, thus reducing the conversation to platitudes or superficial rhetoric?[5]

A helpful answer to this dilemma, in terms of students, is offered by Henry Giroux. He suggests that although White students may become traumatized by these discussions, bringing race and racism out into full view can become a useful pedagogical tool to help them locate themselves and their responsibilities concerning racism.[6] Beverly Tatum has proposed that discussing racism within the framework of racial and cultural identity theory can help focus on how racism negatively affects all people and provide a sense of hope that it can be changed.[7]

What about teachers? Many teachers have had little experience with diversity. Discussions of racism threaten to disrupt their deeply held ideals of fair play and equality. Since most teachers are uneasy with these topics, fruitful classroom discussions about discrimination rarely happen. If this is the case, neither unfair individual behaviors nor institutional policies and practices in schools will change. Students of disempowered groups will continue to bear the brunt of these kinds of inequities.

Multicultural education needs to prepare teachers to confront discrimination of all kinds, and this needs to happen not just in college classrooms but also through inservice education. In one example of the powerful impact that this preparation can have, Sandra Lawrence and Beverly Daniel Tatum described the impact of antiracist professional development on teachers' classroom practice. In their research, they found that many White teachers were apprehensive about engaging in discussions about race with their students because they thought they would degenerate into angry shouting matches. Yet, according to Lawrence and Tatum, after the teachers had participated in an inservice course, most of them took concrete actions in their classrooms and schools that challenged unfair policies and practices, and they were more comfortable in confronting racist behaviors and comments.[8]

---

[5]Marilyn Cochran-Smith, "Uncertain allies: Understanding the boundaries of race and teaching." *Harvard Educational Review*, 65, 4 (Winter, 1995), 541–570.

[6]Henry Giroux, "Rewriting the discourse of racial identity: Towards a pedagogy and politics of whiteness." *Harvard Educational Review*, 67, 2 (Summer, 1997), 285–320.

[7]Beverly Daniel Tatum, *Why are all the black kids sitting together in the cafeteria? and other conversations about race* (New York: Basic Books, 1997).

[8]Sandra M. Lawrence and Beverly Daniel Tatum, "Teachers in transition: The impact of antiracist professional development on classroom practice." *Teachers College Record*, 99, 1 (1997), 162–178.

The focus on policies and practices makes it evident that multicultural education is about more than the perceptions and beliefs of individual teachers and other educators. Multicultural education is antiracist because it exposes the racist and discriminatory practices in schools discussed in preceding chapters. A school truly committed to a multicultural philosophy will closely examine its policies and the attitudes and behaviors of its staff to determine how these might discriminate against some students. How teachers react to their students, whether native language use is permitted in the school, how sorting takes place, and the way in which classroom organization might hurt some students and help others are questions to be considered. In addition, individual teachers will reflect on their own attitudes and practices in the classroom and how they are influenced by their background as well as by their ignorance of students' backgrounds. This soul searching is difficult, but it is a needed step in developing an antiracist multicultural philosophy.

But being antiracist does not mean flailing about in guilt or remorse. One of the reasons schools are reluctant to tackle racism and discrimination is that these are disturbing topics for those who have traditionally benefited by their race, gender, and social class, among other differences. Because such topics place people in the role of either the victimizer or the victimized, an initial and understandable reaction of many White teachers and students is to feel guilty. Although this reaction probably serves a useful purpose initially, it needs to be understood as only one step in the process of becoming multiculturally literate and empowered. If one remains at this level, then guilt only immobilizes. Teachers and students need to move beyond guilt to a stage of energy and confidence, where they take action rather than hide behind feelings of remorse.

Although the primary victims of racism and discrimination are those who suffer its immediate consequences, racism and discrimination are destructive and demeaning to everyone. Keeping this in mind, it is easier for all teachers and students to face these issues. Although not everyone is directly guilty of racism and discrimination, we are all responsible for it. Given this perspective, students and teachers can focus on discrimination as something everyone has a responsibility to change.

In discussing slavery in the United States, for example, it can be presented not simply as slave owners against enslaved Africans. There were many and diverse roles among a great variety of people during this period: enslaved Africans and free Africans, slave owners and poor White farmers, Black abolitionists and White abolitionists, White and Black feminists who fought for both abolition and women's liberation, people of Native American heritage who stood on the side of freedom, and so on. Each of these perspectives should be taught so that children, regardless of ethnic background or gender, see themselves in history in ways that are not simply degrading or guilt-provoking.

I clearly remember the incident told to me by the father of the only Black child in a class whose teacher asked all the students to draw themselves as a character during the Civil War. This child drew a horse, preferring to see himself as an animal rather than as an enslaved man. We can only imagine the deep sense of pain and emptiness that this child felt. I have also heard teachers talk about White students who, after learning about slavery or the internment of the Japanese in our country during World War II, feel tremendous guilt. No child should be made to feel guilt or shame about their background. Providing alternative and empowering roles for all students is another aspect of an antiracist perspective because it creates a sense of hope and purpose.

Multicultural Education Is Basic Education

Given the recurring concern for the "basics" in education, multicultural education must be understood as *basic* education. Multicultural literacy is as indispensable for living in today's world as are reading, writing, arithmetic, and computer literacy.

When multicultural education is peripheral to the core curriculum, it is perceived as irrelevant to basic education. One of the major stumbling blocks to implementing a broadly conceptualized multicultural education is the ossification of the "canon" in our schools. The canon, as understood in contemporary U.S. education, assumes that the knowledge that is most worthwhile is already in place. According to this rather narrow view, the basics have in effect already been defined, and knowledge is inevitably European, male, and upper class in origin and conception. This idea is especially evident in the arts and social sciences. For instance, art history classes rarely leave France, Italy, and sometimes England in considering the "great masters." "Classical music" is another example: What is called classical music is actually *European* classical music. Africa, Asia, and Latin America define their classical music in different ways. This same ethnocentrism is found in our history books, which place Europeans and European Americans as the actors and all others as the recipients, bystanders, or bit players of history. But the canon as it currently stands is unrealistic and incomplete because history is never as one-sided as it appears in most of our schools' curricula. We need to expand what we mean by "basic" by opening up the curriculum to a variety of perspectives and experiences.

The problem that a canon tries to address is a genuine one: Modern-day knowledge is so dispersed and compartmentalized that our young people learn very little that is common. There is no *core* to the knowledge to which they are exposed. But proposing a static list of terms, almost exclusively with European and European American referents, does little to expand our actual common culture.

At the same time, it is unrealistic, for a number of reasons, to expect a perfectly "equal treatment" for all people in the curriculum. A force-fit, which tries to equalize the number of African Americans, women, Jewish Americans, and so on in the curriculum, is not what multicultural education is all about. A great many groups have been denied access in the actual making of history. Their participation has *not* been equal, at least if we consider history in the traditional sense of great movers and shakers, monarchs and despots, and makers of war and peace. But the participation of diverse groups, even within this somewhat narrow view of history, has been appreciable. It therefore deserves to be included. The point is that those who *have* been present in our history, arts, literature, and science should be made visible. Recent literature anthologies are a good example of the inclusion of more voices and perspectives than ever before. Did they become "great writers" overnight, or was it simply that they had been buried for too long?

We are not talking here simply of the "contributions" approach to history, literature, and the arts.[9] Such an approach can easily become patronizing by simply adding bits and pieces to a preconceived canon. Rather, missing from most curricula is a consideration of how generally excluded groups have made history and affected the arts, literature, geography, science, and philosophy *on their own terms.*

The alternative to multicultural education is *monocultural education.* Education reflective of only one reality and biased toward the dominant group, monocultural education is the order of the day in most of our schools. What students learn represents only a fraction of what is available knowledge, and those who decide what is most important make choices that are of necessity influenced by their own limited background, education, and experiences. Because the viewpoints of so many are left out, monocultural education is at best a partial education. It deprives all students of the diversity that is part of our world.

No school can consider that it is doing a proper or complete job unless its students develop multicultural literacy. What such a conception might mean in practice would no doubt differ from school to school. At the very least, we would expect all students to be fluent in a language other than

---

[9]For a discussion of different levels of curriculum integration in multicultural education, see James A. Banks, *Teaching strategies for ethnic studies,* 6th ed. (Boston: Allyn & Bacon, 1997).

their own; aware of the literature and arts of many different peoples; and conversant with the history and geography not only of the United States but also of African, Asian, Latin American, and European countries. Through such an education, we would expect students to develop social and intellectual skills that would help them understand and empathize with a wide diversity of people. Nothing can be more basic than this.

Multicultural Education Is Important for *All* Students

There is a widespread perception that multicultural education is only for students of color, or for urban students, or for so-called disadvantaged students. This belief is probably based on the roots of multicultural education, which grew out of the civil rights and equal education movements of the 1960s. The primary objective of multicultural education was to address the needs of students who historically had been most neglected or miseducated by the schools, especially students of color. Those who promoted multicultural education thought that education should strike more of a balance, and that attention needed to be given to developing curriculum and materials that reflect these students' histories, cultures, and experiences. This thinking was historically necessary and is understandable even today, given the great curricular imbalance that continues to exist in most schools.

More recently a broader conceptualization of multicultural education has gained acceptance. It is that all students are *miseducated* to the extent that they receive only a partial and biased education. The primary victims of biased education are those who are invisible in the curriculum. Females, for example, are absent in most curricula, except in special courses on women's history that are few and far between. Working-class history is also absent in virtually all U.S. curricula. The children of the working class are deprived not only of a more forthright education but, more important, of a place in history, and students of all social class backgrounds are deprived of a more honest and complete view of our history. Likewise, there is a pervasive and inpenetrable silence concerning gays and lesbians in most schools, not just in the curriculum but also in extracurricular activities. The result is that gay and lesbian students are placed at risk in terms of social well being and academic achievement.[10]

Although the primary victims of biased education continue to be those who are invisible in the curriculum, those who figure prominently are victims as well. They receive only a partial education, which legitimates their cultural blinders. European American children, seeing only themselves, learn that they are the norm; everyone else is secondary. The same is true

---

[10]Cathy A. Pohan and Norma J. Bailey, "Opening the closet: Multiculturalism that is truly inclusive." *Multicultural Education*, 5, 1 (Fall, 1997), 12–15.

of males. The children of the wealthy learn that the wealthy and the powerful are the real makers of history, the ones who have left their mark on civilization. Heterosexual students receive the message that gay and lesbian students should be ostracized because they are deviant and immoral. The humanity of all students is jeopardized as a result.

Multicultural education is by definition inclusive. Because it is *about* all people, it is also *for* all people, regardless of their ethnicity, language, sexual orientation, religion, gender, race, class, or other difference. It can even be convincingly argued that students from the dominant culture need multicultural education more than others because they are generally the most miseducated about diversity. For example, European American youths often think that they do not even *have* a culture, at least not in the same sense that clearly culturally identifiable youths do. At the same time, they feel that their ways of living, doing things, believing, and acting are the only acceptable ways. Anything else is ethnic and exotic.

Feeling as they do, these young people are prone to develop an unrealistic view of the world and of their place in it. They learn to think of themselves and their group as the norm and of all others as a deviation. These are the children who learn not to question, for example, the name of "flesh-colored" adhesive strips even though they are not the flesh color of three-quarters of humanity. They do not even have to think about the fact that everyone, Christian or not, gets holidays at Christmas and Easter and that other religious holidays are given little attention in our calendars and school schedules. Whereas children from dominated groups may develop feelings of inferiority based on their schooling, dominant group children may develop feelings of superiority. Both responses are based on incomplete and inaccurate information about the complexity and diversity of the world, and both are harmful.

Despite this, multicultural education continues to be thought of by many educators as education for the "culturally different" or the "disadvantaged." Teachers in predominantly European American schools, for example, may feel it is not important or necessary to teach their students anything about the civil rights movement. Likewise, only in scattered bilingual programs in Mexican American communities are students exposed to literature by Mexican and Mexican American authors, and it is generally just at high schools with a high percentage of students of color that ethnic studies classes are offered. These are ethnocentric interpretations of multicultural education.

The thinking behind these actions is paternalistic as well as misinformed. Because anything remotely digressing from the "regular" (European American) curriculum is automatically considered soft by some educators, the usual response to making a curriculum multicultural is to water it down. Poor pedagogical decisions are then based on the premise that so-called disadvantaged students need a watered-down version of the "real" curriculum, whereas more privileged children can handle the "regular" or more academically challenging curriculum. But rather than dilute it, making a curriculum multicultural makes it more inclusive, inevitably enriching it. All students would be enriched by reading the poetry of Langston Hughes or the stories of Gary Soto, or by being fluent in a second language, or by understanding the history of Islam.

Multicultural Education Is Pervasive

Multicultural education is not something that happens at a set period of the day, or another subject area to be covered. In some school systems, there is even a "multicultural teacher" who goes from class to class in the same way as the music or art teacher. Although the intent of this approach may be to formalize a multicultural perspective in the standard curriculum, it is in the long run self-defeating because it isolates the multicultural philosophy from everything else that happens in the classroom. Having specialists take complete responsibility for multicultural education gives the impression that a multicultural perspective is separate from all other knowledge. The schism between "regular" and "multicultural" education widens. In this kind of arrangement, multicultural education becomes exotic knowledge that is external to the real work that goes on in classrooms. Given this conception of multicultural education, it is little wonder that teachers sometimes decide that it is a frill they cannot afford.

A true multicultural approach is pervasive. It permeates everything: the school climate, physical environment, curriculum, and relationships among teachers and students and community.[11] It is apparent in every lesson, curriculum guide, unit, bulletin board, and letter that is sent home; it can be seen in the process by which books and audiovisual aids are acquired for the library, in the games played during recess, and in the lunch that is served. *Multicultural education is a philosophy, a way of looking at the world, not simply a program or a class or a teacher.* In this comprehensive way, multicultural education helps us rethink school reform.

What might a multicultural philosophy mean in the way that schools are organized? For one, it would probably mean the end of tracking, which inevitably favors some students over others. It would also mean that the complexion of the school, both literally and figuratively, would change. That is, there would be an effort to have the entire school staff be more representative of our nation's diversity. Pervasiveness probably would also

---

[11]A good example of how a multicultural approach can include educators, students, and families is found in *Teaching and learning in a diverse world: Multicultural education for young children*, 2nd ed., by Patricia G. Ramsey (New York: Teachers College Press, 1998).

be apparent in the great variety and creativity of instructional strategies, so that students from all cultural groups, and females as well as males, would benefit from methods other than the traditional. The curriculum would be completely overhauled and would include the histories, viewpoints, and insights of many different peoples and both males and females. Topics usually considered "dangerous" could be talked about in classes, and students would be encouraged to become critical thinkers. Textbooks and other instructional materials would also reflect a pluralistic perspective. Families and other community people would be visible in the schools because they would offer a unique and helpful viewpoint. Teachers, families, and students would have the opportunity to work together to design motivating and multiculturally appropriate curricula.

In other less global but no less important ways, the multicultural school would probably look vastly different as well. For example, the lunchroom might offer a variety of international meals, not because they are exotic delights but because they are the foods people in the community eat daily. Sports and games from all over the world might be played, and not all would be competitive. Letters would be sent home in the languages that parents understand. Children would not be punished for speaking their native language; on the contrary, they would be encouraged to do so and it would be used in their instruction as well. In summary, the school would be a learning environment in which curriculum, pedagogy, and outreach are all consistent with a broadly conceptualized multicultural philosophy.

Multicultural Education Is Education for Social Justice

All good education connects theory with reflection and action, which is what Paulo Freire defined as *praxis*.[12] Developing a multicultural perspective means learning how to think in more inclusive and expansive ways, reflecting on what we learn, and applying that learning to real situations. In this regard, John Dewey maintained that "information severed from thoughtful action is dead, a mind-crushing load."[13] Multicultural education invites students and teachers to put their learning into action for social justice. Whether debating a difficult issue, developing a community newspaper, starting a collaborative program at a local senior center, or organizing a petition for the removal of a potentially dangerous waste treatment plant in the neighborhood, students learn that they have power, collectively and individually, to make change.

---

[12]Paulo Freire, *Pedagogy of the oppressed* (New York: Seabury Press, 1970).

[13]John Dewey, *Democracy and education* (New York: Free Press, 1966; first published 1916), 153.

This aspect of multicultural education fits in particularly well with the developmental level of young people who, starting in the middle elementary grades, are very conscious of what is fair and what is unfair. When their pronounced sense of justice is not channeled appropriately, the result can be anger, resentment, alienation, or dropping out of school physically or psychologically.

Preparing students for active membership in a democracy is the basis of Deweyan philosophy, and it has often been cited by schools as a major educational goal. But few schools serve as a site of apprenticeship for democracy. Policies and practices such as rigid ability grouping, inequitable testing, monocultural curricula, and unimaginative pedagogy mitigate against this lofty aim. The result is that students in many schools perceive the claim of democracy to be a hollow and irrelevant issue. Henry Giroux, for example, has suggested that what he calls "the discourse of democracy" has been trivialized to mean such things as uncritical patriotism and mandatory pledges to the flag.[14] In some schools, democratic practices are found only in textbooks and confined to discussions of the American Revolution, but the chance for students to practice day-to-day democracy is minimal. Social justice becomes an empty concept in this situation.

The fact that power and inequality are rarely discussed in schools should come as no surprise. As institutions, schools are charged with maintaining the status quo, but they are also expected to wipe out inequality. Exposing the contradictions between democratic ideals and actual manifestations of inequality makes many people uncomfortable, and this includes educators. Still, such issues are at the heart of a broadly conceptualized multicultural perspective because the subject matter of schooling is society, with all its wrinkles and warts and contradictions. Ethics and the distribution of power, status, and rewards are basic societal concerns. Education must address them as well.

Although the connection of multicultural education with students' rights and responsibilities in a democracy is unmistakable, many young people do not learn about these responsibilities, the challenges of democracy, or the central role of citizens in ensuring and maintaining the privileges of democracy. Multicultural education can have a great impact in this respect. A multicultural perspective presumes that classrooms should not simply *allow* discussions that focus on social justice, but in fact *welcome* them. These discussions might center on concerns that affect culturally diverse communities—poverty, discrimination, war, the national budget—

---

[14]Henry A. Giroux, "Educational leadership and the crisis of democratic government." *Educational Researcher*, 21, 4 (May 1992), 4–11.

and what students can do to change them. Because all of these concerns are pluralistic, education must of necessity be multicultural.

Multicultural Education Is a Process

Curriculum and materials represent the *content* of multicultural education, but multicultural education is above all a *process*. First, it is ongoing and dynamic. No one ever stops becoming a multicultural person, and knowledge is never complete. This means that there is no established canon that is frozen in cement. Second, multicultural education is a process because it involves primarily relationships among people. The sensitivity and understanding teachers show their students are more crucial in promoting student learning than the facts and figures they may know about different ethnic and cultural groups. Also, multicultural education is a process because it concerns such intangibles as expectations of student achievement, learning environments, students' learning preferences, and other cultural variables that are absolutely essential for schools to understand if they are to become successful with all students.

The dimension of multicultural education as a process is too often relegated to a secondary position, because content is easier to handle and has speedier results. For instance, developing an assembly program on Black History Month is easier than eliminating tracking. Changing a basal reader is easier than developing higher expectations for all students. The first involves changing one book for another; the other involves changing perceptions, behaviors, and knowledge, not an easy task. As a result, the processes of multicultural education are generally more complex, more politically volatile, and more threatening to vested interests than even controversial content.

Multicultural education must be accompanied by unlearning conventional wisdom as well as dismantling policies and practices that are disadvantageous for some students at the expense of others. Teacher education programs, for example, need to be reconceptualized to include awareness of the influence of culture and language on learning, the persistence of racism and discrimination in schools and society, and instructional and curricular strategies that encourage learning among a wide variety of students. Teachers' roles in the school also need to be redefined, because empowered teachers help to empower students. The role of families needs to be expanded so that the insights and values of the community can be more faithfully reflected in the school. Nothing short of a complete restructuring of curriculum and of the organization of schools is called for. The process is complex, problematic, controversial, and time consuming, but it is one in which teachers and schools must engage to make their schools truly multicultural.

Multicultural Education Is Critical Pedagogy

Knowledge is neither neutral nor apolitical, yet it is generally treated by teachers and schools as if it were. Consequently, school knowledge tends to reflect the lowest common denominator: that which is sure to offend the fewest (and the most powerful) and is least controversial. Students may leave school with the impression that all major conflicts have already been resolved. But history, including educational history, is full of great debates, controversies, and ideological struggles. These controversies and conflicts are often left at the schoolhouse door.

Every educational decision made at any level, whether by a teacher or by an entire school system, reflects the political ideology and worldview of the decision maker. Decisions to dismantle tracking, discontinue standardized tests, lengthen the school day, use one textbook rather than another, study the Harlem Renaissance, or use learning centers rather than rows of chairs—all reflect a particular view of learners and of education.

As educators, all the decisions we make, no matter how neutral they may seem, have an impact on the lives and experiences of our students. This is true of the curriculum, books, and other materials we provide for them. State and local guidelines and mandates may limit what particular schools and teachers choose to teach, and this too is a political decision. What is excluded is often as telling as what is included. Much of the literature taught at the high school level, for instance, is still heavily male, European, and European American. The significance of women, people of color, and those who write in other languages is diminished, unintentionally or not.

A major problem with a monocultural curriculum is that it gives students only one way of seeing the world. When reality is presented as static, finished, and flat, the underlying tensions, controversies, passions, and problems faced by people throughout history and today disappear. But to be informed and active participants in a democratic society, students need to understand the complexity of the world and the many perspectives involved. Using a critical perspective, students learn that there is not just one way of seeing things, or even two or three. I use the number 17 facetiously to explain this: There are at least 17 ways of understanding reality, and until we have learned to do that, we have only part of the truth.

What do I mean by "17 ways of understanding reality"? I mean that there are multiple perspectives on every issue. But most of us have learned only the "safe" or standard way of interpreting events and issues. Text-books in all subject areas exclude information about unpopular perspectives, or the perspectives of disempowered groups in our society. These are the "lies my teacher told me" to which James Loewen refers in his powerful critique of U.S. history textbooks.[15] For instance, there are few U.S. history texts that assume the perspective of working-class people, although they were and are the backbone of our country. Likewise, the immigrant experience is generally treated as a romantic and successful odyssey rather than the traumatic, wrenching, and often less-than-idyllic situation it was and continues to be for so many. The experiences of non-European immigrants or those forcibly incorporated into the United States are usually presented as if they were identical to the experiences of Europeans, which they have not at all been. We can also be sure that if the perspectives of women were taken seriously, the school curriculum would be altered dramatically. Unless all students develop the skill to see reality from multiple perspectives, not only the perspective of dominant groups, they will continue to think of it as linear and fixed and to think of themselves as passive in making any changes.

According to James Banks, the main goal of a multicultural curriculum is to help students develop decision-making and social action skills.[16] By doing so, students learn to view events and situations from a variety of perspectives. A multicultural approach values diversity and encourages critical thinking, reflection, and action. Through this process, students can be empowered as well. This is the basis of critical pedagogy. Its opposite is what Paulo Freire called "domesticating education," education that emphasizes passivity, acceptance, and submissiveness.[17] According to Freire, education for domestication is a process of "transferring knowledge," whereas education for liberation is one of "transforming action."[18] Liberating education encourages students to take risks, to be curious, and to question. Rather than expecting students to repeat teachers' words, it expects them to seek their own answers.

How are critical pedagogy and multicultural education connected? They are what Geneva Gay has called "mirror images."[19] That is, they

---

[15]James W. Loewen, *Lies my teacher told me: Everything your American history textbook got wrong* (New York: New Press, 1995).

[16]James A. Banks, *Teaching strategies for ethnic studies*, 6th ed. (Boston: Allyn & Bacon, 1997).

[17]Paulo Freire, *The politics of education: Culture, power, and liberation* (South Hadley, MA: Bergin & Garvey, 1985).

[18]Paulo Freire, *Pedagogy of the oppressed*.

[19]Geneva Gay, "Mirror Images on Common Issues: Parallels Between Multicultural Education and Critical Pedagogy." In *Multicultural education, critical pedagogy, and the politics of difference*, edited by Christine E. Sleeter and Peter L. McLaren (Albany, NY: State University of New York Press, 1995), 155–189.

work together, according to Christine Sleeter, as "a form of resistance to dominant modes of schooling."[20] Critical pedagogy acknowledges rather than suppresses cultural and linguistic diversity. It is not simply the transfer of knowledge from teacher to students, even though that knowledge may challenge what students had learned before. For instance, learning about the internment of Japanese Americans during World War II is not in itself critical pedagogy. It only becomes so when students critically analyze different perspectives and use them to understand and act on the inconsistencies they uncover.

A multicultural perspective does not simply operate on the principle of substituting one "truth" or perspective for another. Rather, it reflects on multiple and contradictory perspectives to understand reality more fully. In addition, it uses the understanding gained from reflection to make changes. Teachers and students sometimes need to learn to respect even those viewpoints with which they may disagree, not to teach what is "politically correct" but to have students develop a critical perspective about what they hear, read, or see.

Consider the hypothetical English literature book previously mentioned. Let us say that students and their teacher have decided to review the textbook to determine whether it fairly represents the voices and perspectives of a number of groups. Finding that it does not is in itself a valuable learning experience. But if nothing more is done with this analysis, it remains academic; it becomes more meaningful if used as the basis for further action. Ira Shor has proposed that critical pedagogy is more difficult precisely because it moves beyond academic discourse: "Testing the limits by practicing theory and theorizing practice in a real context is harder and more risky than theorizing theory without a context."[21] In this sense, critical pedagogy takes courage.

In the example of the English textbooks, students might propose that the English department order a more culturally inclusive anthology for the coming year. They might decide to put together their own book, based on literature with a variety of perspectives. Or they might decide to write a letter to the publisher with their suggestions. Critical pedagogy, however, does not mean that there is a linear process from *knowledge* to *reflection* to *action*. If this were the case, it would become yet another mechanistic strategy.

A few examples of how the typical curriculum discourages students from thinking critically, and what this has to do with a multicultural perspective, are in order. In most schools, students learn that Columbus dis-

---

[20]Christine E. Sleeter, *Multicultural education and social activism* (Albany, NY: State University of New York Press), 2.

[21]Ira Shor, *When students have power: Negotiating authority in a critical pedagogy* (Chicago: University of Chicago Press, 1996), 3.

covered America; that the United States was involved in a heroic westward expansion until the twentieth century; that Puerto Ricans were granted U.S. citizenship in 1917; that enslaved Africans were freed by the Emancipation Proclamation in 1863; that the people who made our country great were the financial barons of the previous century; and if they learn anything about it at all, that Japanese Americans were housed in detention camps during World War II for security reasons.

History, as we know, is generally written by the conquerors, not by the vanquished or by those who benefit least in society. The result is history books skewed in the direction of dominant groups in a society. When American Indian people write history books, they generally say that Columbus invaded rather than discovered this land, and that there was no heroic westward expansion but rather an eastern encroachment. Mexican Americans often include references to Aztlán, the legendary land that was overrun by Europeans during this encroachment. Puerto Ricans usually remove the gratuitous word *granted* that appears in so many textbooks and explain that citizenship was instead *imposed*, and it was opposed by even the two houses of the legislature that existed in Puerto Rico in 1917. African Americans tend to describe the active participation of enslaved Africans in their own liberation and they may include such accounts as slave narratives to describe the rebellion and resistance of their people. Working-class people who know their history usually credit laborers rather than Andrew Carnegie with building the country and the economy. And Japanese Americans frequently cite racist hysteria, economic exploitation, and propaganda as major reasons for their evacuation to concentration camps during World War II.

Critical pedagogy is also an exploder of myths. It helps to expose and demystify as well as demythologize some of the truths that we take for granted and to analyze them critically and carefully. Justice for all, equal treatment under the law, and equal educational opportunity, although certainly ideals worth believing in and striving for, are not always a reality. The problem is that we teach them as if they were always real, always true, with no exceptions. Critical pedagogy allows us to have faith in these ideals without uncritically accepting their reality.

Because critical pedagogy is based on the experiences and viewpoints of students, it is by its very nature multicultural. The most successful education is that which begins with the learner and, when using a multicultural perspective, students themselves become the foundation for the curriculum. But a liberating education also takes students beyond their own particular and therefore limited experiences, no matter what their background.

Critical pedagogy is not new, although it has gone by other terms in other times. In our country, precursors to critical pedagogy can be found in the work of African American educators such as Carter Woodson and

W. E. B. DuBois.[22] In Brazil, the historic work of Paulo Freire influenced literacy and liberation movements throughout the world. Even before Freire, critical pedagogy was being practiced in other parts of the world. Many years ago, Sylvia Ashton-Warner, teaching Maori children in New Zealand, found that the curriculum, materials, viewpoints, and pedagogy used with them were all borrowed from the dominant culture.[23] Because Maori children had been failed dismally by New Zealand schools, Ashton-Warner developed a strategy for literacy based on the children's experiences and interests. Calling it an "organic" approach, she taught children how to read by using the words *they* wanted to learn. Each child would bring in a number of new words each day, learn to read them, and then use them in writing. Because her approach was based on what children knew and wanted to know, it was extraordinarily successful. In contrast, basal readers, having nothing to do with their experiences, were mechanistic instruments that imposed severe limitations on the students' creativity and expressiveness.

Other approaches that have successfully used the experiences of students are worth mentioning: the superb preschool curriculum developed by Louise Derman-Sparks and the Anti-Bias Curriculum Task Force is especially noteworthy. Instructional strategies based on students' languages, cultures, families, and communities are also included in wonderful books by Rethinking Schools and NECA. Stephen May's study of the Richmond Road School in New Zealand offers an inspiring example of multicultural education in practice. Catherine Walsh's culturally affirming work with Puerto Rican youngsters is another good example. Ira Shor's descriptions of the work he does in his own college classroom are further proof of the power of critical pedagogy at all levels. Enid Lee, Deborah Menkart, and Margo Okazawa-Rey have developed an exceptional professional development guide for teachers and preservice teachers.[24]

---

[22]See, for instance, Carter G. Woodson, *The miseducation of the Negro* (Washington, DC: Associated Publishers, 1933); W. E. B. DuBois, "Does the Negro need separate schools?" *Journal of Negro Education*, 4, 3 (July 1935), 328–335. For a historical analysis of multicultural education and critical pedagogy, see James A. Banks, "Multicultural Education."

[23]Sylvia Ashton-Warner, *Teacher* (New York: Simon & Schuster, 1963).

[24]See, for example, Louise Derman-Sparks and the A.B.C. Task Force, *Anti-bias curriculum: Tools for empowering young children* (Washington, DC: National Association for the Education of Young Children, 1989); Bill Bigelow, Linda Christensen, Stanley Karp, Barbara Miner, and Bob Peterson (eds.), *Rethinking our classrooms: Teaching for equity and justice* (Milwaukee, WI: Rethinking Schools, 1994); Catherine E. Walsh, *Pedagogy and the struggle for voice: Issues of language, power, and schooling for Puerto Ricans* (New York: Bergin & Garvey, 1991); Stephen May, *Making multicultural education work* (Clevedon, England: Multilingual Matters, 1994); Ira Shor, *When students have power*; Enid Lee, Deborah Menkart, Margo Okazawa-Rey, *Beyond heroes and holidays: A practical guide to K–12 anti-racist, multicultural education and staff development* (Washington, DC: Network of Educators on the Americas [NECA], 1998).

SUMMARY

In this chapter, we defined multicultural education by these seven characteristics:

Antiracist
Basic
Important for all students
Pervasive
Education for social justice
Process
Critical pedagogy

Multicultural education represents a way of rethinking school reform because it responds to many of the problematic factors leading to school underachievement and failure. When implemented comprehensively, multicultural education can transform and enrich the schooling of all young people. Because multicultural education takes into account the cultures, languages, and experiences of all students, it can go beyond the simple transfer of skills to include those attitudes and critical skills that have the potential to empower students for productive and meaningful lives.

This discussion leads us to an intriguing insight: *In the final analysis, multicultural education as defined here is simply good pedagogy.* That is, all good education takes students seriously, uses their experiences as a basis for further learning, and helps them to develop into critical and empowered citizens. What is multicultural about this? To put it simply, in our multicultural society, all good education needs to take into account the diversity of our student body. Multicultural education is good education for a larger number of our students.

Is multicultural education just as necessary in a monocultural society? We might legitimately ask whether even the most ethnically homogeneous society is truly monocultural, given the diversity of social class, language, sexual orientation, physical ability, and other human and social differences present in all societies. Our world is increasingly interdependent, and all students need to understand their role in a global society and not simply in a nation. Multicultural education is a process that goes beyond the changing demographics in a particular country. It is more effective education for a changing world.

CRITICAL QUESTIONS

1. What do you see as the difference between a *broadly conceptualized multicultural education* and multicultural education as defined in terms of "holidays and heroes"?

2. The definition of multicultural education provided in this chapter is just one way of viewing it. How would you define multicultural education and why? After you've defined it for yourself, get together with some of your classmates and do so collectively. How are these definitions different from mine? the same? Why?

3. As a proponent of multicultural education, you have been asked by the school board in your city to make a public presentation on its benefits. One of the issues that board members are certain to question you about is the conflict between multicultural education and the "basics." Prepare a presentation in which you answer these critics.

Alternatively, you can take on the role of a critic of multicultural education and make a presentation to the school board about why the district's current focus on multicultural education is dangerous and wrong-headed. What arguments will you include and why?

4. Your school has just hired a "multicultural teacher." Although you and a group of colleagues supportive of multicultural education wanted a more pervasive presence in the school than simply one teacher, you are on the hiring committee and have decided to use your influence to determine the job qualifications and job description. What should these be?

ACTIVITIES FOR YOUR CLASSROOM

1. Think of some curriculum ideas that conform to the definition of multicultural education as social justice. How might students be engaged through the curriculum to consider and act on issues of social justice? Give specific examples.

2. With a group of colleagues, design an art, science, or math project that builds on multicultural education as critical pedagogy. How would it do this? In what activities would students be involved? How would these activities motivate them to think critically and become empowered?

3. Speak with your students about multicultural education. Do they know what it is? How do they define it? Do they think it's important? Why or why not? What can you learn from this discussion.

COMMUNITY-BASED ACTIVITIES AND ADVOCACY

1. Does your school have a mission statement? If so, is multicultural education included in a substantive way? If it is not, how might you revise it? Work with colleagues in your school or school system to suggest a change

that emphasizes a multicultural perspective. Present it to your school council or to the central school board.

2. Prepare a workshop for the colleagues in your school in which you present the concepts of multicultural education as defined in this chapter. Work with a colleague or group of colleagues to design it. How would you present it? What materials might you include? What ideas would you focus on? If you feel confident enough to present it, consult with your principal about when it might be done.

SUPPLEMENTARY RESOURCES FOR FURTHER REFLECTION AND STUDY

Banks, James A. & Banks, Cherry A. McGee (1995). *Handbook of research on multicultural education*. New York: Macmillan.

Written by many of the best known scholars in the field, this volume includes almost 50 chapters devoted to the history, philosophy, and implications of multicultural education.

Perry, Theresa & Fraser, James W. (1993). *Freedom's plow: Teaching in the multicultural classroom*. New York: Routledge.

This book contains several chapters that provide a critical understanding of multicultural education. See especially the editors' chapter, "Reconstructing schools as multiracial/multicultural democracies: Toward a theoretical perspective" (pp. 3–24).

Spring, Joel (1997). *Deculturalization and the struggle for equality: A brief history of the education of dominated cultures in the United States*, 2nd ed. New York: McGraw-Hill, Inc.

Spring provides short but compelling histories of the education of Native Americans, African Americans, Asian Americans, Mexican Americans, and Puerto Ricans that can help teachers understand the contemporary issues and problems of students from these groups in U.S. schools.

Wheelock, Anne (1998). *Safe to be smart: Building a culture for standards-based reform in the middle grades*. Columbus, OH: National Middle Schools Association.

Wheelock tackles the issue of how "standards" have been used largely to advance economic purposes. She argues instead that schools and teachers should indeed pursue standards-based reform, but for *educational*, not economic, reasons. She provides many examples for doing so at the middle school level.

Chapter 2

Cultural Difference
and Educational Change
in a Sociopolitical Context

INTRODUCTION

Since the early 1980s, many states, cities, towns, and school systems in the United States have been immersed in educational reform. Increasingly, educational reform is also taking place around the world, not just in our own country. Reform has meant everything from instituting block scheduling to developing site-based management teams to requiring high-stakes tests as gatekeepers for graduation. These reforms have had uneven results, and, as usual, poor students and students from nonmajority backgrounds have been the ones most jeopardized.

Multicultural education is equally a world-wide issue, not just a local or national concern. Due to globalization and the rapidly shrinking world, nations throughout the world are experiencing increasing ethnic, racial, and linguistic diversity. But because diversity has played a small or nonexistent part in reforms taking place in schools in the United States and globally, teachers and schools are often at a loss as to what to do about diversity. In the following chapter, I address what educational reform means in the international arena, and I place change in a sociocultural and sociopolitical framework. This chapter includes specific examples of how students' cultural and linguistic diversity can be used as an asset in the service of their learning.

It is sometimes easier to understand one's own situation by stepping back from it temporarily and focusing on other contexts instead. A certain distance gives us a perspective that is missing when we are totally immersed in our own settings. Learning how diversity is addressed in other countries, for example, may leave us upset or indignant about the little attention it is given—that is, until we realize the same thing may be happening in our own school. As you read this chapter, think about examples of diversity in your own school and community, and how they are approached—or not.

Change and reform became the educational buzzwords of the late twentieth century in many countries throughout the world, especially in highly developed industrialized societies with large immigrant populations. What is meant by reform has differed according to the society in which reform initiatives take place and the effect on various populations within particular societies. Given the dramatic demographic changes taking place in many Western societies at the close of the twentieth century, as well as the history of unequal educational opportunities available to culturally dominated and marginalized students within those societies, it is imperative to pay special attention to the meaning of educational change in a sociopolitical context.

In this chapter, I first briefly define what I mean by cultural difference, educational change, and a sociopolitical context. I will also review some of the relevant research and related literature on cultural differences and educational achievement. Specifically, the chapter will address how a positive perception of student diversity can result in successful learning outcomes. The discussion will center on three general areas: culture and its potential influence on student learning; adaptations of curriculum and pedagogy that can foster academic success; and the impact of school policies and practices on achievement. I conclude the chapter with a number of implications for understanding difference in relation to educational reform.

A note about the scope of this chapter is in order. Although the stated purpose of this volume is to review and highlight educational reform within an international perspective, the term *international* is misleading. If indeed we are concerned with educational change on a global scale, we would be dealing with scores of countries. Yet the literature included in most "international" reviews is limited to a few countries, notably Western, technologically advanced societies where those in power are European or of European descent and English is the dominant language. (A conspicuous exception is Japan, which is also often included under the "international" rubric). Given that the majority of accessible literature has been produced by scholars in this handful of countries, it is also the research from which I will draw most of my examples. I want to emphasize, however, that I do not consider this an international focus, but rather one steeped in Western, European traditions of scholarship. Needless to say, much that is important and enlightening concerning educational change will be missing. Nevertheless, even within this very limited framework, there is much that can be learned because most of the countries generally included in the "international" literature (e.g., the United States, Britain, Australia, New Zealand, and Canada) are also highly diverse, multicultural, and multilingual societies, if not in policy at least in reality.

DEFINING KEY CONCEPTS

There are three key concepts that need further explanation in beginning a discussion of the impact of difference in the arena of educational reform. First, cultural difference and educational change will be defined as they are used in this chapter. Also included is a brief definition of sociopolitical context, since it is the lens through which I view and evaluate educational change efforts.

Cultural Difference

Many discussions of cultural difference are based on limited conceptions of culture that take into account only ethnicity, race, and language. This is understandable given the history of the deplorable educational conditions in which students of non-majority cultures are educated, especially in Western societies. Thus, for example, bilingual, multicultural, intercultural, and antiracist education in the United States, Britain, and the rest of Europe have focused on addressing inequities in educational outcomes for those whose ethnicity, race, and/or language are different from the "mainstream" culture (Allan & Hill, 1995; Banks, 1995; Banks & Lynch, 1986; Figueroa, 1995; Hoff, 1995; Moodley, 1995; Pérez-Domínguez, 1995; Santos Rego, 1994; Skutnabb-Kangas & Toukomaa, 1976). For the purpose of this chapter, I define *culture* as the ever-changing values, traditions, social and political relationships, and worldview created and shared by a group of people bound together by a combination of factors (which can include a common history, geographic location, language, social class, and/or religion), and how these are transformed by those who share them (Nieto, 1996, p. 390). Culture includes not only language, ethnicity, and race, but other crucial dimensions such as social class and gender, because they may be key factors in explaining educational achievement. In fact, the problem is that cultural differences are often separated from one another as if this is how they existed in the real world. Yet differences such as race and social class often combine to place Black and other students of color at a disadvantage for learning; the same is true of ethnicity and gender, and of any number of other combinations.

It is important to mention how race and racial differences will be considered in the discussion of cultural differences. Although the concept of *race* as a biological trait that determines behavior and intelligence has been largely abandoned, the existence and persistence of *racism* as both institutional practices and personal bias, and its corollary, White privilege based on White supremacy, cannot be denied (McIntosh, 1988; Weinberg, 1990). Consequently, it is necessary to consider not racial differences *per se*, but rather *how racial differences are socially constructed*. Racial differences are primarily constructed by the larger society, which often perceives them in only negative ways. Therefore, what is important to remember is that race itself is not what makes a difference in people's attitudes, behaviors, and values, but rather how particular racial groups are valued or devalued by society.

In addition, many students classified as "linguistically and culturally diverse" are in fact also from poor or working class backgrounds; thus, the challenge is to understand the impact of poverty and its connection to how particular cultural differences are perceived in the larger society. That is, sometimes children from non-dominant backgrounds suffer academically not simply because their culture is at odds with the culture of power, but *because their schools and teachers are materially ill-equipped to give them an adequate education*. What often happens in such cases is that a singular focus on race, culture, language, or other differences overshadows the effect of the actual dismal conditions in which these children are educated, including dilapidated buildings and scarce resources (Kozol, 1991). These issues are crucial to understand because it is not *simply* the cultural differences of students, and the negative perception of these differences in the larger society, that places students at risk: They are also placed at risk of academic failure because they are simply not given the minimal resources with which to learn.

As a result, poor teaching methods and approaches are often institutionalized as what children "need," and the result is usually watered-down curriculum, a focus on "basic skills" that never progress to more rigorous standards, and low expectations of students. Knapp (1995), reporting on the first large-scale study in the United States of systematic attempts to enrich the educational experiences of students attending schools in high-poverty areas, found that enrichment efforts yield results superior to those of the conventional practices associated with schools of children who live in poverty. The study, which described and analyzed instructional practices in about 140 classrooms located in 15 schools in low-income communities, discovered that meaning-centered strategies were similar to the goals of current reform movements. In terms of diversity, he also found that teachers who connected learning to students' backgrounds were much more likely to be successful in their efforts.

Finally, it is imperative that culture be understood as dynamic rather than fixed, as process instead of just content, and as historically and socially contextualized rather than insulated. Too often, quaint artifacts or isolated ethnic traditions and folklore are the elements by which culture is defined. When this is the case, educational decisions affecting curriculum, pedagogy, and other school practices are not likely to improve academic achievement. Erickson (1990) maintained that this conception of culture actually supports the status quo, leaving little room for transformative practice. In a cogent criticism of the kinds of superficial implementations of multicultural education that are based on an understanding of culture as frozen traditions and fascinating artifacts, he writes, "A serious danger lies in treating cultural traits in isolation, fragmenting and trivializing our understanding of people's lifeways as we freeze them outside time, outside a world of struggle in concrete history" (p. 34). Instead, Erickson (1990) called for a critical understanding of culture that leads to pedagogy that is genuinely transformative rather than "cosmetically relevant" (p. 23).

Educational Change

From the 1980s and continuing into the 1990s, educational change and reform took center stage in the social and political discourse in many countries. How educational change is defined, however, makes a difference in the kinds of initiatives promoted. For instance, based on educational reform policies in six countries, Beare and Boyd (1993) concluded that there is an almost universal trend towards such reforms as school-based management and other efforts that aim primarily at the control and governance of schools and school systems, that is, the *management* of schools. Yet educational change cannot simply be thought of as a "technical process of managerial efficiency" but must also be considered a political process (Hargreaves, Earl, & Ryan, 1996, p. 233). This means that political considerations as well as structures in schools and communities that either promote or inhibit reform need to be taken into account. Furthermore, given the growing influence of governments and businesses on the enterprise of education, an economic imperative has been at the heart of a majority of school reform initiatives (Beare & Boyd, 1993). The outcome of some of the practices that have emerged (such as increased "high-stakes" testing and the further institutionalization of ability grouping) is that schools, teachers, and students have been the primary targets of blame for poor achievement.

Another consequence of the focus on management in educational change is that issues of pedagogy and curriculum become marginalized. Darling-Hammond (1991), in a review of testing legislation in the United States in terms of equity and diversity, concluded that instead of improving learning outcomes, such legislation was having a negative impact on students who were already disproportionately represented among poor achievers in school, especially African American and Latino youngsters.

Similar findings were reported by Corbett and Wilson (1990) concerning the impact of state-wide testing initiatives in Maryland and Pennsylvania. One reason for negative results was that gross inequities in instructional quality, resources, and other support services are conveniently ignored when testing takes precedence over pedagogy; another is that teachers' creativity is diminished when they have to "teach to the test" and are discouraged from implementing more engaging pedagogical practices. Darling-Hammond (1991) found a decline in the use of teaching and learning methods such as student-centered discussions, essay writing, research projects, and laboratory work when standardized tests were required. Furthermore, Fullan and Stiegelbauer (1991) found that there is a tendency in relatively stable communities to promote innovations that do not favor those who are most disadvantaged (what they call the "bias of neglect," p. 58). Given this situation, students who are already facing substantial obstacles to learning are further jeopardized.

In this chapter, *student learning* will be the lens through which educational reform efforts are judged. In contrast to the focus on management and control, relatively little attention in educational policy has been paid directly to student learning. Yet student learning is at the very center of the purpose of schooling, regardless of country or educational system. Generally missing from reform efforts are questions that focus directly on how and to what extent students of diverse backgrounds best learn, and the implications of these questions for academic achievement (Nieto, 1997). Without this kind of inquiry, educational reform can become just an empty exercise in bureaucratic shuffling or can result in the imposition of national policies that have little impact on the actual learning that goes on in classrooms.

Questions about student learning are especially incisive for societies with heterogeneous populations and those with a history of rampant educational failure among those who are most disadvantaged and powerless. How cultural differences are taken into account in teaching and learning, what the sociopolitical implications of difference are, and what educational change means in such settings are crucial questions for consideration.

Sociopolitical Context

School reform with a focus on diversity needs to begin by addressing what is meant by a *sociopolitical context* (Nieto, 1996). A sociopolitical context takes into account the larger societal and political forces in a particular society and the impact they may have on student learning. A sociopolitical context considers issues of *power* and includes discussions of structural inequality based on stratification due to race, social class, gender, ethnicity, and other differences; it also includes the relative respect or disrespect accorded to particular languages and dialects.

School reform strategies that do not acknowledge macro-level disparities are sometimes little more than wishful thinking because they assume that all students begin their educational experiences on a level playing field. In spite of the rhetoric of meritocracy espoused in most democratic countries, social stratification is based on *groups*, not on individuals (Ogbu, 1994). Given this perspective, educational decisions about such policies as ability grouping, testing, curriculum, pedagogy, and which language to use for instruction are also *political* decisions (Freire, 1985). Embedded within all educational decisions are also assumptions about the nature of learning in general, the worthiness and capability of students from different social groups, and the inherent value of languages other than the dominant one. Thus, even seemingly innocent decisions carry an enormous amount of ideological and philosophical weight, and these are in turn communicated to students either directly or indirectly (Cummins, 1989). Furthermore, education remains a gatekeeper to future opportunities for most youth, and these opportunities are influenced by the quality of education to which students have had access. Consequently, educational changes tend to favor the interests of those who are most powerful in a given society (Hargreaves, Earl, & Ryan, 1996). Corson (1993) describes the impact of such policies and practices on students who tend to be the most disadvantaged in societies: "The members of some social groups, as a result, come to believe that their educational failure, rather than coming from their lowly esteemed social or cultural status, results from their natural inability: their lack of giftedness" (p. 11).

CULTURAL DIFFERENCES AND EDUCATIONAL ACHIEVEMENT

How differences are taken into account when educational reform takes place is a central question for researchers and practitioners to consider because cultural diversity is often either ignored or assumptions about the appropriateness of particular policies or pedagogical strategies are primarily based on the dominant culture in a society. Stubbs (1995), writing about England and Wales, could just as well be speaking about numerous other societies when he describes the unstated premise in much of British educational language policy and planning: "the situation of a monolingual majority should be altered as little as possible" (p. 34). That is, the underlying assumption has generally been that assimilation is both desirable and necessary and most educational reform strategies echo this view. On the other hand, relatively little attention has been paid to how cultural differences, in combination with power differentials, affect student learning.

The foundational work of Cole and associates concerning culture and learning is instructive here (Cole, Gay, Glick, & Sharp, 1971). Although this research is over a quarter century old, it holds important lessons for understanding the learning experiences of children of dominated cultures in Western societies. Cole and his associates were particularly interested in discovering why the Kpelle children of north-central Liberia experienced a great deal of difficulty in Western-style mathematics. First, it is necessary to understand that the Kpelle children's Western-style education generally took place in schools that were physically and culturally separated from the towns in which the children lived. Because of the inherent tensions between tribal traditions and Western-style education, these schools were, in the words of the researchers, "a source of culture contact and culture conflict" (p. 51). It is no surprise, then, that Western-style education represented a tremendous challenge to the children in more ways than one.

When Cole and his associates explored the context of the children's educational and home experiences, they found that while the children did indeed have difficulty in some tasks such as measuring lengths, for example, they were more skilled than American children at other tasks, such as estimating various amounts of rice. Rice farming is, of course, central to their culture and involves a network of related activities. However, measuring lengths is a very specific and isolated activity that depends on what is being measured. Consequently, the metric for cloth is different from the metric for sticks. The axiom that people learn to do best those things that are important to them and which they do often was reinforced. Finally, the researchers suggested that culture and cognition cannot be separated: "To study cognition is to study cognitive behavior in a particular situation and the relation of this behavior to other aspects of the culture" (Cole et al., 1971, p. 18).

In another example of the necessity to understand learning within the context in which it takes place, an early analysis of reading failure among Black students in U.S. schools challenged deficit theories about learning. McDermott (1977) suggested that failing to read is "culturally induced" behavior. That is, because of the conflict between the child's culture and the culture of school, McDermott hypothesized that success in reading and success in social interaction with peers are often mutually exclusive. Thus, *learning not to read* was a necessary adaptation to the cultural conflict. This kind of behavior can be defined as *resistance* (Giroux, 1983; Skutnabb-Kangas, 1988), and it is related not only to ethnic cultural differences, but also to power differentials between students, their teachers, and the institution of school. In the words of McDermott (1977),

> The bicultural child must acquire a sometimes mutually exclusive way of knowing how to act appropriately, one way for when Whites are present and another for when the interaction matrix is all Black. Where code shifting is most difficult is apparently in the bureaucratic setting in which the White code, in addition to being the only acceptable medium of information ex-

change, is also the medium for the expression of host group power and host group access to the essential and even luxurious utilities of contemporary America. (p. 17)

Recently this point has been made even more powerfully by Kohl (1994), who has termed resistance a kind of "creative maladjustment." How students, particularly those from culturally dominated groups, resist learning has serious implications for school policies and practices.

A related issue that has emerged in the past several years is that progressive educational strategies are sometimes used uncritically with students from culturally dominated groups. That is, if such strategies are successful with middle-class mainstream students, the assumption is that they will therefore be appropriate for all children. Although their use may be well-intentioned, uncritically adopting such strategies may result in marginalizing those students whose communities have the least power in society. By using the dominant culture as the standard, educational decisions that affect all children are made. This is the case, for instance, with wholesale applications of process approaches to literacy if they do not take into account the diversity of the student population (Delpit, 1995). In reviewing whole language approaches used with linguistically diverse students, Reyes (1992) also critiqued what she calls "one-size-fits-all" approaches that do not consider students' specific cultural or linguistic characteristics. In another example, an early case study of a progressive primary school in Britain found that the assumptions of "open education" actually worked against children with working class backgrounds (Sharp & Green, 1975). When children failed to thrive in such settings, their home backgrounds were blamed, rather than the educational approach that was used with them. As Fullan and Stiegelbauer (1991) pointed out, innovations often fail because *means* become *ends* in themselves, and the fundamental reasons for change are forgotten. This is especially true where marginalized students are concerned.

It is clear from the above examples that race, culture, language, and other differences, although usually acknowledged to be important considerations in educational reform efforts, are in fact often not taken seriously. A growing number of studies, however, are documenting how taking into account cultural and linguistic diversity in educational reform initiatives, whether at macro or micro levels of implementation, can make a real difference in student learning and achievement.

Using Students' Linguistic, Cultural, and Experiential Backgrounds as Resources

The cultural knowledge and experiences of students from disempowered and culturally dominated communities are frequently dismissed or denied in schools. Perhaps an example from a field unrelated to schools can illustrate how this takes place. Based on several years of ethnographic research, Jordan (1989) described the participation of Mayan midwives in government-sponsored training courses in the Yucatán region of Mexico. She found that the courses, for all their good intentions, generally failed. That is, although the midwives received years of training, their day-to-day practice did not change as a result, partly because the teaching strategies to which they were exposed were based on the unstated premise that they had nothing to contribute to their own learning. Teachers thus tended to dismiss the local culture and its values and practices which would have made learning not only more relevant for the midwives, but also might have provided a challenge to the teachers' imperialistic worldview. Jordan concluded,

> The enterprise of teaching and learning, whether it involves midwives, school children, or an industrial work force, is always an enterprise in the service of multiple agendas. Although it is ostensibly about the transmission of knowledge and skills, in a hierarchically organized society it is also always about the imposition, extension and reproduction of lines of power and authority. (p. 925)

It is not too farfetched to apply this description of cultural imperialism in the training of midwives in the Yucatán to the way children's cultures and life-styles are devalued every day in schools, especially in Western pluralist societies. Although the settings are very different, the process is an all-too-familiar one: the cultures and languages of culturally dominated children are often disregarded and replaced within the school setting.

Bourdieu (1977) was instructive in explaining how this process takes place in schools. Because schools primarily reflect the knowledge and values of economically and culturally dominant groups in any society, they validate and reinforce what Bourdieu called the *cultural capital* that students from such groups bring from home. This validation takes place through the curriculum and environment both overtly and covertly in the school setting, and it represents a *symbolic violence* against devalued groups. The cultural model held up for all, however, is not within easy reach of all; that is, only token members of students from less valued groups can achieve it. If even a few members of disempowered groups learn and take on this cultural capital (usually losing their own culture, language, and values along the way), they may succeed in school. Consequently, the myth of the meritocracy in Western societies is maintained.

In spite of the overwhelming influence of dominant cultural capital, recent research on the education of students whose cultures differ from the mainstream has pointed out that using their cultures, languages, and experiences in their education can lead to academic success. This line of research implies that educational reformers need to learn about cultural and linguistic diversity and become aware of how these can influence learning as a first step in understanding the relevance of diversity in change efforts. Otherwise, their judgments about students' educational potential, if based on incomplete or biased assessments of culture, language, social class and other differences, can actually create or reinforce barriers to achievement. That is, reformers' judgments are often based on societal expectations and criteria where one race, language and culture are afforded higher status, and therefore more credibility, than others. Such judgments become, in effect, the guiding principle of some reform initiatives. Bilingual education is a good example. Although mired in contentious debate and controversy in many countries, research results on an international scale are almost unanimous in their conclusion: children from language minority backgrounds benefit from bilingual programs when their native language plays a major role in their instruction. This is the case in countries such as Mexico, Sweden, and Canada (Moorfield, 1987); the Netherlands (Vallen & Stijnen, 1987), the United States (Ramírez, 1991; Thomas & Collier, 1995), and other countries in Europe and Africa (Skutnabb-Kangas, 1988).

Using students' linguistic, cultural, and experiential backgrounds as resources has proven to be effective in their learning. An important study concerning Latino language-minority students in the United States (Lucas, Henze, & Donato, 1990) documented the positive effect of a shared belief among teachers, counselors, and administrators that all students are capable of high levels of learning. When such beliefs permeate the school climate, concomitant changes are made in policies and practices. In the case of the six high schools studied, researchers found eight features that were especially important in promoting the success of the Latino language-minority students in the schools. One of these, a high value placed on students' language and culture, was epitomized by treating their native language ability as an advantage, encouraging them to continue their study of Spanish and staff members to learn it, and promoting in-depth approaches to affirming cultural diversity rather than superficial "one-shot" professional development workshops or decontextualized diversity programs.

In Auckland, New Zealand, the Richmond Road School is another example of using the cultural and linguistic strengths of children to promote their learning. Rather than a focus on what May (1994) called a "benevolent multicultural education," this school has been internationally recognized for implementing a critically conceived approach to diversity in which total school reform is the goal. The school, with a 48% language minority student and staff population, offers bilingual programs in three languages and supports the biliteracy of all its students. In addition, there is a communal and consensual approach to decision-making, an approach based on the recognition of the cultural appropriateness of this approach for the ethnic minority children who attend the school. More important, however, *both* cultural maintenance *and* access to power (through an emphasis on teaching skills needed to live in the wider society) are at the core of the program (May, 1994).

Although the preceding are noteworthy examples that may hold important lessons concerning school reform, there is an inherent problem with using model schools or programs as examples of transformational change because they represent what have been called an "extreme case of the limitations of school improvement" (Hargreaves, Earl, & Ryan, 1996, p. 238). Often, these schools are built on the reputation, charisma, and vision of individual leaders. When such leaders leave the particular school or program they inspired, the changes they started are usually short-lived. Thus, it is necessary to search for examples of educational transformation that do not rely on single individuals. In the words of Hargreaves, Earl, and Ryan, ". . . while we have learned a lot about how to create exceptional islands of improvement, we know less about how to construct archipelagos and still less about how to build whole continents of successful change" (p. 237).

Nevertheless, the above examples may represent an important beginning to reflect on how to view cultural diversity in order to provide more effective learning opportunities for students. The assumption that students' cultural and linguistic backgrounds can be important resources in their learning can be understood within the framework of what have variously been called *culturally compatible, culturally congruent, culturally responsive, bicultural,* or *culturally relevant pedagogy* (Au & Kawakami, 1994; Darder, 1991; Ladson-Billings, 1994; Hollins, King, & Hayman, 1994). These approaches are based on using students' cultures as an important source of their education, particularly in the case of those whose communities have been omitted or denied in the educational setting. There is, of course, no simple panacea for remedying the wholesale academic failure of students from these communities; nevertheless, culturally responsive approaches offer important insights for understanding it. An exploration of how *cultural motifs* can be successfully incorporated in instruction follows.

Using Cultural Motifs

Family and cultural motifs, that is, the use of values, traditions, and themes central to the lives of nondominant groups, have been found to be effective in a number of situations. In effect, bringing the family culture and practices into classroom instructional and curricular processes can benefit the educational experiences, and therefore the academic success, of students. A powerful example of the use of cultural knowledge can be found in the research in the Piedmont Carolinas by Heath (1983). In exploring the language of African American children at home and at school, she found that different family and cultural ways of using language resulted in certain tensions between the children and their mostly White teachers in the classroom. As a result of becoming aware of these differences, teachers began to experiment with different ways of asking questions, thus helping children bridge the gap between their home and school experiences. Consequently, the children's language use in the classroom and their academic success were enhanced.

Another example can be found in the Kamahameha Elementary Education Program (KEEP) in Hawaii (Vogt, Jordan, & Tharp, 1993). Here, the researchers found that certain cultural discontinuities in instruction were a major problem in the poor academic achievement of Native Hawaiian children. The KEEP Program was established to explore remedies for the children's chronic academic underachievement by changing certain educational practices. For example, teachers changed from a purely phonetic approach to one that emphasized comprehension. In addition, heterogeneous groups were substituted for individual work desks, and individual praise was de-emphasized in favor of more indirect and group praise. These changes more closely paralleled the children's cultural styles. For instance, the move from phonics to comprehension allowed the students to use a speech style called the "talk-story," a familiar linguistic event in the Hawaiian community (Vogt, Jordan, & Tharp, 1993). The KEEP Program has had great success, including significant gains in reading achievement.

Deyhle (1995) investigated the lives of Navajo youth in the United States in and out of school. She found that those youths who had little sense of their Navajo identity and who were not accepted by non-Navajos were most at risk for school failure. Thus, the reservation school was more successful than non-Navajo schools because it helped students to affirm and retain their cultural identity. She concluded:

> For Navajo students, one of the most life-affirming strategies is to embrace reservation life and traditional Navajo culture. Indeed, the students in my study who were able to maintain Navajo/reservation connections gained a solid place in Navajo society and were also more successful in the Anglo world at school and workplace. (Deyhle, 1995, p. 404)

In contrast, Hartle-Schutte (1993), highlighting the experiences of four academically successful Navajo students, found that the school system failed to capitalize on their culture and experiences. Their academic success happened *despite*, rather than *because of*, the instructional and assessment practices of the school. In effect, he found that the four students, who were characterized by what are often considered insurmountable "risk factors" such as poverty and language and cultural differences, had literacy experiences at home that helped them to become successful readers.

Another researcher who has explored Indigenous "ways of going to school" among a number of American Indian nations has concluded that Indigenous schools serve an important role as sites of negotiation between cultures in contact (Stairs, 1994). She also found that Indigenous classrooms are different from traditional U.S. classrooms in a number of ways. In Indigenous classrooms, there tends to be more interaction and collaborative learning and peer teaching, less direct questioning of individual students and little performance in front of the class, more personal narratives, closer physical proximity, and many references to community life and culture. Traditional U.S. classrooms can learn a great deal from these examples of the use of cultural motifs, but Stairs warns of the pitfalls of what she calls the "two-column schemes" characterizing Indigenous learners as compared to others. That is, although these descriptions of Native students' learning styles can be helpful, they can also backfire by characterizing these students with fixed traits within rigid boundaries.

Another example of using cultural motifs in education is provided by Abi-Nader (1993) in a description of a classroom of Latino youths in a large, urban high school in the Northeast United States. She found that interactions between the teacher and his students were largely based on Latino cultural values of *familia* (family): that is, the classroom was characterized by a deep sense of support and affection, students developed collective responsibility for one another through such practices as peer tutoring and mentoring, the teacher acted as a family member and friend to the students, and students were encouraged to do well in order to make their families proud of them. The result: unlike the dramatic dropout rates of Latinos in general, which tend to be the highest in the nation (ASPIRA, 1993), up to 65% of the students in this program went on to college.

Why the use of cultural motifs is effective in promoting educational success may be explained by the fact that students from culturally dominated groups receive, if anything, only negative support for their cultures and languages in the school setting. Consequently, because they are under constant attack, their cultural identities become extremely important to these young people (Corson, 1993). An interesting example of this is found in research on Romani youths ("gypsies") in Hungary (Forray & Hegedüs, 1989). Gender expectations of Romani boys and girls tend to be fairly fixed. Yet because the family is often the only place where most culturally dominated students can positively strengthen their self-image, girls may perceive, quite correctly, that breaking free of even limited expectations of their future life options also results in giving up their ethnic identity. Through questionnaires collected from elementary school teachers of Romani children, the researchers concluded that teachers' negative attitudes and behaviors concerning the differential expectations for boys and girls were at least partly responsible for strengthening the expected gender-based behavior among girls in school. It is conceivable that, had teachers been able to develop a more culturally sensitive approach to their behaviors, the children might have felt safe to explore other options without feeling that they were cultural traitors.

The significance of an emphasis on family motifs is that this framework can be used to weave all instructional strategies together in a way that is easily understood by the students because it is part of their ethnic behavior (Bernal, Knight, Ocampo, Garza, & Cota, 1993). It is true that the actual family lives of some students may be quite different from the ideals expressed in the motifs, especially because of the difficult social and political contexts in which they live. Nevertheless, the students' cultures are important to embody in educational programs and approaches because they allow students to see less of a cultural discontinuity between their homes and schools than is normally the case. Tharp (1989) in a review of the school achievement of learners from culturally dominated groups found that schools consistently supported two major practices in all cases of academic achievement: language development, and contextualized instruction, that is, instruction based on students' previous knowledge and experience.

Delgado-Gaitán and Trueba (1991) have commented on the impressive resilience of youths from culturally dominated backgrounds, and their insights hold lessons for the schools these students attend. Reflecting on their ethnographic research on immigrant students in the United States, they state, "The children's talent for integrating values, priorities, and demands from home and school reveals their significant potential for accomplishing their goals in schools and in life in general" (p. 14). The fact that newcomers, despite being young, feeling isolated, and facing what can be a terrifying situation in an unfamiliar environment, can nonetheless incorporate the cultural motifs of disparate values and behaviors speaks well for them. Schools also can learn to incorporate students' cultural motifs into their policies and practices.

IMPLICATIONS OF CULTURAL DIFFERENCES FOR EDUCATIONAL REFORM

In numerous societies, cultural differences have been generally placed within a framework of cultural deficit. As is evident from the above discussion, a growing body of research is suggesting that the very view of *diversity as deficit* needs to be reframed if educational reformers are serious about affording all students an equal opportunity to learn. A number of implications emerge from the reframing of educational reform that includes a reconceptualization of the salience of diversity. Three implications are briefly addressed.

1. Reform Needs to Take Place in Multiple Contexts

It is becoming increasingly clear that substantive changes in education will occur only through reformation of the *entire learning environment*. This includes not only curriculum and materials, but also institutional norms, attitudes and behaviors of staff, counseling services, and the extent to which families are welcomed in schools.

Positive changes in the learning of individual students or the restructuring of particular classrooms and schools are often used as examples of what might be possible if individual teachers, principals, or other administrators take the leadership in promoting educational success (Abi-Nader, 1993; Lucas, Henze, & Donato, 1990; May, 1994). These are meaningful examples because they point out the salutary effects of pedagogical, attitudinal, and structural changes in specific contexts. In addition, they provide classroom- and school-based models that may contain important lessons for other educators. Nonetheless, in spite of the positive changes that may occur as a result of reform at the individual classroom or school level, a sociopolitical framing of education is needed alongside these examples because it underscores the institutional nature of schools. A good example of how particular classrooms are profoundly influenced by the sociopolitical context can be found in research by Gutierrez, Rymes, and Larson (1995). Analyzing a narrative concerning current events in a 9th grade classroom, the researchers pointed out how students were able to insert their "local knowledge" into a teacher's virtually incontestable script. Students' actions helped create the possibility of a "third space," that is, a context in which various cultures, discourses, and knowledge are made available to all classroom participants, and therefore become resources for mediating learning. In effect, the "third space" is an opening in which the classroom can become a site for social change. Without it, classrooms can remain isolated from their sociopolitical context.

To divorce schools from the societies in which they operate is impossible: although schools may with all good intentions attempt to provide learning environments free from oppressive conditions, once students leave the classroom and building, they are again confronted with inequities in their communities and societies. The implication is that educational reform must take place in multiple contexts: classroom, school, district, nationally, and ideologically. Until this happens, isolated stories of individual hope and inspiration may be the best concrete results of reform we can achieve. Although these stories may be impressive catalysts for further educational reform, they leave most students unaffected.

Educational reform must also take place in the context of professional development, where much remains to be done to prepare teachers to work with students of diverse backgrounds (Banks & Lynch, 1986). Because teachers are drawn primarily from the majority culture in most Western societies, and because schools and colleges of education are slow to analyze their own practices critically, both pre-service and in-service education have been slow to change. Even when multicultural and anti-racist education principles and strategies are addressed, there is often fierce resistance on the part of teachers. For example, a study reported by Solomon (1995) on the perspectives of over 1,000 teachers from five school jurisdictions across Canada found that, although teachers expressed the need for content in diversity, many of them nevertheless resented the implication that they were not adequately prepared to teach students of diverse backgrounds. In addition, White teachers resisted inservice programs that focused on race and ethnicity because of the guilt they experienced as a result. Teachers also resisted addressing issues of race and culture because they felt that such discussions were antithetical to harmonious racial relations.

The result of educators' lack of preparation for teaching students of backgrounds different from their own often results in a serious mismatch between teachers' perceptions of their students' abilities and the actual abilities these students may have. Delgado-Gaitán and Trueba (1991), in discussing the education of immigrant students in the United States, describe the situation in this way:

> The best of intentions on the part of teachers cannot compensate for the way that the teachers' education system fails them. Teachers are not prepared for the challenges of teaching children who, from their perspective seem to be failures, when in fact these children possess a wealth of knowledge and skills which can be harnessed and transformed into creative ideas. (p. 136)

At the national level, pronouncements of reform are frequently couched in the discourse of control rather than in the discourse of equality or social justice (Beare & Boyd, 1993). As a consequence, suggested policies are based on a compensatory framework, that is, on compensating for the supposed shortcomings of students. This is certainly the case with transitional bilingual education approaches that, although encouraging the use of native language in instruction, do so only as a bridge to the second language. A more positive view of cultural differences has yet to be articulated in most educational reform national policy statements.

Troyna (1992), a passionate advocate of anti-racist education, argues nevertheless that anti-racist professional development pays insufficient attention to successful change strategies. Reflecting on how one particular school responded to the recommendation that it should prepare policies that declare a commitment to cultural pluralist ideals, he found that such policies are likely to have a limited impact on the practices of schools unless those involved in their implementation also participate in their formulation. He concluded that it is overly deterministic to suppose that not institutionalizing multicultural education derives completely from the unwitting racist attitudes of teachers. For one, this policy implies ignorance and failure on the part of teachers, and teachers in his study found this to be insulting. The result in the school he studied was the articulation of a watered-down principle that basically absolved staff from a commitment to anti-racist pedagogy. Thus, although teachers may indeed collude with a racist system, blaming teachers alone was an unproductive basis on which to develop effective change in school. Consequently, Troyna concluded that the struggle to achieve racial equality in education is much more complex than is generally assumed.

Given the relatively recent development of anti-racist professional development, little attention has been given to its possible impact. One of the few documented studies concerns the effect of an anti-racist professional development course for White teachers (Lawrence & Tatum, 1997). The course, which was taken by a group of forty teachers and administrators, took place in 3-hour sessions over a period of seven months. Taught by a bi-racial team of instructors, the content included topics such as racism, White privilege, and racial identity development, with specific attention given to the role of Whites as "allies" rather than simply as bearing the entire guilt for racism. The researchers were especially interested in whether White teachers' understanding of their own racial identity influenced their thinking and daily classroom practice. Results indicate that in their essays and reflective papers as well as through interviews with the researchers, the course had a profound impact on most of the participants. Especially important was the influence on the participants' behaviors in their classrooms and schools. For example, teachers began discussing race and race-related topics more frequently with their students, they made a conscious effort to include the experiences and histories of people of color in their curriculum, they changed their teaching practices, and they reconceptualized their relations with parents. Although this study is limited by the fact that it was primarily based on self-reported data, it provides some direction for the positive impact that professional development can have on teachers' attitudes and behaviors.

Finally, a profound shift at the ideological level is needed if educational reform is to work. School policies and practices are the living embodiment of a society's underlying values, educational philosophy, and hopes and dreams for its young people. That is to say, policies and practices in schools—whether curriculum, pedagogical strategies, assessment procedures, disciplinary policies, or grouping practices—do not emerge from thin air, but instead are tangible reminders of a society's beliefs, attitudes, and expectations of students. Thus, for example, retention, ability grouping, and testing are policies laden with value judgments about students' capabilities. It is clear to see, then, that a society's ideology can either promote or retard the kind of learning that prepares students for productive and satisfying lives in a multicultural and democratic society. In practice, this implies that schools can serve as models of pluralism and democracy, or conversely, that they can distort the messages of democracy and pluralism that are conveyed in exalted mission statements and idealized treatments of history in school textbooks.

Similarly, issues of institutional power and privilege in society are played out in daily interactions in a school through its policies and practices. Unfortunately, these issues are rarely made part of the public discourse (Fine, 1991; Freire, 1985). Instead, in modern Western industrialized societies, individual merit, ambition, talent, and intelligence are touted as the sole basis of academic success, with little consideration given to the impact of structural inequality based on race, ethnicity, gender, social class, and other differences. Meritocracy, while a worthy ideal, is far from a reality in most cases. As a consequence, students whose difference may relegate them to a subordinated status in society are often blamed for their lack of achievement (Nieto, 1997). Although it is true that individual differences are also important in explaining relative academic success or failure, they must be understood in tandem with the power and privilege of particular groups in society (McIntosh, 1988). What this means at the ideological level is that until societies believe and act according to the belief that all children are worthy and capable of learning, most students of non-dominant groups will be doomed to academic failure.

2. Both Assimilation and Structural Separation as the Goal of Education Need to Be Contested

Western societies have generally responded in one of two ways to the cultural, racial, and linguistic diversity of students in their schools: either they have emphasized the goal of assimilating these students into the dominant cultural group; or they have supported the goal of structural separation of students who are different from the "mainstream." In general, the first strategy has operated in societies where the students are part of an indigenous or enslaved group, or an immigrant group with intentions to remain in the country (as is usually the case in Canada and the United States). The second strategy has usually operated in Western Europe when immigrants are "guest workers" and expected to leave the country after a specific length of stay. In either case, students from culturally dominated communities learn to feel inferior to the mainstream because their differences are perceived in negative ways. In the words of a young Finn educated in Sweden, "When the idea had eaten itself deeply into my soul that it was despicable to be a Finn, I began to feel ashamed of my origins" (Jalava, 1988, p. 164). If cultural and other differences are to be taken into account in substantive reform efforts, both of these goals need to be challenged.

Assimilation of newcomers into the so-called "mainstream" has been a fundamental goal of education in the United States and, to a lesser extent Canada, for the past century. In the United States, the "melting pot" metaphor has been heralded as proof that assimilation works. Assimilation has operated on the assumption that one must lose something in order to gain something else. Thus, linguistic assimilation has meant not only learning the national language, but also forgetting one's native language; cultural assimilation has meant not only learning the new culture, but also learning to eat, dress, talk, think, and behave like those in the dominant group. To go through this process almost certainly means the inevitable loss of a great part of one's identity. Thus, the process itself poses a wrenching dilemma for culturally dominated youths: either assimilate to a homogeneous model, or resist assimilation and in the long run lose out on the educational and other resources that might provide more enriching life options (Skutnabb-Kangas, 1988).

Studies concerned with the importance of cultural maintenance are beginning to challenge the equation *education = assimilation*. For instance, in a study of successful Punjabi students in the United States (Gibson, 1987), the researcher found that parents consistently admonished their children to maintain their culture, making it clear to them that adopting the values and behaviors of the majority group would dishonor their families and communities. Also in the United States, a study of Southeast Asian students found that higher grade point averages correlated with the maintenance of traditional values, ethnic pride, and close social and cultural ties with members of the same group (Rumbaut & Ima, 1987). Elsewhere, similar results have been reached with reference to bilingual education (Baker, 1993).

The inevitable conclusion that maintaining native languages and cultures will help students in their academic achievement turns on its head not only conventional educational philosophy, but also the policies and practices of schools that have done everything possible to eradicate students' culture and language. Rather than attempt to erase culture and language, recent research is suggesting that schools need to do everything in their power to use, affirm, and encourage them as a foundation for academic success. In order to do this, a constructivist model of teaching and learning needs to be in place whereby students and their teachers begin with what students know, rather than with a transmission model which assumes that students know nothing and need to be "filled up" with knowledge (Cummins, 1994; Freire, 1970).

3. Social Justice Needs to Be Placed at the Center of Educational Reform

A final implication when considering cultural diversity as a central concern in educational reform is that social justice must be at the heart of such efforts. As elegantly expressed by Corson, "Working with minority children is often more than a skill; it is an act of cultural fairness" (Corson, 1993, p. 179). Yet it is too often the case that students from culturally disempowered groups are considered objects of pity or scorn. The result is that the kinds of interventions provided are patronizing and partial because they are located within a model of *diversity as deficit*.

By having a social justice perspective at the center of reform approaches, structural and social inequalities that stand in the way of student achievement can be squarely confronted. For example, a social justice perspective forces reformers to consider how youngsters are *disempowered* by schools and society, rather than simply blaming students, their families, communities, and cultural differences for their supposed deficits. During the 1960s, this was the operating assumption, but it was squarely challenged by Ryan (1972) when he coined the phrase "blaming the victim." Ryan turned the argument of cultural deprivation on its head by suggesting:

> We are dealing, it would seem, not so much with culturally deprived children as with culturally depriving schools. And the task to be accomplished is not to revise, amend, and repair deficient children, but to alter and transform the atmosphere and operations of the schools to which we commit these children. (p. 61)

One way in which social justice is placed at the center of reform, whether in individual classrooms or through more broad-based efforts, is by engaging in what Cummins has called *collaborative relations of power* rather than traditional *coercive relations of power* (Cummins, 1994). This approach operates on the assumption that interpersonal and intergroup relations can serve to empower rather than disempower students. Such a process involves challenging the hegemony of the dominant cultural capital as well as redefining the relationships among students, their families, and the schools. In this way, teachers are encouraged to consider the worthwhile contributions and insights that students and their families can bring to the educational experience. This means that everybody can contribute on an equal basis, but all have to undergo some change, not only students and their families (Skutnabb-Kangas, 1990).

Finally, in order for a social justice agenda to have any meaning in educational reform, students themselves need to be involved. In the words of Fullan and Stiegelbauer (1991): "Students, even little ones, are people too. Unless they have some meaningful (to them) role in the enterprise, most educational change, indeed most education, will fail" (p. 170). Numerous examples of student engagement in their own education, and in the design of school policies and policies that affect their learning on a daily basis, confirm that their views are important and necessary ingredients for educational reform (Nieto, 1994).

CONCLUSION

Educational change strategies are often developed with the best of intentions but with little thought given to the enormous diversity of backgrounds and experiences that students bring to their schooling. When this is the case, educational reform tends to be a prescription for the "remedy of diversity" and those students who have been most severely marginalized and alienated from schools tend to be the ones who once again suffer the most. The perception of diversity as an ailment that needs to be cured is based on the view that in order to be successful in school students need to assimilate and accommodate to the dominant culture. While a certain amount of accommodation and adaptation are indeed necessary, a wholesale assimilation may result in promoting even more academic failure among those who differ from the mainstream. Many reform strategies consequently fail to capitalize on student diversity as a strength to be used in the service of learning. Yet all students have talents, skills, insights, and experiences that can be used to promote learning. Educational reform and change strategies need to take these differences into account in a serious way.

REFERENCES

Abi-Nader, J. (1993). Meeting the needs of multicultural classrooms: Family values and the motivation of minority students. In M. J. O'Hair & S. Odell (Eds.), *Diversity and teaching: Teacher education yearbook* (pp. 212–236). Ft. Worth, TX: Harcourt Brace Jovanovich.

Allan, R., & Hill, B. (1995). Multicultural education in Australia: Historical development and current status. In J. A. Banks & C. A. M. Banks (Eds.), *Handbook of research on multicultural education* (pp. 763–777). New York: Macmillan.

ASPIRA Institute for Policy Research. (1993). *Facing the facts: The state of Hispanic education, 1993.* Washington, DC: Author.

Au, K. A., & Kawakami, A. J. (1994). Cultural congruence in instruction. In E. R. Hollins, J. E. King, & W. C. Hayman (Eds.), *Teaching diverse populations: Formulating a knowledge base* (pp. 5–24). Albany: State University of New York Press.

Baker, C. (1993). *Foundations of bilingual education and bilingualism.* Clevedon, U.K.: Multilingual Matters, Inc.

Banks, J. A. (1995). Multicultural education: Historical development, dimensions, and practice. In J. A. Banks & C. A. M. Banks (Eds.), *Handbook of research on multicultural education* (pp. 3–24). New York: Macmillan.

Banks, J. A. & Lynch, J. (Eds.). (1986). *Multicultural education in Western societies.* London: Holt, Rinehart and Winston.

Beare, H., & Boyd, W. L. (Eds.). (1993). *Restructuring schools: An international perspective on the movement to transform the control and performance of schools.* Washington, DC: The Falmer Press.

Bernal, M., Knight, G., Ocampo, K., Garza, C., & Cota, M. (1993). Development of Mexican American identity. In M. Bernal & G. Knight (Eds.), *Ethnic identity formation and transmission among Hispanics and other minorities* (pp. 31–46). Albany: State University of New York Press.

Bourdieu, P. (1977). *Outline of theory and practice.* Cambridge, Eng.: Cambridge University Press.

Cole, M., Gay, J., Glick, J. A., & Sharp, D. W. (1971). *The cultural context of learning and thinking: An exploration in experimental anthropology.* New York: Basic Books.

Corbett, H. D., & Wilson, B. (1990). *Testing, reform, and rebellion.* Norwood, NY: Ablex.

Corson, D. (1993). *Language, minority education and gender: Linking social justice and power.* Clevedon, England: Multilingual Matters, Ltd.

Cummins, J. (1989). *Empowering minority students.* Sacramento, CA: California Association for Bilingual Education.

Cummins, J. (1994). From coercive to collaborative relations of power in the teaching of literacy. In B. M. Ferdman, R-M. Weber, & A. Ramírez, (Eds.), *Literacy across languages and cultures* (pp. 295–330). Albany: State University of New York Press.

Darder, A. (1991). *Culture and power in the classroom: A critical foundation for bicultural education.* New York: Bergin & Garvey.

Darling-Hammond, L. (1991). The implications of testing policy for quality and equality. *Phi Delta Kappan, 73*(3), 220–225.

Delgado-Gaitán, C., & Trueba, H. (1991). *Crossing cultural borders: Education for immigrant families in America.* London: The Falmer Press.

Delpit, L. (1995). *Other people's children: Cultural conflict in the classroom.* New York: The New Press.

Deyhle, D. (1995). Navajo youth and Anglo racism: Cultural integrity and resistance. *Harvard Educational Review, 65*(3), 403–444.

Erickson, F. (1990). Culture, politics, and educational practice. *Educational Foundations, 4*(2), 21–45.

Figueroa, P. (1995). Multicultural education in the United Kingdom: Historical development and current status. In J. A. Banks & C. A. M. Banks (Eds.), *Handbook of research on multicultural education* (pp. 778–800). New York: Macmillan.

Fine, M. (1991). *Framing dropouts: Notes on the politics of an urban high school.* Albany: State University of New York.

Forray, K. R., & Hegedüs, A. T. (1989). Differences in the upbringing and behavior of Romani boys and girls, as seen by teachers. *Journal of Multilingual and Multicultural Development, 10*(6), 515–528.

Freire, P. (1970). *Pedagogy of the oppressed.* New York: Seabury Press.

Freire, P. (1985). *The politics of education: Culture, power, and liberation.* New York: Bergin & Garvey.

Fullan, M. G., & Stiegelbauer, S. (1991). *The new meaning of educational change* (2nd ed.). New York: Teachers College Press.

Gibson, M. A. (1987). The school performance of immigrant minorities: A comparative view. *Anthropology and Education Quarterly, 18*(4), 262–275.

Giroux, H. A. (1983). *Theory and resistance in education: A pedagogy for the opposition.* New York: Bergin & Garvey.

Gutierrez, K., Rymes, B., & Larson, J. (1995). Script, counterscript, and underlife in the classroom: James Brown versus Brown v. Board of Education. *Harvard Educational Review, 65*(3), 445–471.

Hargreaves, A., Earl, L., & Ryan, J. (1996). *Schooling for change: Educating young adolescents for tomorrow's world.* London and Philadelphia: Falmer Press.

Hartle-Schutte, D. (1993). Literacy development in Navajo homes: Does it lead to success in school? *Language Arts, 70*(8), 643–654.

Heath, S. B. (1983). *Ways with words.* New York: Cambridge University Press.

Hoff, G. R. (1995). Multicultural education in Germany: Historical development and current status. In J. A. Banks & C. A. M. Banks (Eds.). *Handbook of research on multicultural education* (pp. 821–838). New York: Macmillan.

Hollins, E. R., King, J. E., & Hayman, W. C. (Eds.). (1994). *Teaching diverse populations: Formulating a knowledge base.* Albany: State University of New York Press.

Jalava, A. (1988). Mother tongue and identity: Nobody could see that I was a Finn. In T. Skutnabb-Kangas & J. Cummins (Eds.), *Minority education: From shame to struggle* (pp. 161–166). Clevedon, Eng: Multilingual Matters.

Jordan, B. (1989). Cosmopolitan obstetrics: Some insights from the training of traditional midwives. *Social Science and Medicine, 28*(9), 925–944.

Knapp, M. S., Shields, P. M., & Turnbull, B. J. (1995). Academic challenge in high-poverty classrooms. *Phi Delta Kappan, 76*(10), 770–776.

Kohl, H. (1994). *'I won't learn from you' and other thoughts on creative maladjustment.* New York: New Press.

Kozol, J. (1991). *Savage inequalities: Children in America's schools.* New York: Crown.

Ladson-Billings, G. (1994). *The dreamkeepers: Successful teachers of African American children.* San Francisco: Jossey-Bass Publishers.

Lawrence, S. M., & Tatum, B. D. (1997). White educators as allies: Moving from awareness to action. In M. Fine, L. Weis, L. Powell, & M. Wong (Eds.), *Off-White: Critical perspectives on race* (pp. 333–342). New York: Routledge.

Lucas, T., Henze, R., & Donato, R. (1990). Promoting the success of Latino language-minority students: An exploratory study of six high schools. *Harvard Educational Review, 60*(3), 315–340.

May, S. (1994). *Making multicultural education work.* Clevedon, Eng.: Multilingual Matters.

McDermott, R. P. (1977). The cultural context of learning to read. In S. F. Wanat (Ed.), *Papers in applied linguistics* (pp. 10–18). Linguistics and Reading Series: 1. Arlington, VA: Center for Applied Linguistics.

McIntosh, P. (1988). *White privilege and male privilege: A personal account of coming to see correspondences through work in women's studies.* Working paper n. 189. Wellesley, MA: Wellesley College Center for Research on Women.

Moodley, K. A. (1995). Multicultural education in Canada: Historical development and current status. In J. A. Banks & C. A. M. Banks (Eds.). *Handbook of research on multicultural education* (pp. 801–820). New York: Macmillan.

Moorfield, J. (1987). Implications for schools of research findings in bilingual education. In W. Hirsch (Ed.), *Living languages* (pp. 31–43). Auckland: Heinemann.

Nieto, S. (1994). Lessons from students on creating a chance to dream. *Harvard Educational Review, 64*(4), 392–426.

Nieto, S. (1996). *Affirming diversity: The sociopolitical context of multicultural education* (2nd ed.). White Plains, NY: Longman Publishers.

Nieto, S. (1997). School reform and student academic achievement: A multicultural perspective. In J. A. Banks & C. A. M. Banks (Eds.), *Multicultural education: Issues and perspectives*, 3rd ed. (pp. 387–407). Boston: Allyn & Bacon.

Ogbu, J. U. (1994). Racial stratification and education in the United States: Why inequality persists. *Teachers College Record, 96*(2), 264–298.

Pérez-Domínguez, S. (1995). The European dimension in education within cultural and ethnic diversity: The challenge of multi-intercultural education. Paper presented at the conference *1996: A Plan for Europe? Politics, Economics, and Culture*, sponsored by the AIESEC International and the Fountainbleau Youth Foundation, Brussels, September, 1995.

Ramírez, J. D. (1991). *Final report: Longitudinal study of structured English immersion strategy early-exit and late-exit transitional bilingual education programs for language minority children*. Washington, DC: Office of Bilingual Education.

Reyes, M. de la Luz (1992). Challenging venerable assumptions: Literacy instruction for linguistically different students. *Harvard Educational Review, 62*, 427–446.

Rumbaut, R. G., & Ima, K. (1987). *The adaptation of Southeast Asian refugee youth: A comparative study*. Final Report. San Diego, CA: Office of Refugee Resettlement.

Ryan, W. (1972). *Blaming the victim*. New York: Vintage Books.

Santos Rego, M. A. (Ed.). (1994). *Teoría y práctica de la educación intercultural*. Universidade de Santiago de Compostela, España: Promociones y publicaciones universitarias.

Sharp, R., & Green, A. (1975). *Education and social control: A study in progressive primary education*. London: Routledge & Kegan Paul.

Skutnabb-Kangas, T. (1988). Multilingualism and the education of minority children. In T. Skutnabb-Kangas & J. Cummins (Eds.), *Minority education: From shame to struggle* (pp. 9–44). Clevedon, Eng.: Multilingual Matters.

Skutnabb-Kangas, T. (1990). Legitimating or delegitimating new forms of racism: The role of the researcher. *Journal of Multilingual and Multicultural Development, 11*(1 & 2), 77–100.

Skutnabb-Kangas, T., & Toukomaa, P. (1976). *Teaching migrant children's mother tongue and learning the language of the host country in the context of the socio-cultural situation of the migrant family*. Helsinki: Finnish National Commission for UNESCO.

Solomon, R. P. (1995). Beyond prescriptive pedagogy: Teacher inservice education for cultural diversity. *Journal of Teacher Education, 46*(4), 251–258.

Stairs, A. (1994). Indigenous ways to go to school: Exploring many visions. *Journal of Multilingual and Multicultural Development, 15*(1), 63–76.

Stubbs, M. (1995). Educational language planning in England and Wales: Multicultural rhetoric and assimilationist assumptions. In O. Garcia & C. Baker (Eds.), *Policy and practice in bilingual education: Extending the foundations* (pp. 25–39). Clevedon, Eng.: Multilingual Matters.

Tharp, R. G. (1989). Psychocultural variables and constants: Effects on teaching and learning in schools. *American Psychologist, 44*(2), 349–359.

Thomas, W. P. and Collier, V. P. (1995). Language-minority student achievement and program effectiveness studies support native language development *NABE News, 18*(8), 5, 12.

Troyna, B. (1992). *Racism and education*. Buckingham: Open University Press.

Vallen, T., & Stijnen, S. (1987). Language and educational success of indigenous and non-indigenous minority students in the Netherlands. *Language and Education, 1*(2), 109–124.

Vogt, L. A., Jordan, C., & Tharp, R. G. (1993). Explaining school failure, producing school success: Two cases. In E. Jacob & C. Jordan (Eds.), *Minority education: Anthropological Perspectives* (pp. 53–65). Norwood, NJ: Ablex.

Weinberg, M. (1990). *Racism in the United States: A comprehensive classified bibliography*. Westport, CT: Greenwood Press.

CRITICAL QUESTIONS

1. What was new for you in this chapter? What did you learn about educational change in other societies? Discuss this question with a classmate and come up with some of the questions you thought about as a result of reading the chapter.

2. Investigate how poverty and cultural diversity interact in the classroom by interviewing some of your fellow teachers about their thoughts concerning children of diverse backgrounds who live in poverty. Present your conclusions and discuss specific examples of how these issues often become intertwined in the minds of teachers. What are the implications of this situation for reform?

3. One of the central implications derived from this chapter is that *educational reform needs to take place in multiple contexts.* Think of a particular educational reform and describe the various contexts in which it should be addressed. How is cultural difference implied within each context?

ACTIVITIES FOR YOUR CLASSROOM

1. Can you apply what you learned in this chapter to your own situation? Use the two general suggestions outlined in the chapter to develop applications for your classroom:

- Using students' linguistic, cultural, and experiential backgrounds as resources;
- Using cultural motifs

2. Develop a long-distance relationship with a classroom in another country. It can be done via the Internet or simply by mail. This can be an enriching activity for students at all grade levels. One of the benefits of establishing correspondence is that students from both schools can begin to challenge the stereotypes they have about one another. For instance, in many countries around the world, children think of "Americans" as only English-speaking and White; similarly children in the United States generally think of other societies as monolithic. Other inaccurate perceptions may also be challenged by this kind of correspondence. For ideas on how to begin, see *Brave new schools* (listed in *Resources*, following).

COMMUNITY-BASED ACTIVITIES AND ADVOCACY

What are the policies and practices at your school that might chiefly jeopardize students of culturally and linguistically diverse backgrounds? How can they be changed? Get together with a group of colleagues in your school (from your grade level or department) and come up with alternatives to these particular practices. Decide on the best way to bring them up (with the principal, at a school council meeting, etc.) and draw up a plan for doing so.

SUPPLEMENTARY RESOURCES FOR FURTHER REFLECTION AND STUDY

Banks, James A. (1995). The historical reconstruction of knowledge about race: Implications for transformative teaching. *Educational Researcher, 24*(2), 15–25.

Banks uses a historical case study of the understanding of race from the late 19th century to the 1940s to document the ways that cultural, political, and historical contexts influence how knowledge is constructed.

Cummins, Jim & Sayers, Dennis (1995). *Brave new schools: Challenging cultural illiteracy*. New York: St. Martin's Press.

In this book, Cummins and Sayers describe a world in which students are connected globally in order to communicate across geographic and cultural borders. Many examples of actual global networks are provided, with suggestions for teachers and parents on beginning such networks with young people.

Fullan, Michael G. with Stiegelbauer, Suzanne (1991). *The new meaning of educational change*, 2nd. ed. New York: Teachers College Press.

The authors consider the question of what has actually changed in practice as a result of educational reform efforts. They pay special attention to the *goal* of reforms, and why this focus needs to be kept in mind.

Lipman, Pauline (1998). *Race, class, and power in school restructuring*. Albany, NY: SUNY.

In this book, based on her extensive study of one school, Lipman chronicles how race, class, and power are often silent but powerful agents in school reform.

We Speak in Many Tongues:
Language Diversity
and Multicultural Education

INTRODUCTION

Linguistic diversity is a fact of life in many countries around the world, including our own. As a matter of fact, if all native Spanish-speakers in the United States were considered a country, it would be the fifth largest Spanish-speaking country in the world, yet our society is also among the most monolingual on the globe, with a great many people able to speak only English. Because it is the language of power, it is possible to remain monolingual in the United States and yet be successful in life. This is not so in many other countries, where being bilingual or multilingual is essential.

Despite the fact that language diversity is obvious everywhere in our nation—from factories to subways to radio and t.v. stations—schools have been slow to catch up to this reality. As a result, there is a stigma to speaking a language other than English, particularly in public (if it is one's native language). Because of the negative pressure to speak only English, children who speak another language and have the potential to become bilingual frequently end up as monolingual speakers of English. Both individually and collectively, we lose a great national resource when this happens.

The field of multicultural education has been slow to embrace linguistic diversity as a central focus of its work. With the exception of a few scholars who have attended to language issues, most treatments of multicultural education do not consider the significance of language in teaching and learning. Yet the growing immigrant and refugee populations in the

United States makes it more apparent than ever that linguistic diversity is a vital component of an overall understanding of diversity.

In this chapter, I analyze language as a major area of diversity in the United States and I address the responsibility that *all* teachers, not just bilingual or ESL teachers, have for teaching students who speak native languages other than English.

The United States is becoming a more multilingual nation than ever, if not in policy, at least in practice. The number of immigrants entering the United States during the 1970s and 1980s was among the largest in history. Between 1981 and 1990 alone, over 7,300,000 people immigrated to the United States legally, increasing immigration by 63% over the previous decade (U.S. Bureau of the Census, 1994). The new immigrants of 1990 equaled in numbers those of the peak immigration decade in U.S. history, 1900 to 1910 (Portes and Rumbaut, 1996), although the percentage was much smaller (14.7%, compared with 7.9% in 1990). Unlike previous immigrants who were overwhelmingly from Europe, about one-third of the newest immigrants were from Asia and another third from Latin America (U.S. Immigration and Naturalization Service, 1995). The growing immigration has resulted in a concomitant increase in the number of people who speak a native language other than English: according to the 1990 Census, almost 32 million people speak a language other than English at home, with almost half of those speaking Spanish. Not coincidentally, the total number of people claiming to speak a language other than English increased from 23 million (11%) in 1980 to almost 32 million (14%) in 1990 (Portes and Rumbaut, 1996).

Notwithstanding the widespread perspective that English is the sole language of communication in our society, U.S. classrooms, communities, and workplaces are very linguistically diverse. For example, of the nearly 46,000,000 students in public and private schools in the United States, over 3,000,000 (7.4%) are limited in their English proficiency (Macías, 1998). Language minority students are no longer confined to large urban school systems but are also found in small town, suburban, and rural schools throughout the nation. This means that all teachers, not just those who specialize in bilingual and ESL education, need to be prepared to teach students of diverse language backgrounds.

The purpose of this chapter is to propose productive ways that teachers and schools can approach linguistic diversity so that they can teach language minority students to high levels of achievement. Rather than continuing to view linguistic diversity as a problem to be corrected, teachers can learn to think of it as an asset for classrooms and society in general. For that reason, I focus on the importance of native and second language development, and on strategies that all teachers—not simply those who specialize in the education of language minority students—can use to teach them effectively.

LANGUAGE DIVERSITY AND MULTICULTURAL EDUCATION: EXPANDING THE FRAMEWORK

To understand language diversity in a comprehensive and positive way, we need to reconceptualize how we view it. This reconceptualization includes:

- perceiving language diversity as a resource rather than as a deficit.
- understanding the key role that language discrimination has played in U.S. educational history.
- placing language diversity within a multicultural education framework and redefining the benefits of linguistic diversity for all students.
- understanding the crucial role of native language development in school achievement.
- making the education of language minority students the responsibility of *all teachers*.

Viewing Bilingualism as a Resource

In the United States, we have generally been socialized to think of language diversity as a negative rather than positive condition (Crawford, 1992). Yet in most other countries in the world, bilingualism and multilingualism are the order of the day. The prestige accorded to language diversity is a highly complex issue that depends on many factors: the country in question, the region of the country one resides in, the language variety spoken, where and when one has learned to speak specific languages, and of course, the race, ethnicity, and class of the speaker. Sometimes bilingualism is highly valued. This is usually the case with those who are formally educated and have status and power in society. At other times, bilingualism is seen as a sign of low status. This is usually the case with those who are poor and powerless within their society, even if they happen to speak a multitude of languages (Fairclough, 1989; Phillipson, 1992; Corson, 1993). It is evident that issues of status and power must be taken into account in reconceptualizing language diversity. This means developing an awareness that privilege, ethnocentrism, and racism are at the core of policies and practices that limit the use of languages other than officially recognized high-status languages allowed in schools and in the society in general. When particular languages are prohibited or denigrated, the voices of those who speak them are silenced and rejected as well.

English is the language of power in the United States. For those who speak it as a native language—especially if they are also at least middle class and have access to formal education—monolingualism is an asset. At times, bilingualism is considered an asset, but commonly only in the case of those who are native English speakers and have learned another language as a *second* language. Those who speak a native language associated with low prestige and limited power—especially if they do not speak English well, or speak it with an accent—are often regarded as deficient. The *kind* of accent one has is also critical. Speaking French with a Parisian accent, for example, may be regarded as a mark of high status in some parts of the country, while speaking Canadian French or Haitian Creole usually is not. Likewise, speaking Castilian Spanish is regarded more positively than speaking Latin American or Caribbean Spanish, which are generally viewed in our society as inferior varieties of the Spanish language.

For some people, then, bilingualism is perceived to be a handicap. This is usually the case with Latino, American Indian, Asian, and other Caribbean students, those who are also the majority of the language-minority students in our classrooms. Linguistically, there is nothing wrong with the languages they speak; for purposes of communication, one language is as valid as any other. But socially and politically, the languages spoken by most language minority students in the United States are accorded low status. Students who speak these languages are perceived to have a problem, and the problem is defined as fluency in a language other than English. In this case, the major purpose of education becomes the elimination of all signs of the native language. Even well-meaning educators may perceive their students' fluency in another language as a handicap to their learning English.

Developing an Awareness of Linguicism

U.S. educational history is replete with examples of language discrimination or what Tove Skutnabb-Kangas (1988) has called *linguicism*. Specifically, she defines linguicism as "ideologies and structures that are used to legitimate, effectuate, and reproduce an unequal division of power and resources (both material and nonmaterial) between groups that are defined on the basis of language" (p. 13). Entire communities, starting with American Indian nations and enslaved African Americans, have been denied the use of their native languages for either communication or education. This is evident in policies that forbid the use of other languages in schools as well as in the lack of equal educational opportunity for youngsters who cannot understand the language of instruction (Crawford, 1992; Cummins, 1996; Spring, 1997). While linguicism has been particularly evident in racially and economically oppressed communities, it has not been limited to these groups historically, but has in fact been a widespread policy with all languages other than English in our society. The massive obliteration of the German language is a case in point. German was almost on a par with English as a language of communication during the 18th and 19th centuries, and was one of the most common languages used in bilingual programs during parts of our history. But the use of German as a language of instruction was effectively terminated by xenophobic policies immediately prior to and after World War I (Crawford, 1992).

The tremendous pressures to conform to an English-only environment meant that giving up one's native language, although a terrible sacrifice, was accepted as a necessary and inevitable price to pay for the benefits of U.S. citizenship. Educators by and large accepted as one of their primary responsibilities the language assimilation of their students. Even today, it is not uncommon to hear of children punished for speaking their native language, or of notes sent home to parents who barely speak English that ask them not to speak their native language with their children. While today there is more of an awareness of the ethnocentrism of such practices, the fact that they continue to exist is an indication of an ingrained reluctance to perceive language diversity in positive terms. In developing a more accurate understanding of language diversity, it is critical to review how language discrimination has been used to disempower those who speak languages other than English. One implication of this understanding is that language diversity needs to be viewed using the lens of educational equity. That is, it is not simply a question of language difference, but rather of power difference. As such, language diversity is a key part of a multicultural education framework.

The Role of Linguistic Diversity in Multicultural Education

Expanding the framework for language diversity means redefining it as part of multicultural education. Just as race, class, and gender are usually considered integral to multicultural education, language diversity—although it does not fit neatly into any of these categories—should also be taken into account. One of the primary goals of multicultural education is to build on the strengths that students bring to school, but even in multicultural education, language diversity is not always considered an asset. Currently, the most enlightened and inclusive frameworks for multicultural education consider the significance of language differences (Banks & Banks,

1995; Macedo & Bartolomé, 1999), but this was not always the case. While it is true that most language minority students in United States schools are also from racial minority and poor backgrounds, language issues cannot be relegated to either racial or class distinctions alone. Language diversity in and of itself needs to be considered an important difference.

The failure of some supporters of multicultural education to seriously consider linguistic diversity, and the inclination of those in bilingual education to view multicultural education simply as a watering down of bilingual and ethnic studies programs, leads to an artificial separation. This separation often results in the perception that multicultural education is for African American and other students of color who speak English, while bilingual education is only for Latino and other students who speak a language other than English as their native language. These perceptions are reinforced by the fact that each of these fields has its own organizations, publications, conferences, political and research agendas, and networks. This kind of specialization is both necessary and desirable because the concerns of each field are sometimes unique. But the implication that bilingual and multicultural education are fundamentally different and unconnected domains denies their common historical roots and complementary goals. As a result, proponents of bilingual and multicultural education sometimes see one another as enemies with distinct objectives and agendas. Ignorance and hostility may arise, with each scrambling for limited resources.

Language is one of the most salient aspects of culture. Hence, the education of language minority students is part and parcel of multicultural education. The fields of bilingual and multicultural education are inextricably connected, both historically and functionally. If the languages students speak, with all their attendant social meanings and affirmations, are either negated or relegated to a secondary position in their schooling, the possibility of school failure is increased. Because language and culture are intimately connected, and because both bilingual and multicultural approaches seek to involve and empower the most vulnerable students in our schools, it is essential that their natural links be fostered.

Native Language and School Achievement

Effective teaching is based on the fact that learning builds on prior knowledge and experiences. But in the case of language minority students, we seem to forget this fact as schools regularly rob students of access to their prior learning through languages other than English. That this process contradicts how learning takes place and the crucial role of language is well articulated by Jim Cummins (1996), who maintains that "there is general agreement among cognitive psychologists that we learn by integrating new input into our existing cognitive structures or schemata. Our prior experience provides the foundation for interpreting new information. No learner is a blank slate" (p. 17).

When teachers and schools disregard language minority students' native languages and cultures, it is generally for what they believe to be good reasons. Schools often link students' English-language proficiency with their prospective economic and social mobility: that is, students who speak a language other than English are viewed as "handicapped" and they are urged, through subtle and direct means, to abandon their native language. The schools ask parents to speak English to their children at home, they punish children for using their native language, or they simply withhold education until the children have learned English sufficiently well, usually in the name of protecting students' futures. The negative impact of these strategies on language minority students is incalculable. For instance, in her research concerning factors that promoted or impeded academic success for Mexican-descent students in a California high school, Margaret Gibson (1995) found that the school environment stressed English-language monolingualism as a goal, in the process overlooking the benefits of bilingualism. Rather than focus on the native language abilities of students, teachers encouraged them to speak English as much as possible to the exclusion of Spanish. Gibson defined this perception on the part of teachers as "English only attitudes" (Gibson, 1995). David Corson (1993) has suggested that when these kinds of attitudes prevail, students quickly pick up disempowering messages: "The members of some social groups, as a result, come to believe that their educational failure, rather than coming from their lowly esteemed social or cultural status, results from their natural inability: their lack of giftedness" (p. 11).

It is sometimes tempting to point to strategies such as English immersion programs as the solution to the educational problems of language minority students. But the lack of English skills alone cannot explain the poor academic achievement of language minority students. Equating English language acquisition with academic achievement is simplistic at best. For example, a large-scale study of the academic achievement of Mexican American and Puerto Rican students of varying English-language abilities concluded that contrary to the conventional wisdom, Spanish was *not* an impediment to achievement. On the contrary, the researchers found that in some cases, *better English proficiency meant lower academic performance* (Adams et al., 1994). In this case, the researchers theorized that peer pressure mitigated the traditional relationship between English proficiency and academic performance.

In contrast to negative perceptions of bilingualism, a good deal of research confirms the positive influence of knowing another language. Native language maintenance can act as a buffer against academic failure by promoting literacy in children's most developed language. This was the conclusion reached by researchers studying the case of Black English, also called *Ebonics* or *Black dialect*: dialect-speaking four-year-olds enrolled in a Head Start program were able to recall more details with greater accuracy when they retold stories in their cultural dialect rather than in standard English (Williams, 1991). Lourdes Díaz Soto's (1997) research concerning Hispanic families of young children with low and high academic achievement found that parents of the higher achieving children provided native-language home environments more often than did the parents of the lower achieving youngsters. Likewise, Patricia Gándara (1995), in analyzing the impressive academic achievements of Mexican American adults who grew up in poverty, found that only 16% of them came from homes where English was the primary language. The largest percentage of these successful adults grew up in households where *only* Spanish was spoken, and a remarkable two-thirds of them began school speaking *only* Spanish. A similar finding was reported by Ana Celia Zentella (1997) in a study of Puerto Rican families in El Barrio, a low-income community in New York City. She found that the most successful students were enrolled in bilingual programs and they were also the most fluent bilinguals. Moreover, in their review of several research studies concerning the adaptation and school achievement of immigrants of various backgrounds, Alejandro Portes and Rubén Rumbaut (1996) came to a striking conclusion: *students with limited bilingualism are far more likely to leave school than those fluent in both languages.* Rather than an impediment to academic achievement, bilingualism can actually promote learning.

Conclusions such as these contradict the common advice given to language minority parents to "speak English with your children at home." Challenging the prevailing wisdom of this advice, Virginia Collier (1995) has suggested that speaking English only at home among students who are more proficient in another language can slow down cognitive development because it is only when parents and their children speak the language they know best that they are working at their "level of cognitive maturity" (p. 14). Catherine Snow (1997), another respected researcher in literacy and language acquisition, agrees, stating that "the greatest contribution immigrant parents can make to their children's success is to ensure they maintain fluency and continue to develop the home language" (p. 29).

The major problem facing language minority children has often been articulated as one of not knowing English. But the real problem may be what Luis Moll (1992, p. 20) has labeled the "obsession with speaking English," as if learning English would solve all the other dilemmas faced by language minority students, including poverty, racism, poorly financed schools, and the lack of access to excellent education. Rather than supporting the suppression or elimination of native language use at home and school, the research reviewed here supports developing and maintaining native language literacy. If this is the case, then the language dominance of students is not the real issue; rather, *the way in which teachers and schools view students' language may have an even greater influence on their achievement.*

Articulating the issue of the education of language minority students in this way leads to the conclusion that language diversity must be placed within a *sociopolitical context.* That is, more consequential than language difference itself are questions of how language diversity and language use are perceived by schools, and whether or not modifications are made in the curriculum. The prevailing view that bilingualism is a deficit for language minority students but an asset for students from wealthy and privileged backgrounds has to do *not* with the relative merits of the different languages involved, but with the sociopolitical context of education. For example, it is not unusual to find in the same high school the seemingly incongruous situation of one group of students having their native language wiped out while another party of students struggles to learn a foreign language in a contrived and artificial setting. There are more affirming approaches to teaching language minority students, and they need to be used more widely than is currently the case.

Approaches to Teaching Language Minority Students

In the United States, most of the pedagogical approaches currently used with students who speak a language other than English are compensatory in nature. That is, they are premised on the assumption that language diversity is an illness that needs to be cured. As a result, traditional approaches emphasize using the native language as little as possible, if at all, and then only as a bridge to English. When English is learned sufficiently well, the reasoning goes, the bridge can be burned and the students are well on their way to achieving academic success.

There are several problems with this reasoning. First, a compensatory approach assumes that students are only *lacking* in something, rather than that they also possess certain skills and talents. Instead of perceiving fluency in another language as an asset to be cherished, it is seen as something that needs repair. In many schools, using native language literacy as a basis for English language development is not considered a viable option. As a result, students are expected to start their education all over again. Not only do they flounder in English, but they often forget their native language in the process. Even when language minority students are in bilingual programs where their native language is used as a medium of instruction, they are frequently removed too quickly and end up in special education classes (Cummins, 1984).

The most common approaches to teaching language minority students in the past quarter century have been ESL (English as a Second Language) and bilingual education, the latter being far more controversial than the former. In spite of the controversy surrounding it, bilingual education and other programs that support native-language use, even if only as a transition to English, are generally more effective than programs such as ESL alone. This is true not only in terms of learning content in the native language, but in learning English as well. This seeming contradiction can be understood if one considers the fact that students in bilingual programs are provided with continued education in content areas along with structured instruction in English. In addition, these programs build on students' previous literacy so that it becomes what W. E. Lambert (1975) has called an *additive* form of bilingual education. *Subtractive* bilingual education, on the other hand, frequently occurs when one language is substituted for another; as a result, true literacy is not achieved in either. This may happen in programs where the students' native language is eliminated and English grammar, phonics, and other language features are taught out of context with the way in which real day-to-day language is used.

There is a substantial relationship between bilingual education and equity. That is, bilingual education is viewed by many language-minority communities as vital to the educational achievement of their children. Although frequently addressed as simply an issue of language, it can be argued that bilingual education is a civil rights issue because it is the only guarantee that children who do not speak English will be provided education in a language they understand. Without it, millions of children may be doomed to educational underachievement and limited occupational choices in the future.

This connection was recognized by the U.S. Supreme Court in 1974. Plaintiffs representing 1,800 Chinese-speaking students sued the San Francisco Unified School District in 1969 for failing to provide students who did not speak English with an equal chance to learn. They lost their case in San Francisco, but by 1974 they had taken it all the way to the Supreme Court. In the landmark *Lau v. Nichols* case, the Court ruled unanimously that the civil rights of students who did not understand the language of instruction were indeed being violated. The Court stated, in part: "There is no equality of treatment merely by providing students with the same facilities, textbooks, teachers, and curriculum; for students who do not understand English are effectively foreclosed from any meaningful education" (*Lau v. Nichols*, 414, U.S. 563, 1974).

Although the decision did not impose any particular remedy, its results were immediate and extensive. By 1975, the Office for Civil Rights and the Department of Health, Education, and Welfare issued a document called "The *Lau* Remedies," which then served as the basis for providing school systems with guidance in identifying students with a limited proficiency in English, assessing their language abilities, and providing appropriate programs. Bilingual programs have been the common remedy in many school systems.

There are numerous program models and definitions of bilingual education (Ovando & Collier, 1998), but in general terms, bilingual education can be defined as *an educational program that involves the use of two languages of instruction at some point in a student's school career.* This definition is broad enough to include many program variations. A primary objective of all bilingual programs is to develop proficiency and literacy in the English language. ESL is an integral and necessary component of all bilingual programs, but when provided in isolation, it is not bilingual education because the child's native language is not used in instruction. While they are learning to communicate in English, students in ESL programs may be languishing in their other subject areas because they do not understand the language of instruction.

Probably the most common model of bilingual education in the United States is the *transitional bilingual education* approach. In this approach, students are taught content area instruction in their native language while also learning English as a second language. As soon as they are thought to be ready to benefit from the monolingual English-language curriculum, they are "exited" or "mainstreamed" out of the program. The rationale behind this model is that native-language services should serve only as a transition to English. Therefore, there is a limit on the time a student may be in a bilingual program, usually three years. *Developmental* or *maintenance bilingual education* is a more comprehensive and long-term model. As in the transitional approach, students receive content area instruction in their native language while learning English as a second language. The difference is that generally no limit is set on the time students can be in the program. The objective is to develop fluency in both languages by using both for instruction.

Two-way bilingual education (Christian, 1994) is a program model that integrates students whose native language is English with students for whom English is a second language. Two-way bilingual programs validate both languages of instruction, and their primary goals are to develop bilingual proficiency, academic achievement, and positive cross-cultural attitudes and behaviors among all students. Students in these programs not only learn through two languages, but they also learn to appreciate the language and culture of others, and to empathize with their peers in the difficult process of developing fluency in a language not their own (Christian et al., 1997). This approach lends itself to cooperative learning and peer tutoring, and it holds the promise of expanding our nation's linguistic resources and improving relationships between majority and minority language groups.

What Works With Language Minority Students?

Research concerning the most effective programs for language minority students points to the benefits of native language development. Students generally need between five and seven years to make a successful transition from their native language to English (Cummins, 1981; Thomas & Collier, 1997). But because bilingual education, and especially native-language instruction, challenges the assimilationist nature of education in our society, it has been the most controversial program. Ironically, when students fail to achieve after being removed from bilingual programs too early, the blame is placed on bilingual programs, rather than on their premature exit from those very programs that could have helped them.

The fact is that bilingual education has generally been found to be more effective than other programs such as ESL alone, even for English language development. This finding has been reiterated in many studies over the years, most recently in a 1998 summary of research conducted by the Center for Research on Education, Diversity, and Excellence (National Association for Bilingual Education, 1998). Even in the anti-bilingual climate of California in 1998, surprising results were found: achievement test scores from San Francisco and San Jose found that students who completed bilingual education generally performed better than native English-speaking children in reading, math, language, and spelling (Asimov, 1998). Many of the gains were impressive. This situation was reported just one month after the passage of Proposition 227, which virtually outlawed the use of bilingual education in the state.

Research by Wayne Thomas and Virginia Collier (1997) has confirmed once again the benefits of bilingual education. In a comprehensive investigation of the records of 700,000 language minority students in five large school systems from 1982 to 1996, the researchers found that language minority students who received bilingual education finished their schooling with average scores that reached or exceeded the 50th national percentile in all content areas. In contrast, language minority students who received even well-implemented ESL-pullout instruction—a very common program type—typically finished school, if they graduated at all, with average scores between the 10th and 18th national percentiles. Thomas and Collier also found that two-way developmental bilingual education was the most successful program model of all. Unfortunately, this is the least common program model in the United States.

Bilingual programs also may have secondary salutary effects, such as motivating students to remain in school rather than dropping out, making school more meaningful, and in general making the school experience more enjoyable. A related phenomenon is that bilingual education may reinforce close relationships among children and their family members, promoting more communication than would be the case if they were instructed solely in English and lost their native language. This is what Lily Wong Fillmore (1991) found through interviews with immigrant parents when their preschool children were placed in English-only settings. Not only did the children lose their first language, but more significantly, they lost the ability to communicate with their parents and families. In the process, they also lost the academic advantage that fluency and literacy in a language would give them when they begin school.

In my own research with academically successful students (Nieto, 2000a), I found that maintaining language and culture were essential in supporting and sustaining academic achievement. In a series of in-depth interviews with linguistically and culturally diverse students, one of the salient features that accounted for school success was a strong-willed determination to hold onto their culture and native language. Although their pride in culture and language was not without conflict, the steadfastness with which they maintained their culture and language in spite of widespread negative messages about them was surprising.

An intriguing conclusion from research on the importance of language and culture on academic achievement is that cultural and linguistic maintenance seem to have a positive impact on academic success. This is obviously not true in all cases, and it cannot be overstated. But the benefits of cultural and linguistic maintenance challenge the "melting pot" ideology that has dominated U.S. schools and society throughout the last century. We can even say that when their language and culture are reinforced both at home and school, students seem to develop less confusion and ambiguity about their ability to learn. Regardless of the sometimes harsh attacks on their culture and language—as is the case in communities that have strident campaigns to pass English-only legislation—students whose language and culture are valued in the school setting pick up affirming messages about their worth. The notion that assimilation is a necessary prerequisite for success in school and society is severely tested by current research.

In spite of the evidence that some form of bilingual education is most effective for teaching language minority students, most students who could benefit are not in such programs. This is due to both political and pragmatic considerations. For one, in many school systems, there are not enough trained teachers for such programs. In addition, the numbers of students who speak the same language is generally too small to require an entire program. Furthermore, the segregation that bilingual education presupposes poses a genuine dilemma. It is also true, however, that every bilingual program has numerous opportunities for integrating students more meaningfully than is currently the case. Moreover, the bilingual program can be more structurally integrated into the school instead of separated in a wing of the building so that teachers from both bilingual and nonbilingual classrooms can work on collaborative projects with their students. This kind of collaboration does not happen often enough. Besides being physically separated from other teachers—often in the basement, an apt metaphor (Nieto, 2000b)—bilingual teachers bear the burden of the "bilingual" label in the same way as their students: They may be seen as less intelligent, less academically prepared, and less able than nonbilingual teachers—this in spite of the fact that they are usually fluent in two languages and have a wide range of pedagogical approaches for teaching a diverse student body. Because many bilingual teachers are from the same cultural and linguistic backgrounds as the students they teach, they bring a necessary element of diversity into the school. But many schools have not found a way to benefit from their presence.

Two-way bilingual programs provide another opportunity for integration and enhanced academic achievement for all students. For example, research on a Spanish–English two-way program in Cambridge, Massachusetts, found both groups of children progressing well in all subject matters and neither group declining in its native language development. Researchers also found that children at all grade levels selected their best friend without an ethnic or racial bias, that the self-esteem of children from both groups was enhanced, and that there was much less segregation than before the program—all worthy social and educational goals (Cazabon, Lambert, & Hall, 1993). But two-way bilingual education is not always an option. This is because not all languages have the same appeal of Spanish, which is spoken in many places in the world, for English-speaking students and their families.

Other approaches for integrating students of diverse language backgrounds include setting aside times for joint instruction and developing bilingual options in desegregation plans and magnet schools. But much remains to be done in expanding options such as these. Perhaps the most noteworthy change that can take place is a shift in thinking so that bilingual classrooms, teachers, and students are seen as rich resources for nonbilingual classrooms, teachers, and students. When this shift happens, schools will have taken the first step in making bilingualism and even multilingualism central educational goals for all students. This is hardly the case right now. On the contrary, English language acquisition for language minority students is often pursued at the expense of native language development. Even for monolingual English students, the goal of bilingualism is an elusive one because foreign language courses are ineffective in that they are usually delayed until secondary school. But if language diversity were to become an option for all students, the low status and persistent underfunding of bilingual education might be eliminated.

IMPLICATIONS FOR TEACHING LANGUAGE MINORITY STUDENTS

The dramatic increase in the number of language minority students in our country in the past three decades means that every classroom in every city and town has already been or will soon be affected. The responsibility for educating language minority students can no longer fall only on those teachers who have been trained specifically to provide bilingual education and ESL services; this responsibility needs to be shared by *all* teachers and *all* schools. Yet most teachers have had little training in language acquisition and other language-related issues: even in bilingual classrooms, only 10% of teachers serving English language learners are certified in bilingual education (August & Hakuta, 1998).

In what follows, I suggest a number of steps that all educators can take to more effectively educate language minority students. But first let me emphasize that while learning new approaches and techniques may be very helpful, *teaching language minority students successfully means above all changing one's attitudes towards the students, their languages and cultures, and their communities* (Cummins, 1996; Nieto, 1999). Having said this, however, there are necessary bodies of knowledge and approaches that all teachers need to develop if they are to be successful with the growing number of language minority students in our schools: (1) All teachers need to understand how language is learned. (2) Teachers need to develop an additive perspective concerning bilingualism. (3) Teachers and schools can learn to consciously foster native language literacy.

All Teachers Need to Understand How Language Is Learned

This includes both native and subsequent languages. For example, Stephen Krashen's (1981) theories of second language acquisition and his recommendations that teachers provide students for whom English is a second language with *comprehensible input* by including engaging and contextualized cues in their instruction is useful for all teachers who have language minority students in their classrooms. Likewise, related knowledge in curriculum and instruction, linguistics, sociology, and history are all critical for teachers of language minority students.

The following suggestions should be helpful for all teachers. (For a more detailed discussion, see Nieto, 2000b).

- first and second language acquisition.
- the sociocultural and sociopolitical context of education for language minority students.
- the history of immigration in the United States, with particular attention to language policies and practices throughout that history.
- the history and experiences of specific groups of people, especially those who are residents of the city, town, and state where they are teaching.
- the ability to adapt curriculum for students whose first language is other than English.
- competence in pedagogical approaches suitable for culturally and linguistically heterogeneous classrooms.
- experience with teachers of diverse backgrounds and the ability to develop collaborative relationships with colleagues that promote the learning of language minority students.
- the ability to communicate effectively with parents of diverse language, culture, and social class backgrounds.

Because many teachers have not had access to this kind of knowledge during their teacher preparation, they may need to acquire it on their own. They can do this by attending conferences in literacy, bilingual education, multicultural education, and ESL; participating in professional development opportunities in their district and beyond; subscribing to journals and newsletters in these fields; setting up study groups with colleagues to discuss and practice different strategies; and returning to graduate school to take relevant courses or seek advanced degrees.

Teachers Need to Develop an Additive Perspective Concerning Bilingualism

An additive perspective (Lambert, 1975) is radically different from the traditional expectation that immigrants need to exchange their native language for their new language, English. The terrible psychic costs of abandoning one's native language, not to mention the concurrent loss of linguistic resources to the nation, is now being questioned. An additive bilingualism supports the notion that English *plus* other languages can make us stronger individually and as a society.

In their research, María Fránquiz and María de la luz Reyes (1998) set out to answer the question, "If I am not fluent in the languages my students speak, how can I effectively teach English language arts to a linguistically diverse class?" They found that teachers do not have to be fluent in the native languages of their students to support their use in the classroom. Rather, they discovered that encouraging students to use their native languages and cultural knowledge as resources for learning is frequently more important than knowing the students' languages. What does this mean in practice? In their research, Fránquiz and Reyes provide examples of teachers "who are not paralyzed by their own monolingualism" (p. 217). They document, for example, the positive results of teachers' acceptance of a range of language registers and codes, from standard to more colloquial forms of speech, and from monolingual to more mixed language speech. These language forms are often prohibited in classroom discourse, but allowing them to flourish is a way of using students' current knowledge to build future knowledge.

Teachers and Schools Can Learn to Consciously Foster Native Language Literacy

Teachers can actively support the native language literacy of their students by providing them the time and space to work with their peers, or with tutors or mentors, who speak the same native language. In her work with immigrant students, for instance, Cristina Igoa (1995) reserves the last period of the day three times a week for students to listen to stories or to read in their native languages. Because she does not speak all the languages of her students who come from numerous language backgrounds, she recruits college students who are fluent in various languages to help out.

Teachers can also make a commitment to learn at least one of the languages of their students. When they become second language learners, teachers develop a new appreciation for the struggles experienced by language minority students—including exhaustion, frustration, and withdrawal—when they are learning English. This was what happened to Bill Dunn, a doctoral student of mine and a veteran teacher who decided to "come out of the closet as a Spanish speaker" (Nieto, 1999). He realized that, after teaching for 20 years in a largely Puerto Rican community, he understood a great deal of Spanish, so he decided to study it formally and to keep a journal of his experiences. Although he had always been a wonderful and caring teacher, putting himself in the place of his students helped him understand a great many things more clearly, from students' grammatical errors in English to their boredom and misbehavior when they could not understand the language of instruction.

The responsibility to create excellent learning environments for language minority students should not rest with individual teachers alone, however. Entire schools can develop such environments. Catherine Minicucci and her associates (1995) analyzed eight exemplary school reform efforts for language minority students and they found that all of the schools shared the following common characteristics, among others:

- They had a schoolwide vision of excellence that incorporated students of limited English proficiency.
- They created a community of learners engaged in active discovery.
- They designed programs to develop both the English and native-language skills of language minority students.
- They made a conscious effort to recruit and hire bilingual staff members.
- They communicated frequently with parents in their native languages.
- They honored the multicultural quality of the student population.

The researchers concluded that the success of schools with these attributes challenges the conventional assumption that students need to learn English *before* they can learn grade-level content in social studies, math, or anything else.

CONCLUSION

Language is one of the fundamentals signs of our humanity. It is "the palette from which people color their lives and culture" (Allman, 1990). Although linguistic diversity is a fact of life in American schools and society, many languages are not accorded the respect and visibility they deserve. But given recent trends in immigration, the shrinking of our world, and the subsequent necessity to learn to communicate with larger numbers of people, a reconceptualization of the role of languages other than English in our schools and society is in order. Given this kind of reconceptualization, current school policies and practices need to be reexamined. Those that build on students' diversity need to be strengthened, while those that focus on differences as deficits must be eliminated. This means, at the very least, that bilingual and multicultural programs for all students have to be comprehensively defined, adequately funded, and strongly supported.

The issue of what to do about language minority students goes much deeper than simple language diversity. Above all, it is an issue of educational equity. Whether bilingual education, ESL, or other approaches and support services are offered, they need to be developed with an eye toward promoting, rather than limiting, educational opportunities for all students. Given the increasing number of students who enter schools speaking a native language other than English, it is clear that attending to the unique condition of language minority students is the responsibility of all educators. For students with limited English proficiency, suitable approaches geared to their particular situation are not frills, but basic education. For English monolingual students, too, learning to appreciate and communicate in other languages is a gift to be cherished. When we approach language diversity as a resource that is respected and fostered, all students benefit.

REFERENCES

Adams, D., Astone, B., Nuñez-Wormack, E., & Smodlaka, I. (1994). Predicting the academic achievement of Puerto Rican and Mexican-American ninth-grade students. *The Urban Review, 26*(1), 1–14.

Allman, W. F. (1990, November 5). The mother tongue. *U.S. News and World Report.*

Asimov, N. (1998, July 7). Bilingual surprise in state testing. *San Francisco Chronicle*, A1.

August, D., & Hakuta, K. (Eds.) (1998). *Educating language-minority children.* Commission on Behavioral and Social Sciences and Education, National Research Council, Institute of Medicine. Washington, DC: National Academy Press.

Banks, J. A., & Banks, C. A. M. (Eds.) (1995). *Handbook of research on multicultural education.* New York: Macmillan.

Cazabon, M., Lambert, W. E., & Hall, G. (1993). *Two-way bilingual education: A progress report on the Amigos Program.* Santa Cruz, CA: National Center for Research in Cultural Diversity and Second Language Learning.

Christian, D. (1994). *Two-way bilingual education: Students learning through two languages.* Santa Cruz, CA: National Center for Research on Cultural Diversity and Second Language Learning.

Christian, D., Montone, C., Lindholm, K. J., & Carranza, I. (1997). *Profiles in two-way immersion education.* McHenry, IL: Delta Systems.

Collier, V. P. (1995). *Promoting academic success for ESL students: Understanding second language acquisition at school.* Elizabeth, NJ: New Jersey Teachers of English to Speakers of Other Languages–Bilingual Educators.

Corson, D. (1993). *Language, minority education and gender: Linking social justice and power.* Clevedon, Eng.: Multilingual Matters.

Crawford, J. (1992). *Hold your tongue: Bilingualism and the politics of "English only."* Reading, MA: Addison-Wesley.

Cummins, J. (1981). The role of primary language development in promoting educational success for language minority students. In Office of Bilingual Bicultural Education, *Schooling and language minority students: A theoretical framework.* Sacramento, CA: Evaluation, Dissemination, and Assessment Center, California State University, Los Angeles.

Cummins, J. (1984). *Bilingualism and special education.* Clevedon, Eng.: Multilingual Matters.

Cummins, J. (1996). *Negotiating identities: Education for empowerment in a diverse society.* Ontario: California Association for Bilingual Education.

Fairclough, N. (1989). *Language and power.* New York: Longman.

Fránquiz, M. E., & de la luz Reyes, M. (1998). Creating inclusive learning communities through English language arts: From *chanclas* to *canicas. Language Arts, 75*(3), 211–220.

Gándara, P. (1995). *Over the ivy walls: The educational mobility of low-income Chicanos.* Albany: State University of New York Press.

Gibson, M. A. (1995). Perspectives on acculturation and school performance. *Focus on Diversity* (Newsletter of the National Center for Research on Cultural Diversity and Second Language Learning), *5*(3), 8–10.

Igoa, C. (1995). *The inner world of the immigrant child*. New York: St. Martin's.

Krashen, S. (1981). *Second language acquisition and second language learning*. New York: Pergamon.

Lambert, W. E. (1975). Culture and language as factors in learning and education. In A. Wolfgang (Ed.), *Education of immigrant students*. Toronto: OISE.

Lau v. Nichols, 414 U.S. 563 (1974).

Macedo, D., & Bartolomé, L. I. (1999). *Dancing with bigotry: Beyond the politics of difference*. New York: St. Martin's.

Macías, R. R., et al. (1998). *Summary report of the survey of the states' limited English proficient students and available educational programs and services, 1996–97*. Washington, DC: National Clearinghouse of Bilingual Education.

Minicucci, C., Berman, P., McLaughlin, B., McLeod, B., Nelson, B., & Woodworth, K. (1995). School reform and student diversity. *Phi Delta Kappan, 77*(1), 77–80.

Moll, L. C. (1992). Bilingual classroom studies and community analysis: Some recent trends. *Educational Researcher, 21*(2), 20–24.

National Association for Bilingual Education. (1998, May 1). Findings of the effectiveness of bilingual education. *NABE News*, 5.

Nieto, S. (1999). *The light in their eyes: Creating multicultural learning communities*. New York: Teachers College Press.

Nieto, S. (2000a). *Affirming diversity: The sociopolitical context of multicultural education* (3rd ed.). New York: Longman.

Nieto, S. (2000b). Bringing bilingual education out of the basement, and other imperatives for teacher education. In Z. Beykont (Ed.), *Lifting every voice: Pedagogy and politics of bilingual education* (pp. 187–207). Cambridge, MA: Harvard Education Publishing Group.

Ovando, C. J., & Collier, V. P. (1998). *Bilingual and ESL classrooms: Teaching in multicultural contexts* (2nd ed.). New York: McGraw-Hill.

Phillipson, R. (1992). *Linguistic imperialism*. Oxford, Eng: Oxford University Press.

Portes, A., & Rumbaut, R. G. (1996). *Immigrant America: A portrait* (2nd ed.). Berkeley: University of California Press.

Skutnabb-Kangas, T. (1988). Multilingualism and the education of minority children. In T. Skutnabb-Kangas & J. Cummins (Eds.), *Minority language: From shame to struggle* (pp. 9–44). Clevedon, Eng.: Multilingual Matters.

Snow, C. (1997). The myths around bilingual education. *NABE News, 21*(2), 29.

Soto, L. D. (1997). *Language, culture, and power: Bilingual families and the struggle for quality education*. Albany: State University of New York Press.

Spring, J. (1997). *Deculturization and the struggle for equality: A brief history of the education of dominated cultures in the United States* (2nd ed.). New York: McGraw-Hill.

Thomas, W. P., & Collier, V. P. (1997). *School effectiveness for language minority students*. Washington, DC: National Clearinghouse for Bilingual Education.

U.S. Bureau of the Census. (1994). *Statistical abstract of the United States* (114th ed, p. 11). Washington, DC: U.S. Government Printing Office.

U.S. Immigration and Naturalization Service. (1995). *Statistical yearbook of the immigration and naturalization service*. Washington, DC: U.S. Government Printing Office.

Williams, S. W. (1991). Classroom use of African American Language: Educational tool or social weapon? In C. E. Sleeter (Ed.), *Empowerment through multicultural education* (pp. 199–215). Albany: State University of New York Press.

Wong Fillmore, L. (1991). When learning a second language means losing the first. *Early Childhood Research Quarterly, 6*, 323–346.

Zentella, Ana Celia (1997). *Growing up bilingual: Puerto Rican children in New York*. Malden, MA: Blackwell.

CRITICAL QUESTIONS

1. Research the "English-Only" movement. Do you consider it an example of linguicism? Why or why not?

2. The argument that "My folks made it without bilingual education; why give other folks special treatment?" has often been made, particularly by descendants of European American immigrants. Do you think this is a compelling argument? Why or why not? (You may want to do some research on the "Nativist Movement" of the nineteenth century as background for this discussion).

3. If you were the principal of a school with a large population of language-minority students, what would you do to address this situation? What if you were a parent of one of those children? or a teacher? If you were one of the students, what kind of help might you want?

4. What preparation have you had to teach students of linguistically diverse backgrounds in your teacher education program? What would you like to have learned? What would most have helped you be effective with students who speak languages other than English?

COMMUNITY-BASED ADVOCACY

What are the policies and practices concerning language minority students in your school? How could language minority students be better served? Along with a group of interested parents and teachers, think about policies and practices that would be most appropriate and beneficial for these students (and that might also benefit English-speaking monolingual students). Draw up a list of suggestions that you can give to the school council, parent group, or principal.

SUPPLEMENTARY RESOURCES FOR FURTHER REFLECTION AND STUDY

Corson, David (1993). *Language, minority education and gender: Linking social justice and power*. Clevedon, England: Multilingual Matters Ltd.

    The author links issues of language with ethnicity and gender in a substantive way, and discusses why teachers need to understand them within a social justice framework.

Krashen, Stephen (1996). *Under attack: The case against bilingual education*. Culver City, CA: Language Education Associates.

In this short monograph, the author presents a comprehensive and lively counterpoint to arguments against bilingual education.

Portes, Alejandro & Rumbaut, Rubén G. (1996). *Immigrant America: A portrait*, 2nd ed. University of California Press.

In this extensively documented text, the authors describe the changing demographics of the United States by analyzing the rapidly growing immigrant population as well as research that has been done about it.

Part II

IDENTITY AND BELONGING

One might well ask what a student's identity has to do with learning. After all, isn't learning neutral with respect to students' ethnicities and native languages? Although many approaches to learning have been based on just such a universal approach, the previous chapters have made clear that students' identities and whether they are acknowledged, respected, or dismissed can indeed be noteworthy factors in promoting or hindering learning. As much as we may resist the idea, students' identities play a role in whether they are welcomed or rejected as learners in our schools.

The chapters that follow center on identity and belonging as key issues in learning and teaching. Chapter 4 tackles the complex question of what it means to be an American and why the question is a meaningful one for teachers to ponder. Chapter 5 is based on research I did a number of years ago on young peoples' responses to interviews that centered on culture, identity, and learning. Young people of diverse backgrounds have many lessons for teachers and schools, and these lessons have implications that reach far beyond their own identities. In Chapter 6, I discuss what it means to "write for real" by reflecting on using the experiences of students' "words and worlds."

On Becoming American:
An Exploratory Essay

INTRODUCTION

The question I pose in this chapter began as a personal quandary. It is a question I have thought about for my entire life, and one that I am still answering. If this is the case for me—a seasoned, self-confident, and highly educated professional—it is even more true for young people who frequently feel isolated and marginalized in schools because of their very identities. For them, "becoming American" very often means abandoning their families and forgetting their past. But as I make clear in this chapter, "either–or" responses can be limiting and destructive, not just for the young people involved but for our society in general. These are excruciating choices that we are asking young people to make. In the essay you are about to read, I ask educators to think of a better and more humane way to bring young people, and all newcomers, into the fold.

Many of us come from an immigrant past. All others in our country were either brought here by force, as in the case with African Americans, or, in the case of Native Americans and Mexican Americans, colonized within their own land. Yet the memories and stories of our past are frequently silenced as we travel through the generations. This historical amnesia is especially true for those of European descent, the people who make up the great majority of teachers in our public schools today. If teachers are to develop vital relationships with their students of culturally and linguistically diverse backgrounds, they need to at the very least try to understand what it is like to be an "outsider" and how the pressures to conform weigh heavily on them. One way to do this is by uncovering some of the stories and memories that have been long forgotten, another suggestion I make in the chapter that follows.

What does it mean to be an American? This is in some ways the quintessential American dilemma, yet it has not historically invited a deep or sustained critical analysis. In spite of repeated attempts to answer the question throughout the successive generations of both newcomers and old-timers that have characterized the building of our nation, either easy speculation or pat answers have been the usual result. Why is this? For one, there is in place an unstated assumption of what it means to be an American; for another, questioning the assumed definition seems almost heretical because a number of troubling contradictions challenge the taken-for-granted definition. Yet for many, it is a deeply troubling issue that, it seems to me, is at the root of much of the continuing disunity in our country.

The question of becoming an American is one that has haunted me for many years, but until recently I have not focused on it in any deliberate or conscious way. My intense fascination with this question is motivated by my own background: Even though I was born in this country and have spent my entire life here, even though I was formed and educated and lead a productive professional life in the United States, when I am asked the inevitable question, "What are you?" I always answer "Puerto Rican." Why is it that for me being an American seems inherently to conflict with being a Puerto Rican? Ironically, I myself recognize that I am in some ways undeniably American; that is, my experiences, tastes, and even values immediately define me to most onlookers as "American," albeit with a deep connection to my Puerto Rican heritage. Several years ago, I was jarred when speaking with an island-born Puerto Rican who commented that he could tell at first glance that I was born and raised in the United States simply by looking at my body language! Here I was, convinced that I was as Puerto Rican as any Puerto Rican, that I had *"la mancha del plátano"* (the stain of the plantain) firmly imprinted on my face and body, and yet he saw my American roots through it all.

I must also admit that the unprecedented opportunities I have been given in the United States have made it possible for me to far transcend what my possibilities might have been had I not been raised and educated here. Although it is true that these opportunities are not held out to the majority of Puerto Ricans, among many others, and that our society has a long way to go before fulfilling its ideals of equal access and opportunity for all, it is nevertheless true that the fact that the ideals exist *at all* has made a dramatic difference in the lives of many people. My life as a fairly successful academic, teacher, and writer would probably have been impossible if I had been raised on the island in the working-class family with little formal education from which I came. Yet I resist being defined as

American, and this is troubling for me because on some deep level I understand that I deserve the right to claim this identity if I mean to work to change what it means.

I am not alone in the quandary concerning my identity. I have met a great many people over the years who have similar feelings. Many of us who are what can be called "bicultural" (not necessarily because we have chosen to be so, but because of our circumstances) have faced the same dilemma (Darder, 1991). Is one an American by the mere fact of being born here? Can one be born elsewhere and still be an American? How many generations does it take? Do we belong here or there, in neither place, or in both? Does being an American have to erase or diminish automatically our accents, our values, our hues and textures? Where does our language, which sometimes is unacceptable both in our communities of origin and in the larger society, fit in? Do we have to "trade in" our identity, much as we would an old car, to acquire the shiny new image of American? How can we reconcile the sometimes dramatically differing value systems, languages, expectations of appropriate behavior, and the contradictory activities that take place in our everyday lives?

The question of identity is reverberating with more meaning and currency than ever in the twenty-first century. Our nation is becoming more diverse and also more divided along lines of race, ethnicity, language use, social class, and other differences, although it can be argued that this division is not due necessarily to our growing diversity but rather to our inability to deal with it. Addressing issues that arise as a result of increased diversity demands both insight and care rather than arrogance and simplistic notions of unity. It is my purpose in this exploratory essay to reflect on the question of what it means to be, or as I have stated it in the title of this chapter, to *become* American, not only as it might be answered in a personal way for me, but also how as a society we might think about it.

DICHOTOMIES AS ANSWERS

In my own life, I had often come across a simple answer to the question of being an American: One is either an American or one is not. Simplistic *either/or* formulations are commonplace in our society, and problems such as these generally get answered in terms of dichotomies. Maxine Greene's work has provided me with both insight and hope in trying to answer the question of becoming American, so I begin this essay by referring to her thoughts on dichotomies. Rather than considering *community* and *pluralism* as necessarily or deterministically irreconcilable, she has instead challenged the respective boundaries and rigid parameters of both of these concepts. For example, she has written, "I want to break through, whenever possible, the persisting either/ors. There is, after all, a dialectical relation marking every human situation. The relation between subject and object, individual and environment, living consciousness and phenomenal world. This relation exists between two different, apparently opposite poles; but it presupposes a mediation between them" (1988, p. 8).

The traditional boundaries of fixed identities became clear to me when I was doing research in preparation for my first book several years ago (Nieto, 1992). Extensive interviews with ten academically successful students from a variety of cultural backgrounds revealed to me the familiar image of my own persistent dilemmas with identity. This was somewhat surprising because these young people were about three decades younger than I, but the same kinds of challenges were apparent in their lives as had been in mine when I was growing up in Brooklyn in the 1940s and '50s. I thought that surely by now this issue would be resolved one way or another; what I found instead was that the students were in the tumultuous midst of developing their identities in an ever-changing and even more complex world than was mine. Yet the students, unlike me, were also tentatively challenging the assumption that one must sacrifice culture and identity to become an American.

Although we had not asked these young people to lay claim to an exclusive identity, many of them chose to do so and often they defined themselves as either American or as a member of their national origin group. Underlying this choice seemed to be a recognition that our society demanded complete allegiance in return for the privilege of becoming an American. These young people were not always willing to pay the price. Take, for instance, Manuel, a young Cape Verdean man of nineteen who was the youngest of eleven children and the first to graduate from high school, an accomplishment that he must have known might not have been possible had he and his family remained in Cape Verde. Yet in his eyes, the price in loss of identity that is frequently paid for the privilege of an education, success, and "fitting in" may be simply too high. Manuel stated the problem in this way: "That's something that a lot of kids do when they come to America. They change their names. Say you're Carlos, they say, 'I'm Carl.' They wanna be American; they're not Cape Verdean. . . . That's wrong. They're fooling themselves. . . . I identify myself as Cape Verdean. I'm Cape Verdean. I cannot be an American because I'm not an American. That's it" (Nieto, 1992, p. 176).

James, a Lebanese Christian (Maronite), faced a similar dilemma. Although by all outward appearances James was "American" in tastes, habits, and future goals, he too felt the pressure of difference. Born and raised in the United States, he had learned from his parents to cherish the Arabic language he spoke, the religion he practiced, and the culture they still maintained. This was not easy, however, in a school where he was a mem-

ber of a minority so invisible that it did not even make the school cookbook, the international fair, or the foreign-language-month celebration,
the few indications of the school's response to a growing multicultural student body. What other students knew about his background was thus
mired in a web of superstitions and stereotypes. Try as he might to dismiss
these as unimportant, it was clear that they had an impact on him: "Some
people call me, you know, 'cause I'm Lebanese, so people say, 'Look out
for the terrorist! Don't mess with him or he'll blow up your house!' or
some stuff like that. But they're just joking around, though. . . . I don't
think anybody's serious, 'cause I wouldn't blow up anybody's house—and
they know that. . . . I don't care. It doesn't matter what people say. . . . I
just want everybody to know that, you know, it's not true" (Nieto, 1992, p.
134).

Nevertheless, rather than hide behind the identity "American," which
he could certainly claim and which might prove far easier to negotiate,
this is what James said about who he is: "First thing I'd say is I'm Lebanese. . . . I'm just proud to be Lebanese. If somebody asked me, 'What are
you?' . . . everybody else would answer, 'I'm American,' but I'd say, 'I'm
Lebanese' and I feel proud of it" (p. 136). Further reflecting on this complicated issue of identity, James used the example of his idol, the biking
star Greg LeMond, as a critique of forced assimilation: "Even though
somebody might have the last name like LeMond or something, he's considered American. But you know, LeMond is a French name, so his culture
must be French. His background is French. But, you know, they're considered Americans. But I'd like to be considered Lebanese" (p. 136).

One of the youngest students to be interviewed, thirteen-year-old
Yolanda, who self-identified as Mexican, also talked about the saliency of
her background. Although aware of the low status of Mexicans in the general population and of the conflict that might lead other young people to
either hide, change, or erase their identity, she stated, "I feel proud of myself. I see some other kids that they say, like they'd say they're Colombian
or something. They try to make themselves look cool in front of everybody. . . . I don't feel bad like if they say, 'Ooh, she's Mexican' or anything. . . . For me, it's good. For other people, some other guys and girls,
don't think it's nice, it's like, 'Oh, man, I should've been born here instead
of being over there.' Not me, it's O.K. for me being born over there 'cause
I feel proud of myself. I feel proud of my culture" (p. 184).

In this research, one of the most consistent, although unexpected, outcomes was the striking combination of *pride* and *shame* that these young
people felt about their culture. That is, the great pride they felt was not
sustained without great conflict, hesitation, and contradiction. For these
young people, pride in culture was neither uniform nor easy. Upon closer
reflection, this was an understandable response: After all, a positive sense

of cultural identity flies in the face of the assimilation model held out as the prize for sacrificing ethnicity, language, and even family loyalties. But the internal conflicts that resulted were also quite apparent.

Sometimes the conflict and pain are too great and, rather than attempt to somehow reconcile cultural differences, the choice may be made to become an American on traditional terms. The alienation from family and culture as chronicled by Richard Rodriguez in *Hunger of Memory* is a case in point. In the following reflection from his book, Rodriguez speaks with tremendous nostalgia about losing his native language, but also with absolute certainty about the folly of providing such programs as bilingual education as a bridge or buffer for children to learn to fit into what he called the "public world" of school and society:

> Without question, it would have pleased me to hear my teachers address me in Spanish when I entered the classroom. I would have felt much less afraid. I would have trusted them and responded with ease. But I would have delayed—for how long postponed?—having to learn the language of public society. I would have evaded—and for how long could I have afforded the delay?—learning the great lesson of school, that I had a public identity. . . . I continued to mumble. I resisted the teacher's demands. (Did I somehow suspect that once I learned the public language my pleasing family life would be changed?). (1982, pp. 19–20)

Nowhere can a more poignant reminder of the wholesale acceptance of the "either/ors" to which Maxine Greene refers be found. Rodriguez's dilemma, that is, was predicated on a difficult choice: either lose your "private language" to become a public person, with all the benefits it entails; or retain your "private language" and forfeit a public identity. Rather than *English plus Spanish*, the formulation was *English or Spanish*. The result, in Rodriguez's formulation, was learning English and accomplishing a high level of academic achievement. However, as we see from his autobiography, this kind of "success" is often accompanied by tormented musings on what might have been lost in the process. The idea that one can be *both* successful *and* maintain one's cultural and linguistic identity is not part of this formula.

An alternative approach, also in the "either/or" paradigm, is to resist assimilation and instead maintain one's native language and culture. This approach operates on a continuum, ranging from retaining an idealized and pure image of the native culture, to a more pragmatic approach where learning the second language and becoming more or less familiar with the host culture is the outcome. The more extreme form of this cultural maintenance, that is, complete isolation and rigid nationalism, in the short run provides a shield against assimilation and can be seen as a healthy response to the violent stripping away of identity that is characteristic of what it has meant to become an American. In the long run, however, it is unworkable and unrealistic in today's complex and interdependent world. In speaking about the more extreme forms of Afrocentrism, it is what Cornel West has called "a gallant yet misguided attempt," (1993, p.4) because to believe that any culture will remain intact and static when placed on new ground is hopelessly romantic at best. Culture, writes Thomas Bender, "is not an emblem of achievement to be worn; it is a resource to be used. It is not fixed and permanent. Cultures change as they are used as resources for addressing new experiences that history presents to us" (1992, p. 13). Thus, culture is dialectical, responding with inventive new creations to both the positive and negative influences of transplanted migrations and immigrations.

In the end, a static cultural maintenance is both implausible and exclusionary and this realization may help explain my impatience with "cultural purists." In some gatherings of Latinos, for instance, there is sometimes a fervent insistence that only Spanish be spoken (almost the flip side of the "English-Only" insistence, but without its institutionalized and hegemonic power). Ironically, this kind of purism may in the process alienate further those second-, third-, and even fourth-generation Latinos who happen not to speak Spanish. Or my anger when Spanish-speaking elitist intellectuals, for example, disdainful in their rejection of U.S.-based artists, state unequivocally that Latino literature can be *only* that literature written in Spanish. For them, English, Spanish and English, Spanglish, or any of the other creative combinations used by U.S.-based artists, are simply out of the question because they represent a corruption of what it means to be a Latino. These kinds of definitions, whether of Latino or of American, fall back on simplistic notions of culture as static and fixed and are thus flawed and untrue to reality. That is, they fail to acknowledge that culture must be mediated in human interactions. Rather than a bounded box of artifacts and values, culture is more like an amoebae that changes shape with every move. Either/or dichotomies are unsatisfactory in either case.

CHALLENGING THE "EITHER/ORS"

If one is to eschew either/or positions, that is, if one cannot either wholly maintain native culture, nor accept assimilation as inevitable, what is to be done? The young people who we interviewed for my study offered a range of possibilities, although in most cases culture was still perceived as immutable. Some of them, although feeling quite proud of their culture, of their ability to function effectively in at least two worlds, and of their bilingualism, also learned to feel ashamed of their culture and of those who represented it. Sometimes, it was clear they blamed their parents or others in the community for perceived failures, and they absolved the school of any wrongdoing. For others, the conflict was too great and led, among other things, to reaching the conclusion that one could not be both American and Cape Verdean (as in the case of Manuel); that "Puerto Ricans are way badder than Whites" (as in the case of Marisol, a Puerto Rican girl who nevertheless loudly proclaimed her pride at being Puerto Rican); or that their culture should not necessarily be important in the school, although it is in the home (as in the case of James, whose culture was so invisible in his school).

The pressures of assimilation proved too great for Vinh, who talked at length about what was apparently a depression he had suffered: "I've been here for three years, but the first two years I didn't learn anything. I got sick, mental. I got mental. Because when I came to the United States, I missed my [parents], my family and my friends, and my Vietnam. . . . I am a very sad person. Sometimes, I just want to be alone to think about myself. . . . Before I got mental, okay, I feel very good about myself, like I am smart. . . . But after I got mental, I don't get any enjoyment. . . . I'm not smart anymore" (Nieto, 1992, p. 146).

The choices made by most of the young people were based on hard-learned lessons concerning the price of cultural assimilation. Forced to make a choice, they were generally making it in favor of their heritage. This decision can also be problematic because, although a courageous stance in light of the negative messages of ethnicity and culture that they hear and see daily, it may limit their possibilities. That is, in choosing *not* to be American, they may have also decided that they are not deserving or entitled to help shape and change their society. Making the choice to have no attachment, they may feel also that they have no rights or responsibilities.

Needless to say, questions of race, colonial status, and social class (in sum, issues of power or powerlessness) are at the very heart of the conflicts I have described. In particular, the weight of a history of white supremacy and racist ideology, unacknowledged but unmistakable in their impact, are a continuing legacy in our notions of who is most likely to be defined as American. Most Europeans, even relatively new immigrants, can be accommodated into the cultural mainstream almost immediately because of their white skin privilege, their status as more or less "voluntary immigrants," and also often because of their middle-class or professional backgrounds. Although they may face the pain and alienation of all new immigrants, they, and certainly their children and grandchildren, rarely have to contend with even making a choice; it is made for them. They almost immediately become "American," fitting into the mainstream of race and class that has been defined as such. Asians and Latinos, and ironically even American Indians, on the other hand, may have been on this soil for many generations but are still asked the inevitable "Where are you from?" reserved for outsiders. Their faces or accents are constant and unmistakable reminders of their roots in Africa, Asia, Latin America, and even Indigenous America, and this question once again belies our society's claim to accept all people on an equal basis.

BECOMING AMERICAN: A NEW PROPOSITION

Departing from either/or formulations, some new directions are being proposed, both by theorists who think about marginalized ethnicities and cultures, and by those who live these realities every day. What if we were to insist that everyone needed to *become American*, rather than begin with the premise that they need to *be American*, so that all of us, including those from the dominant cultural group, found it necessary to renegotiate identity on a continuous basis, to be formed and reformed every day?

This new formulation would lead to Maxine Greene's "passions of pluralism," where the newly conceived "great community" of which she speaks might become a true possibility (Greene, 1993). Community, of course, without the informed consent of its constituents becomes simply an imposed and bureaucratic identity, and those who have not had a hand in constructing it chafe under its definition. This is what has happened with so many of us who resist the label "American" because we have had no hand in determining what it means. Redefining American means not reconstituting it as much as searching into what is already there, recapturing the living and breathing cultures so apparent in our cities and towns, and in our schools and homes. Creating "the expanding community," in the words of Maxine Greene, requires this kind of search: "Something life-affirming in diversity must be discovered and rediscovered, as what is held in common becomes always more many-faceted—open and inclusive, drawn to untapped possibility" (1993, p. 17).

The insistence on the untapped possibility of pluralism is where the redefinition of becoming American must begin. But a redefinition that ossifies a new canon is not what is called for. Examples of a new, monolithic multicultural canon are apparent in programs of "pablum multiculturalism" defined in an "everybody is beautiful, let's celebrate diversity" way, or multiculturalism as an uncontested, unconflicted, smooth road to upward mobility that refuses to tackle the difficult realities of structural inequality.

As Maxine Greene reminds us, diversity must be problematized, studied, and understood as a dialectic rather than simply "celebrated." This means rejecting the "sunny-side-up diversity" that attempts to paper over important differences. A more critical multiculturalism is based on *agency*, that is, the power and the ability to create culture. Being cultural beings implies that we are also cultural creators and negotiators and cultural critics, struggling to develop identities that retain important insights and values while also challenging the limitations that both our native and adopted cultures may impose on us.

Creating a new culture also does not mean inserting ethnic tidbits into an already existing culture, thus replicating what James Banks has called the "contributions approach" (1991) to American culture and history that is the favorite of too many programs in multicultural education. All cultures exist in relation to one another, and that is what a process of renegotiation needs to consider. In terms of learning a new language, for instance, this might mean injecting it into the old and creating something new, and this complex process is described by Eva Hoffman in this way: "Each language modifies the other, crossbreeds with it, fertilizes it. Each language makes the other relative. Like everybody, I am the sum of my languages—the language of my family and childhood, and education and friendship, and love, and the larger, changing world—though perhaps I tend to be more aware than most of the fractures between them, and of the building blocks" (1989, p. 273). More aggressively, Gloria Anzaldúa speaks of the "borderlands" inhabited by Chicanos and the crucial role that language plays in this creation:

> For a people who are neither Spanish nor live in a country in which Spanish is the first language; for a people who live in a country in which English is the reigning tongue but who are not Anglo; for a people who cannot entirely identify with either standard (formal, Castilian) Spanish nor standard English, what recourse is left to them but to create their own language? A language which they can connect their identity to, one capable of communicating the realities and values true to themselves—a language with terms that are neither *español ni inglés*, but both. We speak a patois, a forked tongue, a variation of two languages. (1987, p. 55)

Language is an important symbol of cultural identity, and the stubborn resistance to accepting wholesale a language of imposition is evident in the research of Juan Flores, John Attinasi, and Pedro Pedraza on the language use and attitudes of residents of El Barrio, a Puerto Rican community in New York City:

> By virtual consensus, Puerto Ricans want to maintain Spanish. This is true even for young people who admit to not knowing much Spanish. The feeling is that Spanish should be audible and visible wherever Puerto Rican culture exists, an attitude that connects to both observed language use and the postulated life cycle of language competence.... Puerto Ricans also want to learn English; for most, a person who is more fluent in English than in Spanish is neither a paradox nor an anomaly, much less a case of deliberate or unwitting cultural betrayal. These findings reveal that both linguistic and

cultural identity are changing in response to economic and social transfor-
mations, and that interpenetrating bilingualism is the idiom in which these
cultural changes are expressed. (1993, p. 167)

The process of re-creation must concern and involve all of us, but young
people who feel marginalized are particularly important in the creation of
a new culture. In a new conception of American, native cultures do not
simply disappear, as schools or society might expect or want them to.
Rather, aspects of them are retained, modified, and reinserted into different contexts to become valid and workable. But the process of creating a
new culture is generally neither conscious nor planned. It is instead the inevitable conclusion of cultures co-existing in uneasy, conflicted, but also
rewarding ways. Neither assimilation nor cultural purity is the result. Hip
hop, break dancing, and any number of new music forms are good examples of this process, as are the English/Spanish/"Spanglish" poetry of urban Latinos and the redefined murals of the inner city. By changing the
complexion, attitudes, behaviors, and values of society, we can all experience the comfort of the known as well as the pain and dislocation of the
unknown.

The process of *becoming American* is not merely an academic exercise,
but must connect to schools in fundamental ways. Students and teachers
need to learn how to construct curricula that affirm all students while also
challenging the idea of fixed or idealized identities. They need to search
for new sources of knowledge to create a shifting canon that includes all
students and communities. And they also need to develop the "great community" to which Maxine Greene refers, not in a mechanical or unproblematic way, but through constant negotiation and renegotiation.

LIVING WITH CONFLICTED DEFINITIONS

I am left then with the question with which I began this essay: What does it
mean to become American? In the case of Puerto Ricans, the example
closest to my heart, it remains a riveting and defining question. I close
with a reflection on the Puerto Rican experience, not just because of my
own self-interest, but also because it may help enlighten others for whom
the questions of belonging, identity, and fitting in are so central. Roberto
Márquez discusses these concerns in an elegant essay on the experiences,
dilemmas, and challenges of Puerto Ricans in the United States:

> What emerges from all this is the biculturally and binationally problematic,
> inventive, intrinsically challenging nature of this "new" Puerto Rican who, in
> a very important sense, is in fact no longer an (im)migrant at all, but is also,
> unmistakably, the historical product and extension of the "old" Puerto Ri-

can (im)migrant and clings as fiercely to his island roots. No less an inveter-
ate commuter, this Puerto Rican's *place* is now both *here* and *there* and, invariably, neither *here* nor *there*. Between *one* and *the other*, it is no longer the
termination points or patrolled borders but the syncretic results of con-
stantly moving between and beyond them that becomes central; it is the os-
cillating intensity of being both fixed and in constant motion that nourishes
a creatively defiant endurance and dynamic vitality. (1995, p. 114)

This reflection on what it means to become American, mired as it is in
both contradictions and complexities, will not make it any simpler to answer the other inevitable question I am asked when meeting someone for
the first time: "Where are you from?" they may ask (sometimes a substitute
for "What are you?"). I usually pause for a long second before answering
with my own series of questions, "Do you mean where was I born? Or what
is my ethnic background? How do I identify? Or where do I live?" All these
are possible answers, but it would be much easier to answer, without hesitation, "I am an American." But because "American" does not yet include
me in any significant way, I am not able to do this. I cannot even yet say, "I
am a Puerto Rican-American" because I cannot bring myself to live as a
hyphenated person. And I particularly refuse to be included when those
who, with an arrogance so complete that they are not even aware of their
own ignorance, attempt to include me under taken-for-granted definitions into the "club" on their terms (at the conclusion of an unresolved
conversation about differences, they may say, winking broadly at me, "After all, we're all Americans, aren't we?").

I hope that, if not for my children, at least for my grandchildren the answer will be a less conflicted one. But I hope that it will not come too easily
either. If being an American means that they must leave behind or forget
their own multiple identities, they will have lost something precious in the
answer. For my daughters, the answer is already even more difficult in
some ways than it has been for me. My older daughter, half Puerto Rican
and half Spanish, and with a deep sense of her Latino heritage, also has to
think before answering. For my younger daughter, adopted, with a Puerto
Rican, Canadian European, and American Indian heritage, it is even more
problematic given current definitions. And for my little granddaughter,
who is all that and also African American, I can only hope that being
American develops to mean all of this and more.

As long as there are newcomers, as long as there are those who refuse to
be included in a definition that denies them both their individual and
group identities, the question of becoming American will be with us. The
challenge for us as a society is to make room for all of them. Maxine
Greene refers to these people when she says, "There are always strangers,
people with their own cultural memories, with voices aching to be heard"
(1988, p. 87). Perhaps by making room for these cultural memories, these

achings to be heard, our society as a whole can begin constructing a new definition of becoming American.

REFERENCES

Anzaldúa, G. (1987). *Borderlands*/La frontera: *The new mestiza*. San Francisco: Aunt Lute Books.

Banks, J. (1991). *Teaching strategies for ethnic studies* (5th ed.), Boston: Allyn & Bacon.

Bender, T. (1992). Negotiating public culture: Inclusion and synthesis in American history. *Liberal Education, 78*(2), 10–15.

Darder, A. (1991). *Culture and power in the classroom: A critical foundation for bicultural education*. New York: Bergin & Garvey.

Flores, J., Attinasi, J., & Pedraza, P. (1993). La Carreta made a U-turn: Puerto Rican language and culture in the United States. In J. Flores (Ed.), *Divided borders: Essays on Puerto Rican identity*. Houston, TX: Arte Público Press, pp. 157–181.

Greene, M. (1988). *The dialectic of freedom*. New York: Teachers College Press.

Greene, M. (1993). The passions of pluralism: Multiculturalism and the expanding community. *Educational Researcher, 22*(1), 13–18.

Hoffman, E. (1989). *Lost in translation: A life in a new language*. New York: E. P. Dutton.

Márquez, R. (1995). Sojourners, settlers, castaways and creators: A recollection of Puerto Rico past and Puerto Ricans present. *The Massachusetts Review, XXXVI*(1), 94–118.

Nieto, S. (1992). *Affirming diversity: The sociopolitical context of multicultural education* (1st ed.) White Plains, NY: Longman Publishing Group.

Rodriguez, R. (1982). *Hunger of memory: The education of Richard Rodriguez*. Boston: David R. Godine.

West, C. (1993). *Race matters*. Boston: Beacon Press.

CRITICAL QUESTIONS

1. How would you respond to the first question in this essay, "What does it mean to be an American?" Ask a number of students of various backgrounds the same question. How do their responses differ from yours? from one another's?

2. Read over the quote from Richard Rodriguez on p. 108. Do you agree or disagree with him? Why?

3. On p. 113 it says, "The process of *becoming American* is not merely an academic exercise, but must connect to schools in fundamental ways. Students and teachers need to learn how to construct curricula that affirm all students while also challenging the idea of fixed or idealized identities." How might you include the topic of assimilation in your curriculum? What materials would you use? What activities? How would you use your students' experiences?

COMMUNITY-BASED ACTIVITIES AND ADVOCACY

1. Ask your students to do an oral history of a family or community member who is a newcomer to this country. How do they identify and why? How would they like their children, if they have any, to identify? Share the results in class.

2. Invite guests from various countries around the world to visit your classroom. They may be students' family members or not. In the younger grades, you may ask them simply to talk about their experiences in our country. For older students, you may want to prepare them with information about the guests' countries of origin, the experiences they had prior to coming here, and so on. It would be best if you included people with different perspectives on the question posed in this essay.

3. Related to the topic of identity (even though they may not be immigrants), gay and lesbian students are often marginalized in schools. In the words of John Anderson (see reference below), "We do little—in most cases nothing—to prepare them for a world that reviles them or to support them in a school environment in which they are called faggots and dykes" (p. 151). What can you and your colleagues do to prepare all students to learn to respect gay and lesbian students, and all others who may be different from themselves? Draw up an action plan and present it to your school council and principal.

SUPPLEMENTARY RESOURCES FOR FURTHER REFLECTION AND STUDY

Anderson, John D. (1994). School climate for gay and lesbian students and staff members. *Phi Delta Kappan, 76*(2), 151–154.

Anderson suggests five approaches that schools can use to help gay and lesbian students feel a sense of safety and belonging.

Glasser, Ruth (1997). *Aquí me quedo: Puerto Ricans in Connecticut*. Middletown, CT: Connecticut Humanities Council.

Based on interviews with Puerto Ricans of all ages and backgrounds who live in Connecticut, this curriculum for young people focuses on their reasons for migrating, stories of adaptation, and some of the struggles in which they've engaged. The curriculum is accompanied by a video and a teacher's guide.

Olsen, Laurie (1997). *Made in America: Immigrant students in our public schools*. New York: The New Press.

In this ethnographic study, Laurie Olsen takes an in-depth look at the lives of the new immigrant students in our nation's schools by focusing on "Madison High School," the pseudonym she uses for a comprehensive high school in California in which over a fifth of the students were born in another country and over a third speak a language other than English.

How we feel: Hispanic students speak out.

This half-hour video, developed by Virginia Vogel Zanger, highlights students in a Boston high school and their thoughts about identity, what it means to learn English as a second language, and teachers' responsibilities to teach them. Although it highlights Hispanics, the issues they discuss concern students of many backgrounds. The video is available from Landmark Films, Inc., Falls Church, VA. Their phone number is (800) 342-4336.

Lessons From Students on Creating a Chance to Dream

INTRODUCTION

For the most part, discussions about developing strategies to solve educational problems lack the perspectives of one of the very groups they most affect: students, especially those students who are categorized as "problems" and are most oppressed by traditional educational structures and procedures. In this chapter, I use interviews of young people from a wide variety of ethnic, racial, linguistic, and social-class backgrounds to present their ideas about the kinds of schools that would have been most affirming for them.

By focusing on students' thoughts about school policies and practices and on the effects of racism and other kinds of discrimination on their education, the article explores what characteristics of these students' specific experiences helped them remain and succeed in school, despite the obstacles. In essence, these are lessons from students because students need to be included in the dialogue if educators are to reflect critically on school reform.

How does it come about that the one institution that is said to be the gateway to opportunity, the school, is the very one that is most effective in perpetuating an oppressed and impoverished status in society? —(Stein, 1971, p. 178)

The poignant question above was posed in this very journal (Harvard Educational Review) almost a quarter of a century ago by Annie Stein, a consistent critic of the schools and a relentless advocate for social justice. This question shall serve as the central motif of this article because, in many ways, it remains to be answered and continues to be a fundamental dilemma standing in the way of our society's stated ideals of equity and equal educational opportunity. Annie Stein's observations about the New York City public schools ring true today in too many school systems throughout the country and can be used to examine some of the same policies and practices she decried in her 1971 article.

It is my purpose in this article to suggest that successfully educating all students in U.S. schools must begin by challenging school policies and practices that place roadblocks in the way of academic achievement for too many young people. Educating students today is, of course, a far different and more complex proposition than it has been in the past. Young people face innumerable personal, social, and political challenges, not to mention massive economic structural changes not even dreamed about by other generations of youth in previous centuries. In spite of the tensions that such challenges may pose, U.S. society has nevertheless historically had a social contract to educate *all* youngsters, not simply those who happen to be European American, English speaking, economically privileged, and, in the current educational reform jargon, "ready to learn."[1] Yet, our schools have traditionally failed some youngsters, especially those from racially and culturally dominated and economically oppressed backgrounds. Research over the past half century has documented a disheartening legacy of failure for many students of all backgrounds, but especially children of Latino, African American, and Native American families, as well as poor European American families and, more recently, Asian and Pacific American immigrant students. Responding to the wholesale failure of so many youngsters within our public schools, educational theorists, sociologists, and psychologists devised elaborate theories of genetic inferiority, cultural deprivation, and the limits of "throwing money" at educational problems. Such theories held sway in particular during the 1960s and 1970s, but their influence is still apparent in educational policies and practices today.[2]

The fact that many youngsters live in difficult, sometimes oppressive conditions is not at issue here. Some may live in ruthless poverty and face

---

[1]I recognize that overarching terms, such as "European American," "African American," "Latino," etc., are problematic. Nevertheless, "European American" is more explicit than "White" with regard to culture and ethnicity, and thus challenges Whites also to think of themselves in ethnic terms, something they usually reserve for those from more clearly identifiable groups (generally, people of color). I have a more in-depth discussion of this issue in chapter two of my book, *Affirming Diversity* (1992).

[2]The early arguments for cultural deprivation are well expressed by Carl Bereiter and Siegfried Englemann (1966) and by Frank Reissman (1962). A thorough review of a range of deficit theories can be found in Herbert Ginsburg (1986).

the challenges of dilapidated housing, inadequate health care, and even abuse and neglect. They and their families may be subject to racism and other oppressive institutional barriers. They may have difficult personal, psychological, medical, or other kinds of problems. These are real concerns that should not be discounted. But, despite what may seem to be insurmountable obstacles to learning and teaching, some schools are nevertheless successful with young people who live in these situations. In addition, many children who live in otherwise onerous situations also have loving families willing to sacrifice what it takes to give their children the chance they never had during their own childhoods. Thus, poverty, single-parent households, and even homelessness, while they may be tremendous hardships, do not in and of themselves doom children to academic failure (see, among others, Clark, 1983; Lucas, Henze, & Donato, 1990; Mehan & Villanueva, 1993; Moll, 1992; Taylor & Dorsey-Gaines, 1988). These and similar studies point out that schools that have made up their minds that their students deserve the chance to learn do find the ways to educate them successfully in spite of what may seem to be overwhelming odds.

Educators may consider students difficult to teach simply because they come from families that do not fit neatly into what has been defined as "the mainstream." Some of them speak no English; many come from cultures that seem to be at odds with the dominant culture of U.S. society that is inevitably reflected in the school; others begin their schooling without the benefit of early experiences that could help prepare them for the cognitive demands they will face. Assumptions are often made about how such situations may negatively affect student achievement and, as a consequence, some children are condemned to failure before they begin. In a study by Nitza Hidalgo, a teacher's description of the students at an urban high school speaks to this condemnation: "Students are generally poor, uneducated and come from broken families who do not value school. Those conditions that produce achievers are somewhere else, not here. We get street people" (Hidalgo, 1991, p. 58). When such viewpoints guide teachers' and schools' behaviors and expectations, little progress can be expected in student achievement.

On the other hand, a growing number of studies suggest that teachers and schools need to build on rather than tear down what students bring to school. That is, they need to understand and incorporate cultural, linguistic, and experiential differences, as well as differences in social class, into the learning process (Abi-Nader, 1993; Hollins, King, & Hayman, 1994; Lucas et al., 1990; Moll & Díaz, 1993). The results of such efforts often provide inspiring examples of success because they begin with a belief that all students deserve a chance to learn. In this article, I will highlight these efforts by exploring the stories of some academically successful young people in order to suggest how the policies and practices of schools can be transformed to create environments in which all children are capable of learning.

It is too convenient to fall back on deficit theories and continue the practice of blaming students, their families, and their communities for educational failure. Instead, schools need to focus on where they *can* make a difference, namely, their own instructional policies and practices. A number of recent studies, for example, have concluded that a combination of factors, including characteristics of schools as opposed to only student background and actions, can explain differences between high- and low-achieving students. School characteristics that have been found to make a positive difference in these studies include an enriched and more demanding curriculum, respect for students' languages and cultures, high expectations for all students, and encouragement for parental involvement in their children's education (Lee, Winfield, & Wilson, 1991; Lucas et al., 1990; Moll, 1992). This would suggest that we need to shift from a single-minded focus on low- or high-achieving students to the conditions that create low- or high-achieving schools. If we understand school policies and practices as being enmeshed in societal values, we can better understand the manifestations of these values in schools as well. Thus, for example, "tracked" schools, rather than reflecting a school practice that exists in isolation from society, reflect a society that is itself tracked along racial, gender, and social-class lines. In the same way, "teacher expectations" do not come from thin air, but reflect and support expectations of students that are deeply ingrained in societal and ideological values.

Reforming school structures alone will not lead to substantive differences in student achievement, however, if such changes are not also accompanied by profound changes in how we as educators think about our students; that is, in what we believe they deserve and are capable of achieving. Put another way, changing policies and practices is a necessary but insufficient condition for total school transformation. For example, in a study of six high schools in which Latino students have been successful, Tamara Lucas, Rosemary Henze, and Rubén Donato (1990) found that the most crucial element is a shared belief among teachers, counselors, and administrators that all students are capable of learning. This means that concomitant changes are needed in policies and practices *and* in our individual and collective will to educate all students. Fred Newmann (1993), in an important analysis of educational restructuring, underlines this point by emphasizing that reform efforts will fail unless they are accompanied by a set of particular commitments and competencies to guide them, including a commitment to the success of all students, the creation of new roles for teachers, and the development of schools as caring communities.

Another crucial consideration in undertaking educational change is a focus on what Jim Cummins (1994) has called the "relations of power" in schools. In proposing a shift from coercive to collaborative relations of power, Cummins argues that traditional teacher-centered transmission models can limit the potential for critical thinking on the part of both teachers and students, but especially for students from dominated communities whose cultures and languages have been devalued by the dominant canon.[3] By encouraging collaborative relations of power, schools and teachers can begin to recognize other sources of legitimate knowledge that have been overlooked, negated, or minimized because they are not part of the dominant discourse in schools.

Focusing on concerns such as the limits of school reform without concomitant changes in educators' attitudes towards students and their families, and the crucial role of power relationships in schools may help rescue current reform efforts from simplistic technical responses to what are essentially moral and political dilemmas. That is, such technical changes as tinkering with the length of the school day, substituting one textbook for another, or adding curricular requirements may do little to change student outcomes unless these changes are part and parcel of a more comprehensive conceptualization of school reform. When such issues are considered fundamental to the changes that must be made in schools, we might more precisely speak about *transformation* rather than simply about reform. But educational transformation cannot take place without the inclusion of the voices of students, among others, in the dialogue.

WHY LISTEN TO STUDENTS?

One way to begin the process of changing school policies and practices is to listen to students' views about them; however, research that focuses on student voices is relatively recent and scarce. For example, student perspectives are for the most part missing in discussions concerning strategies for confronting educational problems. In addition, the voices of students are rarely heard in the debates about school failure and success, and the perspectives of students from disempowered and dominated communities are even more invisible. In this article, I will draw primarily on the words of students I interviewed for a previous research study (Nieto, 1992). I used the interviews to develop case studies of young people from a wide

---

[3]"Critical thinking," as used here, is not meant in the sense that it has come to be used conventionally to imply, for example, higher order thinking skills in math and science as disconnected from a political awareness. Rather, it means developing, in the Freirian (1970) sense, a consciousness of oneself as a critical agent in learning and transforming one's reality.

variety of ethnic, racial, linguistic, and social-class backgrounds who were at the time students in junior or senior high school. These ten young people lived in communities as diverse as large urban areas and small rural hamlets, and belonged to families ranging from single-parent households to large, extended families. The one common element in all of their experiences turned out to be something we as researchers had neither planned nor expected: they were all successful students.[4]

The students were selected in a number of ways, but primarily through community contacts. Most were interviewed at home or in another setting of their choice outside of school. The only requirement that my colleagues and I determined for selecting students was that they reflect a variety of ethnic and racial backgrounds, in order to give us the diversity for which we were looking. The students selected self-identified as Black, African American, Mexican, Native American, Black and White American (biracial), Vietnamese, Jewish, Lebanese, Puerto Rican, and Cape Verdean. The one European American was the only student who had a hard time defining herself, other than as "American" (for a further analysis of this issue, see Nieto, 1992). That these particular students were academically successful was quite serendipitous. We defined them as such for the following reasons: they were all either still in school or just graduating; they all planned to complete at least high school, and most hoped to go to college; they had good grades, although they were not all at the top of their class; they had thought about their future and had made some plans for it; they generally enjoyed school and felt engaged in it (but they were also critical of their own school experiences and that of their peers, as we shall see); and most described themselves as successful. Although it had not been our initial intention to focus exclusively on academically successful students, on closer reflection it seemed logical that such students would be more likely to want to talk about their experiences than those who were not successful. It was at that point that I decided to explore what it was about these students' specific experiences that helped them succeed in school.

Therefore, the fact that these students saw themselves as successful helped further define the study, whose original purpose was to determine the benefits of multicultural education for students of diverse backgrounds. I was particularly interested in developing a way of looking at multicultural education that went beyond the typical "Holidays and Heroes" approach, which is too superficial to have any lasting impact in

---

[4]I was assisted in doing the interviews by a wonderful group of colleagues, most of whom contacted the students, interviewed them, and gave me much of the background information that helped me craft the case studies. I am grateful for the insights and help the following colleagues provided: Carlie Collins Tartakov, Paula Elliott, Haydée Font, Maya Gillingham, Mac Lee Morante, Diane Sweet, and Carol Shea.

schools (Banks, 1991; Sleeter, 1991).[5] By exploring such issues as racism and low expectations of student achievement, as well as school policies and practices such as curriculum, pedagogy, testing, and tracking, I set about developing an understanding of multicultural education as antiracist, comprehensive, pervasive, and rooted in social justice. Students were interviewed to find out what it meant to be from a particular background, how this influenced their school experience, and what about that experience they would change if they could. Although they were not asked specifically about the policies and practices in their schools, they nevertheless reflected on them in their answers to questions ranging from identifying their favorite subjects to describing the importance of getting an education. In this article, I will revisit the interviews to focus on students' thoughts about a number of school policies and practices and on the effects of racism and other forms of discrimination on their education.

The insights provided by the students were far richer than we had first thought. Although we expected numerous criticisms of schools and some concrete suggestions, we were surprised at the depth of awareness and analysis the students shared with us. They had a lot to say about the teachers they liked, as well as those they disliked, and they were able to explain the differences between them; they talked about grades and how these had become overly important in determining curriculum and pedagogy; they discussed their parents' lack of involvement, in most cases, in traditional school activities such as P.T.O. membership and bake sales, but otherwise passionate support for their children's academic success; they mused about what schools could do to encourage more students to learn; they spoke with feeling about their cultures, languages, and communities, and what schools could do to capitalize on these factors; and they gave us concrete suggestions for improving schools for young people of all backgrounds. This experience confirmed my belief that educators can benefit from hearing students' critical perspectives, which might cause them to modify how they approach curriculum, pedagogy, and other school practices. Since doing this research, I have come across other studies that also focus on young people's perspectives and provide additional powerful examples of the lessons we can learn from them. This article thus begins with "lessons from students," an approach that takes the perspective proposed

---

[5]"Holidays and Heroes" refers to an approach in which multicultural education is understood as consisting primarily of ethnic celebrations and the acknowledgment of "great men" in the history of particular cultures. Deeper structures of cultures, including values and lifestyle differences, and an explicit emphasis on power differentials as they affect particular cultural groups, are not addressed in this approach. Thus, this approach is correctly perceived as one that tends to romanticize culture and treat it in an artificial way. In contrast, multicultural education as empowering and liberating pedagogy confronts such structural issues and power differentials quite directly.

by Paulo Freire, that teachers need to become students just as students need to become teachers in order for education to become reciprocal and empowering for both (Freire, 1970).

This focus on students is not meant to suggest that their ideas should be the final and conclusive word in how schools need to change. Nobody has all the answers, and suggesting that students' views should be adopted wholesale is to accept a romantic view of students that is just as partial and condescending as excluding them completely from the discussion. I am instead suggesting that if we believe schools must provide an equal and quality education for all, students need to be included in the dialogue, and that their views, just as those of others, should be problematized and used to reflect critically on school reform.

SELECTED POLICIES AND PRACTICES AND STUDENTS' VIEWS ABOUT THEM

School policies and practices need to be understood within the sociopolitical context of our society in general, rather than simply within individual schools' or teachers' attitudes and practices. This is important to remember for a number of reasons. First, although "teacher bashing" provides an easy target for complex problems, it fails to take into account the fact that teachers function within particular societal and institutional structures. In addition, it results in placing an inordinate amount of blame on some of those who care most deeply about students and who struggle every day to help them learn. That some teachers are racist, classist, and mean-spirited and that others have lost all creativity and caring is not in question here, and I begin with the assumption that the majority of teachers are not consciously so. I do suggest, however, that although many teachers are hardworking, supportive of their students, and talented educators, many of these same teachers are also burned out, frustrated, and negatively influenced by societal views about the students they teach. Teachers could benefit from knowing more about their students' families and experiences, as well as about students' views on school and how it could be improved.

How do students feel about the curriculum they must learn? What do they think about the pedagogical strategies their teachers use? Is student involvement a meaningful issue for them? Are their own identities important considerations in how they view school? What about tracking and testing and disciplinary policies? These are crucial questions to consider when reflecting on what teachers and schools can learn from students, but we know very little about students' responses. When asked, students seem surprised and excited about being included in the conversation, and what they have to say is often compelling and eloquent. In fact, Patricia Phelan,

Ann Locke Davidson, and Hanh Thanh Cao (1992), in a two-year research project designed to identify students' thoughts about school, discovered that students' views on teaching and learning were remarkably consistent with those of current theorists concerned with learning theory, cognitive science, and the sociology of work. This should come as no surprise when we consider that students spend more time in schools than anybody else except teachers (who are also omitted in most discussions of school reform, but that is a topic for another article). In the following sections, I will focus on students' perceptions concerning the curriculum, pedagogy, tracking, and grades in their schools. I will also discuss their attitudes about racism and other biases, how these are manifested in their schools and classrooms, and what effect they may have on students' learning and participation in school.

Curriculum. The curriculum in schools is at odds with the experiences, backgrounds, hopes, and wishes of many students. This is true of both the tangible curriculum as expressed through books, other materials, and the actual written curriculum guides, as well as in the less tangible and "hidden" curriculum as seen in the bulletin boards, extracurricular activities, and messages given to students about their abilities and talents. For instance, Christine Sleeter and Carl Grant (1991) found that a third of the students in a desegregated junior high school they studied said that *none* of the class content related to their lives outside class. Those who indicated some relevancy cited only current events, oral history, money and banking, and multicultural content (because it dealt with prejudice) as being relevant. The same was true in a study by Mary Poplin and Joseph Weeres (1992), who found that students frequently reported being bored in school and seeing little relevance in what was taught for their lives or their futures. The authors concluded that students became more disengaged as the curriculum, texts, and assignments became more standardized. Thus, in contrast to Ira Shor's (1992) suggestion that "What students bring to class is where learning begins. It starts there and goes places" (p. 44), there is often a tremendous mismatch between students' cultures and the culture of the school. In many schools, learning starts not with what students bring to class, but with what is considered high-status knowledge; that is, the "canon," with its overemphasis on European and European American history, arts, and values. This seldom includes the backgrounds, experiences, and talents of the majority of students in U.S. schools. Rather than "going elsewhere," their learning therefore often goes nowhere.

That students' backgrounds and experiences are missing in many schools is particularly evident where the native language of most of the students is not English. In such settings, it is not unusual to see little or no representation of those students' language in the curriculum. In fact, there is often an insistence that students "speak only English" in these schools, which sends a powerful message to young people struggling to maintain an identity in the face of overpowering messages that they must assimilate. This was certainly the case for Marisol, a Puerto Rican girl of sixteen participating in my research, who said:

> I used to have a lot of problems with one of my teachers 'cause she didn't want us to talk Spanish in class and I thought that was like an insult to us, you know? Just telling us not to talk Spanish, 'cause they were Puerto Ricans and, you know, we're free to talk whatever we want, . . . I could never stay quiet and talk only English, 'cause sometimes . . . words slip in Spanish. You know, I think they should understand that.

Practices such as not allowing students to speak their native tongue are certain to influence negatively students' identities and their views of what constitutes important knowledge. For example, when asked if she would be interested in taking a course on Puerto Rican history, Marisol was quick to answer: "I don't think [it's] important. . . . I'm proud of myself and my culture, but I think I know what I should know about the culture already, so I wouldn't take the course." Ironically, it was evident to me after speaking with her on several occasions that Marisol knew virtually nothing about Puerto Rican history. However, she had already learned another lesson well: given what she said about the courses she needed to take, she made it clear that "important" history is U.S. history, which rarely includes anything about Puerto Rico.

Messages about culture and language and how they are valued or devalued in society are communicated not only or even primarily by schools, but by the media and community as a whole. The sociopolitical context of the particular city where Marisol lived, and of its school system, is important to understand: there had been an attempt to pass an ordinance restricting the number of Puerto Ricans coming into town based on the argument that they placed an undue burden on the welfare rolls and other social services. In addition, the "English Only" debate had become an issue when the mayor had ordered all municipal workers to speak only English on the job. Furthermore, although the school system had a student body that was 65 percent Puerto Rican, there was only a one-semester course on Puerto Rican history that had just recently been approved for the bilingual program. In contrast, there were two courses, which although rarely taught were on the books, that focused on apartheid and the Holocaust, despite the fact that both the African American and Jewish communities in the town were quite small. That such courses should be part of a comprehensive multicultural program is not being questioned; however, it is ironic that the largest population in the school was ignored in the general curriculum.

In a similar vein, Nancy Commins's (1989) research with four first-generation Mexican American fifth-grade students focused on how these students made decisions about their education, both consciously and unconsciously, based on their determination of what counted as important knowledge. Her research suggests that the classroom setting and curriculum can support or hinder students' perceptions of themselves as learners based on the languages they speak and their cultural backgrounds. She found that although the homes of these four students provided rich environments for a variety of language uses and literacy, the school did little to capitalize on these strengths. In their classroom, for instance, these children rarely used Spanish, commenting that it was the language of the "dumb kids." As a result, Commins states: "Their reluctance to use Spanish in an academic context also limited their opportunities to practice talking about abstract ideas and to use higher level cognitive skills in Spanish" (p. 35). She also found that the content of the curriculum was almost completely divorced from the experiences of these youngsters, since the problems of poverty, racism, and discrimination, which were prominent in their lives, were not addressed in the curriculum.

In spite of teachers' reluctance to address such concerns, they are often compelling to students, particularly those who are otherwise invisible in the curriculum. Vinh, an 18-year-old Vietnamese student attending a high school in a culturally heterogeneous town, lived with his uncle and younger brothers and sisters. Although grateful for the education he was receiving, Vinh expressed concern about what he saw as insensitivity on the part of some of his teachers to the difficulties of adjusting to a new culture and learning English:

> [Teachers] have to know about our culture. . . . From the second language, it
> is very difficult for me and for other people.

Vinh's concern was echoed by Manuel, a nineteen-year-old Cape Verdean senior who, at the time of the interviews, was just getting ready to graduate, the first in his family of eleven children to do so:

> I was kind of afraid of school, you know, 'cause it's different when you're
> learning the language. . . . It's kind of scary at first, especially if you don't
> know the language and like if you don't have friends here.

In Manuel's case, the Cape Verdean Crioulo bilingual program served as a linguistic and cultural mediator, negotiating difficult experiences that he faced in school so that, by the time he reached high school, he had learned enough English to "speak up." Another positive curricular experience was the theater workshop he took as a sophomore. There, students created and acted in skits focusing on their lived experiences. He recalled with great enthusiasm, for example, a monologue he did about a student going to a new school, because it was based on his personal experience.

Sometimes a school's curriculum is unconsciously disrespectful of students' cultures and experiences. James, a student who proudly identified himself as Lebanese American, found that he was invisible in the curriculum, even in supposedly multicultural curricular and extracurricular activities. He mentioned a language fair, a multicultural festival, and a school cookbook, all of which omitted references to the Arabic language and to Lebanese people. About the cookbook, he said:

> They made this cookbook of all these different recipes from all over the world. And I would've brought in some Lebanese recipes if somebody'd let me know. And I didn't hear about it until the week before they started selling them. . . . I asked one of the teachers to look at it and there was nothing Lebanese in there.

James made an effort to dismiss this oversight, and although he said that it didn't matter, he seemed to be struggling with the growing realization that it mattered very much indeed:

> I don't know, I guess there's not that many Lebanese people in . . . I don't know; you don't hear really that much. . . . Well, you hear it in the news a lot, but I mean, I don't know, there's not a lot of Lebanese kids in our school. . . . I don't mind, 'cause I mean, I don't know, just I don't mind it. . . . It's not really important. It *is* important for me. It would be important for me to see a Lebanese flag.

Lebanese people were mentioned in the media, although usually in negative ways, and these were the only images of James's ethnic group that made their way into the school. He spoke, for example, about how the Lebanese were characterized by his peers:

> Some people call me, you know, 'cause I'm Lebanese, so people say, "Look out for the terrorist! Don't mess with him or he'll blow up your house!" or some stuff like that. . . . But they're just joking around, though. . . . I don't think anybody's serious 'cause I wouldn't blow up anybody's house—and they know that. . . . I don't care. It doesn't matter what people say. . . . I just want everybody to know that, you know, it's not true.

Cultural ambivalence, both pride and shame, were evident in the responses of many of the students. Although almost all of them were quite clear that their culture was important to them, they were also confronted with debilitating messages about it from society in general. How to make sense of these contradictions was a dilemma for many of these young people.

Fern, who identified herself as Native American, was, at thirteen, one of the youngest students interviewed. She reflected on the constant challenges she faced in the history curriculum in her junior high school. Her father was active in their school and community and he gave her a great deal of support for defending her position, but she was the only Native American student in her entire school in this mid-size city in Iowa. She said:

> If there's something in the history book that's wrong, my dad always taught me that if it's wrong, I should tell them that it is wrong. And the only time I ever do is if I know it's *exactly* wrong. Like we were reading about Native Americans and scalping. Well, the French are really the ones that made them do it so they could get money. And my teacher would not believe me. I finally just shut up because he just would not believe me.

Fern also mentioned that her sister had come home angry one day because somebody in school had said "Geronimo was a stupid chief riding that stupid horse." The connection between an unresponsive curriculum and dropping out of school was not lost on Fern, and she talked about this incident as she wondered aloud why other Native Americans had dropped out of the town's schools. Similar sentiments were reported by students in Virginia Vogel Zanger's (1994) study of twenty Latinos from a Boston high school who took part in a panel discussion in which they reflected on their experiences in school. Some of the students who decided to stay in school claimed that dropping out among their peers was a direct consequence of the school's attempts to "monoculture" them.

Fern was self-confident and strong in expressing her views, despite her young age. Yet she too was silenced by the way the curriculum was presented in class. This is because schools often avoid bringing up difficult, contentious, or conflicting issues in the curriculum, especially when these contradict the sanctioned views of the standard curriculum, resulting in what Michelle Fine has called "silencing." According to Fine: "Silencing is about who can speak, what can and cannot be spoken, and whose discourse must be controlled" (1991, p. 33). Two topics in particular that appear to have great saliency for many students, regardless of their backgrounds, are bias and discrimination, yet these are among the issues most avoided in classrooms. Perhaps this is because the majority of teachers are European Americans who are unaccustomed, afraid, or uncomfortable in discussing these issues (Sleeter, 1994); perhaps it is due to the pressure teachers feel to "cover the material"; maybe it has to do with the tradition of presenting information in schools as if it were free of conflict and controversy (Kohl, 1993); or, most likely, it is a combination of all these things. In any event, both students and teachers soon pick up the message that racism, discrimination, and other dangerous topics are not supposed to be discussed in school. We also need to keep in mind that these issues have disparate meanings for people of different backgrounds, and are often perceived as particularly threatening to those from dominant cultural and racial groups. Deidre, one of the young African American women in Fine's 1991 study of an urban high school, explained it this way: "White people might feel like everything's over and OK, but we remember" (p. 33).

Another reason that teachers may avoid bringing up potentially contentious issues in the curriculum is their feeling that doing so may create or exacerbate animosity and hostility among students. They may even believe, as did the reading teacher in Jonathan Kozol's 1967 classic book on the Boston Public Schools, *Death at an Early Age*, that discussing slavery in the context of U.S. history was just too complicated for children to understand, not to mention uncomfortable for teachers to explain. Kozol writes of the reading teacher:

> She said, with the very opposite of malice but only with an expression of the most intense and honest affection for the children in the class: "I don't want these children to have to think back on this year later on and to have to remember that we were the ones who told them they were Negro." (p. 68)

More than a quarter of a century later, the same kinds of disclaimers are being made for the failure to include in the curriculum the very issues that would engage students in learning. Fine (1991) found that although over half of the students in the urban high school she interviewed described experiences with racism, teachers were reluctant to discuss it in class, explaining, in the words of one teacher, "It would demoralize the students, they need to feel positive and optimistic—like they have a chance. Racism is just an excuse they use to not try harder" (p. 37). Some of these concerns may be sincere expressions of protectiveness towards students, but others are merely self-serving and manifest teachers' discomfort with discussing racism.

The few relevant studies I have found concerning the inclusion of issues of racism and discrimination in the curriculum suggest that discussions about these topics can be immensely constructive if they are approached with sensitivity and understanding. This was the case in Melinda Fine's description of the "Facing History and Ourselves" (FHAO) curriculum, a project that started in the Brookline (Massachusetts) Public Schools almost two decades ago (Fine, 1993). FHAO provides a model for teaching history that encourages students to reflect critically on a variety of contemporary social, moral, and political issues. Using the Holocaust as a case study, students learn to think critically about such issues as scapegoating, racism, and personal and collective responsibility. Fine suggests that moral dilemmas do not disappear simply because teachers refuse to bring them into the schools. On the contrary, when these realities are separated from the curriculum, young people learn that school knowledge is unrelated to their lives, and once again, they are poorly prepared to face the challenges that society has in store for them.

A good case in point is Vanessa, a young European American woman in my study who was intrigued by "difference" yet was uncomfortable and reluctant to discuss it; although she was active in a peer education group that focused on such concerns as peer pressure, discrimination, and exclusion, these were rarely discussed in the formal curriculum. Vanessa, therefore, had no language with which to talk about these issues. In thinking about U.S. history, she mused about some of the contradictions that were rarely addressed in school:

> It seems weird . . . because people came from Europe and they wanted to get away from all the stuff that was over there. And then they came here and set up all the stuff like slavery, and I don't know, it seems the opposite of what they would have done.

The curriculum, then, can act to either enable or handicap students in their learning. Given the kind of curriculum that draws on their experiences and energizes them because it focuses precisely on those things that are most important in their lives, students can either soar or sink in our schools. Curriculum can provide what María Torres-Guzmán (1992) refers to as "cognitive empowerment," encouraging students to become confident, active critical thinkers who learn that their background experiences are important tools for further learning. The connection of the curriculum to real life and their future was mentioned by several of the students interviewed in my study. Avi, a Jewish boy of sixteen who often felt a schism between his school and home lives, for instance, spoke about the importance of school: "If you don't go to school, then you can't learn about life, or you can't learn about things that you need to progress [in] your life." And Vanessa, who seemed to yearn for a more socially conscious curriculum in her school, summed up why education was important to her: "A good education is like when you personally learn something . . . like growing, expanding your mind and your views."

Pedagogy. If curriculum is primarily the *what* of education, then pedagogy concerns the *why* and *how*. No matter how interesting and relevant the curriculum may be, the way in which it is presented is what will make it engaging or dull to students. Students' views echo those of educational researchers who have found that teaching methods in most classrooms, and particularly those in secondary schools, vary little from traditional "chalk and talk" methods; that textbooks are the dominant teaching materials used; that routine and rote learning are generally favored over creativity and critical thinking; and that teacher-centered transmission models prevail (Cummins, 1994; Goodlad, 1984; McNeil, 1986). Martin Haberman is especially critical of what he calls "the pedagogy of poverty," that is, a basic urban pedagogy used with children who live in poverty and which consists primarily of giving instructions, asking questions, giving directions, making assignments, and monitoring seat work. Such pedagogy is based on the assumption that before students can be engaged in creative or critical work, they must first master "the basics." Nevertheless, Haberman asserts that this pedagogy does not work and, furthermore, that it actually gets in the way of real teaching and learning. He suggests instead that we look at exemplary pedagogy in urban schools that actively involves students in real-life situations, which allows them to reflect on their own lives. He finds that good teaching is taking place when teachers welcome difficult issues and events and use human difference as the basis for the curriculum; design collaborative activities for heterogeneous groups; and help students apply ideals of fairness, equity, and justice to their world (Haberman, 1991).

Students in my study had more to say about pedagogy than about anything else, and they were especially critical of the lack of imagination that led to boring classes. Linda, who was just graduating as the valedictorian of her class in an urban high school, is a case in point. Her academic experiences had not always been smooth sailing. For example, she had failed both seventh and eighth grade twice, for a combination of reasons, including academic and medical problems. Consequently, she had experienced both exhilarating and devastating educational experiences. Linda had this to say about pedagogy:

> I think you have to be creative to be a teacher, you have to make it interesting. You can't just go in and say, "Yeah, I'm going to teach the kids just that; I'm gonna teach them right out of the book and that's the way it is, and don't ask questions." Because I know there were plenty of classes where I lost complete interest. But those were all because the teachers just, "Open the books to this page." They never made up problems out of their head. Everything came out of the book. You didn't ask questions. If you asked them questions, then the answer was "in the book." And if you asked the question and the answer *wasn't* in the book, then you shouldn't have asked that question!

Rich, a young Black man, planned to attend pharmacy school after graduation, primarily because of the interest he had developed in chemistry. He too talked about the importance of making classes "interesting":

I believe a teacher, by the way he introduces different things to you, can make a class interesting. Not like a normal teacher that gets up, gives you a lecture, or there's teachers that just pass out the work, you do the work, pass it in, get a grade, good-bye!

Students were especially critical of teachers' reliance on textbooks and blackboards, a sad indictment of much of the teaching that encourages student passivity. Avi, for instance, felt that some teachers get along better when they teach from the point of view of the students: "They don't just come out and say, 'All right, do this, blah, blah, blah.' . . . They're not so *one-tone voice*." Yolanda said that her English teacher didn't get along with the students. In her words, "She just does the things and sits down." James mentioned that some teachers just don't seem to care: "They just teach the stuff. 'Here,' write a couple of things on the board, 'see, that's how you do it. Go ahead, page 25.' " And Vinh added his voice to those of the students who clearly saw the connection between pedagogy and caring: "Some teachers, they just go inside and go to the blackboard. . . . They don't care."

Students did more than criticize teachers' pedagogy, however; they also praised teachers who were interesting, creative, and caring. Linda, in a particularly moving testimony to her first-grade teacher, whom she called her mentor, mentioned that she would be "following in her footsteps" and studying elementary education. She added:

She's always been there for me. After the first or second grade, if I had a problem, I could always go back to her. Through the whole rest of my life, I've been able to go back and talk to her. . . . She's a Golden Apple Award winner, which is a very high award for elementary school teachers. . . . She keeps me on my toes. . . . When I start getting down . . . she peps me back up and I get on my feet.

Vinh talked with feeling about teachers who allowed him to speak Vietnamese with other students in class. Vinh loved working in groups. He particularly remembered a teacher who always asked students to discuss important issues, rather than focusing only on learning what he called "the word's meaning" by writing and memorizing lists of words. The important issues concerned U.S. history, the students' histories and cultures, and other engaging topics that were central to their lives. Students' preference for group work has been mentioned by other educators as well. Phelan et al. (1992), in their research on students' perspectives concerning school, found that both high- and low-achieving students of all backgrounds expressed a strong preference for working in groups because it helped them generate ideas and participate actively in class.

James also appreciated teachers who explained things and let everybody ask questions because, as he said, "There could be someone sitting in the back of the class that has the same question you have. Might as well bring it out." Fern contrasted classes where she felt like falling asleep because they're just "blah," to chorus, where the teacher used a rap song to teach history and involve all the students. And Avi, who liked most of his teachers, singled out a particular math teacher he had had in ninth grade for praise:

> 'Cause I never really did good in math until I had him. And he showed me that it wasn't so bad, and after that I've been doing pretty good in math and I enjoy it.

Yolanda had been particularly fortunate to have many teachers she felt understood and supported her, whether they commented on her bilingual ability, or referred to her membership in a folkloric Mexican dance group, or simply talked with her and the other students about their lives. She added:

> I really got along with the teachers a lot. . . . Actually, 'cause I had some teachers, and they were always calling my mom, like I did a great job. Or they would start talking to me, or they kinda like pulled me up some grades, or moved me to other classes, or took me somewhere. And they were always congratulating me.

Such support, however, rarely represented only individual effort on the part of some teachers, but rather was often manifested by the school as a whole; that is, it was integral to the school's practices and policies. For instance, Yolanda had recently been selected "Student of the Month" and her picture had been prominently displayed in her school's main hall. In addition, she received a certificate and was taken out to dinner by the principal. Although Linda's first-grade teacher was her special favorite, she had others who also created an educational context in which all students felt welcomed and connected. The entire Tremont Elementary School had been special for Linda, and thus the context of the school, including its leadership and commitment, were the major ingredients that made it successful:

> All of my teachers were wonderful. I don't think there's a teacher at the whole Tremont School that I didn't like. . . . It's just a feeling you have. You know that they really care for you. You just know it; you can tell. Teachers who don't have you in any of their classes or haven't ever had you, they still know who you are. . . . The Tremont School in itself is a community. . . . I love that school! I want to teach there.

Vanessa talked about how teachers used their students' lives and experiences in their teaching. For her, this made them especially good teachers:

> [Most teachers] are really caring and supportive and are willing to share their lives and are willing to listen to mine. They don't just want to talk about what they're teaching you; they also want to know you.

Aside from criticism and praise, students in this study also offered their teachers many thoughtful suggestions for making their classrooms more engaging places. Rich, for instance, said that he would "put more activities into the day that can make it interesting." Fern recommended that teachers involve students more actively in learning: "More like making the whole class be involved, not making only the two smartest people up here do the whole work for the whole class." Vanessa added, "You could have games that could teach anything that they're trying to teach through notes or lectures." She suggested that in learning Spanish, for instance, students could act out the words, making them easier to remember. She also thought that other books should be required "just to show some points of view," a response no doubt to the bland quality of so many of the textbooks and other teaching materials available in schools. Avi thought that teachers who make themselves available to students ("You know, I'm here after school. Come and get help.") were most helpful.

Vinh was very specific in his suggestions, and he touched on important cultural issues. Because he came from Vietnam when he was fifteen, learning English was a difficult challenge for Vinh, and he tended to be very hard on himself, saying such things as "I'm not really good, but I'm trying" when asked to describe himself as a student. Although he had considered himself smart in Vietnam, he felt that because his English was not perfect, he wasn't smart anymore. His teachers often showered him with praise for his efforts, but Vinh criticized this approach:

> Sometimes, the English teachers, they don't understand about us. Because something we not do good, like my English is not good. And she say, "Oh, your English is great!" But that's the way the American culture is. But my culture is not like that. . . . If my English is not good, she has to say, "Your English is not good. So you have to go home and study." And she tell me what to study and how to study and get better. But some Americans, you know, they don't understand about myself. So they just say, Oh! You're doing a good job! You're doing great! Everything is great! Teachers talk like that, but my culture is different. . . . They say, "You have to do better."

This is an important lesson not only because it challenges the overuse of praise, a practice among those that María de la Luz Reyes (1992) has called "venerable assumptions," but also because it cautions teachers to take into account both cultural and individual differences. In this case, the practice of praising was perceived by Vinh as hollow, and therefore insincere. Linda referred to the lesson she learned when she failed seventh and eighth grade and "blew two years":

> I learned a lot from it. As a matter of fact, one of my college essays was on the fact that from that experience, I learned that I don't need to hear other people's praise to get by. . . . All I need to know is in here [pointing to her heart] whether I tried or not.

Students have important messages for teachers about what works and what doesn't. It is important, however, not to fall back on what Lilia Bartolomé (1994) has aptly termed the "methods fetish," that is, a simplistic belief that particular methods will automatically resolve complex problems of underachievement. According to Bartolomé, such a myopic approach results in teachers avoiding the central issue of why some students succeed and others fail in school and how political inequality is at the heart of this dilemma. Rather than using this or that method, Bartolomé suggests that teachers develop what she calls a "humanizing pedagogy" in which students' languages and cultures are central. There is also the problem that Reyes (1992) has called a "one-size-fits all" approach, where students' cultural and other differences may be denied even if teachers' methods are based on well-meaning and progressive pedagogy. The point here is that no method can become a sacred cow uncritically accepted and used simply because it is the latest fad. It is probably fair to say that teachers who use more traditional methods but care about their students and believe they deserve the chance to dream may have more of a positive effect than those who know the latest methods but do not share these beliefs. Students need more than such innovations as heterogeneous grouping, peer tutoring, or cooperative groups. Although these may in fact be excellent and effective teaching methods, they will do little by themselves unless accompanied by changes in teachers' attitudes and behaviors.

The students quoted above are not looking for one magic solution or method. In fact, they have many, sometimes contradictory, suggestions to make about pedagogy. While rarely speaking with one voice, they nevertheless have similar overriding concerns: too many classrooms are boring, alienating, and disempowering. There is a complex interplay of policies, practices, and attitudes that cause such pedagogy to continue. Tracking and testing are two powerful forces implicated in this interplay.

Tracking/Ability Grouping/Grades and Expectations of Student Achievement.

> It is not low income that matters but low status. And status is always created and imposed by the ones on top. (Stein, 1971, p. 158)

In her 1971 article, Annie Stein cited a New York City study in which kindergarten teachers were asked to list in order of importance the things a child should learn in order to prepare for first grade. Their responses were coded according to whether they were primarily socialization or educational goals. In the schools with large Puerto Rican and African American student populations, the socialization goals were always predominant; in the mixed schools, the educational goals were first. Concluded Stein, "In fact, in a list of six or seven goals, several teachers in the minority-group kindergartens forgot to mention any educational goals at all" (p. 167). A kind of tracking, in which students' educational goals were being sacrificed for social aims, was taking place in these schools, and its effects were already evident in kindergarten.

Most recent research on tracking has found it to be problematic, especially among middle- and low-achieving students, and suggestions for detracking schools have gained growing support (Oakes, 1992; Wheelock, 1992). Nevertheless, although many tracking decisions are made on the most tenuous grounds, they are supported by ideological norms in our society about the nature of intelligence and the distribution of ability. The long-term effects of ability grouping can be devastating for the life chances of young people. John Goodlad (1984) found that first- or second-grade children tracked by teachers' judgments of their reading and math ability or by testing are likely to remain in their assigned track *for the rest of their schooling*. In addition, he found that poor children and children of color are more likely to face the negative effects of tracking than are other youngsters. For example, a recent research project by Hugh Mehan and Irene Villanueva (1993) found that when low-achieving high school students are detracked, they tend to benefit academically. The study focused on low-achieving students in the San Diego City Schools. When these students, mostly Latinos and African Americans, were removed from a low track and placed in college-bound courses with high-achieving students, they benefitted in a number of ways, including significantly higher college enrollment. The researchers concluded that a rigorous academic program serves the educational and social interests of such students more effectively than remedial and compensatory programs.

Most of the young people in my study did not mention tracking or ability grouping by name, but almost all referred to it circuitously, and usually in negative ways. Although by and large academically successful themselves, they were quick to point out that teachers' expectations often doomed their peers to failure. Yolanda, for instance, when asked what suggestions she would give teachers, said, "I'd say to teachers, 'Get along more with the kids that are not really into themselves. . . . Have more communication with them.' " When asked what she would like teachers to know about other Mexican American students, she quickly said, "They try real hard, that's one thing I know." She also criticized teachers for having low expectations of students, claiming that materials used in the classes were "too low." She added, "We are supposed to be doing higher things. And like they take us too slow, see, step by step. And that's why everybody takes it as a joke." Fern, although she enjoyed being at the "top of my class," did not like to be treated differently. She spoke about a school she attended previously where "you were all the same and you all got pushed the same and you were all helped the same. And one thing I've noticed in Springdale is they kind of teach 25 percent and they kinda leave 75 percent out." She added that, if students were receiving bad grades, teachers did not help them as much: "In Springdale, I've noticed if you're getting D's and F's, they don't look up to you; they look down. And you're always the last on the list for special activities, you know?"

These young people also referred to expectations teachers had of students based on cultural or class differences. Vanessa said that some teachers based their expectations of students on bad reputations, and found least helpful those teachers who "kind of just move really fast, just trying to get across to you what they're trying to teach you. Not willing to slow down because they need to get in what they want to get in." Rich, who attended a predominately Black school, felt that some teachers there did not expect as much as they should from the Black students: "Many of the White teachers there don't push. . . . Their expectations don't seem to be as high as they should be. . . . I know that some Black teachers, their expectations are higher than White teachers. . . . They just do it, because they know how it was for them. . . . Actually, I'd say, you have to be in Black shoes to know how it is." Little did Rich know that he was reaching the same conclusion as a major research study on fostering high achievement for African American students. In this study, Janine Bempechat determined that "across all schools, it seems that achievement is fostered by high expectations and standards" (Bempechat, 1992, p. 43).

Virginia Vogel Zanger's research with Latino and Latina students in a Boston high school focused on what can be called "social tracking." Although the students she interviewed were high-achieving and tracked in a college-bound course, they too felt the sting of alienation. In a linguistic analysis of their comments, she found that students conveyed a strong sense of marginalization, using terms such as "left out," "below," "under," and "not joined in" to reflect their feelings about school (Zanger, 1993). Although these were clearly academically successful students, they perceived tracking in the subordinate status they were assigned based on their cultural backgrounds and on the racist climate established in the school. Similarly, in a study on dropping out among Puerto Rican students, my colleague Manuel Frau-Ramos and I found some of the same kind of language. José, who had dropped out in eleventh grade, explained, "I was alone. . . . I was an outsider" (Frau-Ramos & Nieto, 1993, p. 156). Pedro, a young man who had actually graduated, nevertheless felt the same kind of alienation. When asked what the school could do to help Puerto Ricans stay in school, he said, *"Hacer algo para que los boricuas no se sientan aparte"* (Do something so that the Puerto Ricans wouldn't feel so separate; p. 157).

Grading policies have also been mentioned in relation to tracking and expectations of achievement. One study, for example, found that when teachers de-emphasized grades and standardized testing, the status of their African American and White students became more equal, and White students made more cross-race friendship choices (Hallinan & Teixeira, 1987). In my own research, I found a somewhat surprising revelation: although the students were achieving successfully in school, most did not feel that grades were very helpful. Of course, for the most part they enjoyed receiving good grades, but it was not always for the expected reason. Fern, for instance, wanted good grades because they were one guarantee that teachers would pay attention to her. Marisol talked about the "nice report cards" that she and her siblings in this family of eight children received, and said, "and, usually, we do this for my mother. We like to see her the way she wants to be, you know, to see her happy."

But they were also quick to downplay the importance of grades. Linda, for instance, gave as an example her computer teacher, who she felt had been the least helpful in her high school:

> I have no idea about computer literacy. I got A's in that course. Just because he saw that I had A's, and that my name was all around the school for all the "wonderful things" I do, he just automatically assumed. He didn't really pay attention to who I was. The grade I think I deserved in that class was at least a C, but I got A just because everybody else gave me A's. . . . He didn't help me at all because he didn't challenge me.

She added,

> To me, they're just something on a piece of paper. . . . [My parents] feel just about the same way. If they ask me, "Honestly, did you try your best?" and I tell them yes, then they'll look at the grades and say okay.

Rich stated that, although grades were important to his mother, "I'm comfortable setting my own standards." James said, without arrogance, that he was "probably the smartest kid in my class." Learning was important to him and, unlike other students who also did the assignments, he liked to "really get into the work and stuff." He added,

> If you don't get involved with it, even if you do get, if you get perfect scores and stuff . . . it's not like really gonna sink in. . . . You can memorize the

words, you know, on a test . . . but you know, if you memorize them, it's not going to do you any good. You have to *learn* them, you know?

Most of the students made similar comments, and their perceptions challenge schools to think more deeply about the real meaning of education. Linda was not alone when she said that the reason for going to school was to "make yourself a better person." She loved learning, and commented that "I just want to keep continuously learning, because when you stop learning, then you start dying." Yolanda used the metaphor of nutrition to talk about learning: "[Education] is good for you. . . . It's like when you eat. It's like if you don't eat in a whole day, you feel weird. That's the same thing for me." Vanessa, also an enthusiastic student, spoke pensively about success and happiness: "I'm happy. Success is being happy to me, it's not like having a job that gives you a zillion dollars. It's just having self-happiness."

Finally, Vinh spoke extensively about the meaning of education, contrasting the difference between what he felt it meant in the United States and what it meant in his home culture:

> In Vietnam, we go to school because we want to become educated people. But in the United States, most people, they say, "Oh, we go to school because we want to get a good job." But my idea, I don't think so. I say, if we go to school, we want a good job *also*, but we want to become a good person.
>
> [Grades] are not important to me. Important to me is education. . . . I not so concerned about [test scores] very much. . . . I just know I do my exam very good. But I don't need to know I got A or B. I have to learn more and more.
>
> Some people, they got a good education. They go to school, they got master's, they got doctorate, but they're just helping *themselves*. So that's not good. I don't care much about money. So, I just want to have a normal job that I can take care of myself and my family. So that's enough. I don't want to climb up compared to other people.

Racism and Discrimination

> The facts are clear to behold, but the BIG LIE of racism blinds all but its victims. (Stein, 1971, p. 179)

An increasing number of formal research studies, as well as informal accounts and anecdotes, attest to the lasting legacy of various forms of institutional discrimination in the schools based on race, ethnicity, religion, gender, social class, language, and sexual orientation. Yet, as Annie Stein wrote in 1971, these are rarely addressed directly. The major reason for this may be that institutional discrimination flies in the face of our stated ideals of justice and fair play and of the philosophy that individual hard work is the road to success. Beverly Daniel Tatum, in discussing the myth of meritocracy, explains why racism is so often denied, downplayed, or dismissed: "An understanding of racism as a system of advantage presents a serious challenge to the notion of the United States as a just society where rewards are based solely on one's merits" (Tatum, 1992, p. 6).

Recent studies point out numerous ways in which racism and other forms of discrimination affect students and their learning. For instance, Angela Taylor found that, to the extent that teachers harbor negative racial stereotypes, the African American child's race *alone* is probably sufficient to place him or her at risk for negative school outcomes (Taylor, 1991). Many teachers, of course, see it differently, preferring to think instead that students' lack of academic achievement is due solely to conditions inside their homes or communities. But the occurrence of discriminatory actions in schools, both by other students and by teachers and other staff, has been widely documented. A 1990 study of Boston high school students found that while 57 percent had witnessed a racial attack and 47 percent would either join in or feel that the group being attacked deserved it, only a quarter of those interviewed said they would report a racial incident to school officials (Ribadeneira, 1990). It should not be surprising, then, that in a report about immigrant students in California, most believed that Americans felt negatively and unwelcoming toward them. In fact, almost every immigrant student interviewed reported that they had at one time or another been spat upon, and tricked, teased, and laughed at because of their race, accent, or the way they dressed. More than half also indicated that they had been the victims of teachers' prejudice, citing instances where they were punished, publicly embarrassed, or made fun of because of improper use of English. They also reported that teachers had made derogatory comments about immigrant groups in front of the class, or had avoided particular students because of the language difficulty (Olsen, 1988). Most of the middle and high school students interviewed by Mary Poplin and Joseph Weeres (1992) had also witnessed incidents of racism in school. In Karen Donaldson's study in an urban high school where students used the racism they experienced as the content of a peer education program, over 80 percent of students surveyed said that they had perceived racism to exist in school (Donaldson, 1994).

Marietta Saravia-Shore and Herminio Martínez found similar results in their ethnographic study of Puerto Rican young people who had dropped out of school and were currently participating in an alternative high school program. These adolescents felt that their former teachers were, in their words, "against Puerto Ricans and Blacks" and had openly discriminated against them. One reported that a teacher had said, "Do you want to be like the other Puerto Rican women who never got an education? Do you want to be like the rest of your family and never go to school?" (Saravia-Shore & Martínez, 1992, p. 242). In Virginia Vogel Zanger's study of high-achieving Latino and Latina Boston high school students, one young man described his shock when his teacher called him "spic" right in class; although the teacher was later suspended, this incident had left its mark on him (Zanger, 1993). Unfortunately, incidents such as these are more frequent than schools care to admit or acknowledge. Students, however, seem eager to address these issues, but are rarely given a forum in which such discussions can take place.

How do students feel about the racism and other aspects of discrimination that they see around them and experience? What effect does it have on them? In interviews with students, Karen Donaldson found three major ways in which they said they were affected: White students experienced guilt and embarrassment when they became aware of the racism to which their peers were subjected; students of color sometimes felt they needed to overcompensate and overachieve to prove they were equal to their White classmates; and students of color also mentioned that discrimination had a negative impact on their self-esteem (Donaldson, 1994). The issue of self-esteem is a complicated one and may include many variables. Children's self-esteem does not come fully formed out of the blue, but is *created* within particular contexts and responds to conditions that vary from situation to situation, and teachers' and schools' complicity in creating negative self-esteem certainly cannot be discounted. This was understood by Lillian, one of the young women in Nitza Hidalgo's study of an urban high school, who commented, "That's another problem I have, teachers, they are always talking about how we have no type of self-esteem or anything like that. . . . But they're the people that's putting us down. That's why our self-esteem is so low" (Hidalgo, 1991, p. 95).

The students in my research also mentioned examples of discrimination based on their race, ethnicity, culture, religion, and language. Some, like Manuel, felt it from fellow students. As an immigrant from Cape Verde who came to the United States at the age of eleven, he found the adjustment difficult:

> When American students see you, it's kinda hard [to] get along with them when you have a different culture, a different way of dressing and stuff like that. So kids really look at you and laugh, you know, at the beginning.

Avi spoke of anti-Semitism in his school. The majority of residents in his town were European American and Christian. The Jewish community had dwindled significantly over the years, and there were now very few Jewish students in his school. On one occasion, a student had walked by him saying, "Are you ready for the second Holocaust?" He described another incident in some detail:

I was in a woods class, and there was another boy in there, my age, and he was in my grade. He's also Jewish and he used to come to the temple sometimes and went to Hebrew school. But then, of course, he started hanging around with the wrong people and some of these people were in my class, and I guess they were . . . making fun of him. And a few of them starting making swastikas out of wood. . . . So I saw one and I said to some kid, "What are you doing?" and the kid said to me, "Don't worry. It's not for you, it's for him." And I said to him, "What?!"

Other students talked about discrimination on the part of teachers. Both Marisol and Vinh specifically mentioned language discrimination as a problem. For Marisol, it had happened when a particular teacher did not allow Spanish to be spoken in her room. For Vinh, it concerned teachers' attitudes about his language: "Some teachers don't understand about the language. So sometimes, my language, they say it sounds funny." Rich spoke of the differences between the expectations of White and Black teachers, and concluded that all teachers should teach the curriculum *as if they were in an all-White school*, meaning that then expectations would be high for everybody. Other students were the object of teasing, but some, including James, even welcomed it, perhaps because it at least made his culture visible. He spoke of Mr. Miller, an elementary teacher he had been particularly fond of, who had called him "Gonzo" because he had a big nose and "Klinger" after the *M.A.S.H.* character who was Lebanese. James said, "And then everybody called me Klinger from then on. . . . I liked it, kind of . . . everybody laughing at me."

It was Linda who had the most to say about racism. As a young woman who identified herself as mixed because her mother was White and her father Black, Linda had faced discrimination or confusion on the part of both students and teachers. For example, she resented the fact that when teachers had to indicate her race, they came to their own conclusions without bothering to ask her. She explained what it was like:

[Teachers should not] try to make us one or the other. And God forbid you should make us something we're totally not. . . . Don't write down that I'm Hispanic when I'm not. Some people actually think I'm Chinese when I smile. . . . Find out. Don't just make your judgments. . . . If you're filling out someone's report card and you need to know, then ask.

She went on to say:

I've had people tell me, "Well, you're Black." I'm not Black; I'm Black and White. I'm Black and White American. "Well, you're Black!" No, I'm not! I'm both. . . . I mean, I'm not ashamed of being Black, but I'm not ashamed of being White either, and if I'm both, I want to be part of both. And I think teachers need to be sensitive to that.

Linda did not restrict her criticisms to White teachers, but also spoke of a Black teacher in her high school. Besides Mr. Benson, her favorite teacher of all, there was another Black teacher in the school:

> The other Black teacher, he was a racist, and I didn't like him. I belonged to the Black Students Association, and he was the advisor. And he just made it so obvious: he was all for Black supremacy. . . . A lot of times, whether they deserved it or not, his Black students passed, and his White students, if they deserved an A, they got a B. . . . He was insistent that only Hispanics and Blacks be allowed in the club. He had a very hard time letting me in because I'm not all Black. . . . I just really wasn't that welcome there. . . . He never found out what I was about. He just made his judgments from afar.

It was clear that racism was a particularly compelling issue for Linda, and she thought and talked about it a great deal, The weight of racism on her mind was evident when she said, "It's hard. I look at history and I feel really bad for what some of my ancestors did to some of my other ancestors. Unless you're mixed, you don't know what it's like to be mixed." She even wrote a poem about it, which ended like this:

> But all that I wonder is who ever gave
> them the right to tell me
> What I can and can't do
> Who I can and can't be
> God made each one of us
> Just like the other
> the only difference is,
> I'm darker in color.

Implications of Students' Views for Transformation of Schools

Numerous lessons are contained within the narratives above. But what are the implications of these lessons for the school's curriculum, pedagogy, and tracking? How can we use what students have taught us about racism and discrimination? How can schools' policies and practices be informed through dialogue with students about what works and doesn't work? Although the students in my study never mentioned multicultural education by name, they were deeply concerned with whether and in what ways they and their families and communities were respected and represented in their schools. Two implications that are inherently multicultural come to mind, and I would suggest that both can have a major impact on school policies and practices. It is important that I first make explicit my own view of multicultural education: It is my understanding that multicultural education should be *basic for all students, pervasive in the curriculum and pedagogy, grounded in social justice, and based on critical pedagogy* (Nieto, 1992). Given this interpretation of multicultural education, we can see that it goes beyond the "tolerance" called for in numerous proclamations about diversity. It is also a far cry from the "cultural sensitivity" that is the focus of many professional development workshops (Nieto, 1994). In fact, "cultural sensitivity" can become little more than a condescending "bandaid" response to diversity, because it often does little to solve deep-seated problems of inequity. Thus, a focus on cultural sensitivity in and of itself can be superficial if it fails to take into account the structural and institutional barriers that reflect and reproduce power differentials in society. Rather than promoting cultural sensitivity, I would suggest that multicultural education needs to be understood as "arrogance reduction"; that is, as encompassing *both* individual *and* structural changes that squarely confront the individual biases, attitudes, and behaviors of educators, as well as the policies and practices in schools that emanate from them.

Affirming Students' Languages, Cultures, and Experiences. Over twenty years ago, Annie Stein reported asking a kindergarten teacher to explain why she had ranked four of her students at the bottom of her list, noting that they were "mute." " 'Yes,' she said, 'they have not said one word for six months and they don't appear to hear anything I say.' 'Do they ever talk to the other children?' we asked. 'Sure,' was her reply. 'They cackle to each other in Spanish all day.' " (Stein, 1971, p. 161). These young children, although quite vocal in their own language, were not heard by their teacher because the language they spoke was bereft of all significance in the school. The children were not, however, blank slates; on the contrary, they came to school with a language, culture, and experiences that could have been important in their learning. Thus, we need to look not only at the individual weaknesses or strengths of particular students, but also at the way in which schools assign status to entire groups of students based on the sociopolitical and linguistic context in which they live. Jim Cummins addressed this concern in relation to the kinds of superficial antidotes frequently proposed to solve the problem of functional illiteracy among students from culturally and economically dominated groups: "A remedial focus only on technical aspects of functional illiteracy is inadequate because the causes of educational underachievement and 'illiteracy' among subordinated groups are rooted in the systematic devaluation of culture and denial of access to power and resources by the dominant group" (1994, pp. 307–308). As we have seen in many of the examples cited throughout this article, when culture and language are acknowledged by the school, students are able to reclaim the voice they need to continue their education successfully.

Nevertheless, the situation is complicated by the competing messages that students pick up from their schools and society at large. The research that I have reviewed makes it clear that, although students' cultures are important to them personally and in their families, they are also problematic because they are rarely valued or acknowledged by schools. The decisions young people make about their identities are frequently contradictory and mired in the tensions and struggles concerning diversity that are reflected in our society. Schools are not immune to such debates. There are numerous ways in which students' languages and cultures are excluded in schools: they are invisible, as with James, denigrated, as in Marisol's case, or simply not known, as happened with Vinh. It is no wonder then that these young people had conflicted feelings about their backgrounds. In spite of this, all of them spoke about the strength they derived from family and culture, and the steps they took to maintain it. James and Marisol mentioned that they continued to speak their native languages at home; Fern discussed her father's many efforts to maintain their Native American heritage; Manuel made it clear that he would always consider himself first and foremost Cape Verdean. Vinh spoke movingly about what his culture meant to him, and said that only Vietnamese was allowed in the home and that his sisters and brothers wrote to their parents in Vietnamese weekly. Most of these young people also maintained solid ties with their religion and places of worship as an important link to their heritage.

Much of the recent literature on educating culturally diverse students is helping to provide a radically different paradigm that contests the equation *education* = *assimilation* (Trueba, 1989). This research challenges the old assumptions about the role of the school as primarily an assimilationist agent, and provides a foundation for policy recommendations that focus on using students' cultural background values to promote academic achievement. In the case of Asian Pacific American youth, Peter Kiang and Vivian Wai-Fun Lee state the following:

> It is ironic that strengths and cultural values of family support which are so often praised as explanations for the academic achievement of Asian Pacific American students are severely undercut by the lack of programmatic and policy support for broad-based bilingual instruction and native language development, particularly in early childhood education. (Kiang & Lee, 1993, p. 39)

A study by Jeannette Abi-Nader of a program for Hispanic youth provides an example of how this can work. In the large urban high school she studied, students' cultural values, especially those concerned with *familia*, were the basis of everyday classroom interactions. Unlike the dismal dropout statistics prevalent in so many other Hispanic communities, up to 65 percent of the high school graduates in this program went on to college. Furthermore, the youth attributed their academic success to the program, and made enthusiastic statements about it, including this one written on a survey: "The best thing I like about this class is that we all work together and we all participate and try to help each other. We're family!" (Abi-Nader, 1993, p. 213).

The students in my research also provided impassioned examples of the effect that affirming their languages and cultures had on them and, conversely, on how negating their languages and cultures negated a part of them as well. The attitudes and behaviors of the teachers in Yolanda's school, for example, were reflected in policies that seemed to be based on an appreciation for student diversity. Given the support of her teachers and their affirmation of her language and her culture, Yolanda concluded, "Actually, it's fun around here if you really get into learning. . . . I like learning. I like really getting my mind working." Manuel also commented on how crucial it was for teachers to become aware of students' cultural values and backgrounds. This was especially important for Manuel, since his parents were immigrants unfamiliar with U.S. schools and society, and although they gave him important moral support, they could do little to help him in school. He said of his teachers:

> If you don't know a student there's no way to influence him. If you don't know his background, there's no way you are going to get in touch with him. There's no way you're going to influence him if you don't know where he's been.

Fern, on the other hand, as the only Native American student in her school, spoke about how difficult it was to discuss values that were different from those of the majority. She specifically mentioned a discussion about abortion in which she was trying to express that for Native Americans, the fetus is alive: "And, so, when I try to tell them, they just, 'Oh, well, we're out of time.' They cut me off, and we've still got half an hour!" And Avi, although he felt that teachers tried to be understanding of his religion, also longed for more cultural affirmation. He would have welcomed, for example, the support of the one Jewish teacher at school who Avi felt was trying to hide his Jewishness.

On the contrary, in Linda's case, Mr. Benson, her English teacher, who was also her favorite teacher, provided just that kind of affirmation. Because he was racially mixed like Linda, she felt that he could relate to the kinds of problems she confronted. He became, in the words of Esteban

Díaz and his colleagues, a "sociocultural mediator" for Linda by assigning her identity, language, and culture important roles in the learning environment (Díaz, Flores, Cousin, & Soo Hoo, 1992). Although Linda spoke English as her native language, she gave a wonderful example of how Mr. Benson encouraged her to be "bilingual," using what she referred to as her "street talk." Below is her description of Mr. Benson and the role he played in her education:

> I've enjoyed all my English teachers at Jefferson. But Mr. Benson, my English Honors teacher, he just threw me for a whirl! I wasn't going to college until I met this man. . . . He was one of the few teachers I could talk to . . . 'cause Mr. Benson, he says, I can go into Harvard and converse with those people, and I can go out in the street and "rap with y'all." It's that type of thing. I love it. I try and be like that myself. I have my street talk. I get out in the street and I say "ain't" this and "ain't" that and "your momma" or "wha's up?" But I get somewhere where I know the people aren't familiar with that language or aren't accepting that language, and I will talk properly. . . . I walk into a place and I listen to how people are talking and it just automatically comes to me.

Providing time in the curriculum for students and teachers to engage in discussions about how the language use of students from dominated groups is discriminated against would go a long way in affirming the legitimacy of the discourse of *all* students (Delpit, 1992). According to Margaret Gibson (1991), much recent research has confirmed that schooling may unintentionally contribute to the educational problems of students from culturally dominated groups by pressuring them to assimilate against their wishes. The conventional wisdom that assimilation is the answer to academic underachievement is thus severely challenged. One intriguing implication is that the more students are involved in resisting assimilation while maintaining their culture and language, the more successful they will be in school. That is, maintaining culture and language, although a conflicted decision, seems to have a positive impact on academic success. In any case, it seems to be a far healthier response than adopting an oppositional identity that effectively limits the possibility of academic success (Fordham & Ogbu, 1986; Skutnabb-Kangas, 1988). Although it is important not to overstate this conslusion, it is indeed a real possibility, one that tests the "melting pot" ideology that continues to dominate U.S. schools and society.

We know, of course, that cultural maintenance is not true in all cases of academic success, and everybody can come up with examples of students who felt they needed to assimilate to be successful in school. But the question remains whether this kind of assimilation is healthy or necessary. For instance, in one large-scale study, immigrant students clearly expressed a strong desire to maintain their native languages and cultures and to pass them on to their children (Olsen, 1988). Other research has found that bilingual students specifically appreciate hearing their native language in school, and want the opportunity to learn in that language (Poplin & Weeres, 1992). In addition, an intriguing study of Cambodian refugee children by the Metropolitan Indochinese Children and Adolescent Service found that the more successful they became at modeling their behavior to be like U.S. children, the more their emotional adjustment worsened (National Coalition, 1988). Furthermore, a study of Southeast Asian students found a significant connection between grades and culture: in this research, higher grade point averages correlated with the *maintenance* of traditional values, ethnic pride, and close social and cultural ties with members of the same ethnic group (Rumbaut & Ima, 1987).

All of the above suggests that it is time to look critically at policies and practices that encourage students to leave their cultures and languages at the schoolhouse door. It also suggests that schools and teachers need to affirm, maintain, and value the differences that students bring to school as a foundation for their learning. It is still too common to hear teachers urging parents to "speak only English," as my parents were encouraged to do with my sister and me (luckily, our parents never paid attention). The ample literature cited throughout this article concerning diverse student populations is calling such practices into question. What we are learning is that teachers instead need to encourage parents to speak their *native* language, not English, at home with their children. We are also learning that they should emphasize the importance of family values, not in the rigid and limiting way that this term has been used in the past to create a sense of superiority for those who are culturally dominant, but rather by accepting the strong ethical values that all cultural groups and all kinds of families cherish. As an initial step, however, teachers and schools must first learn more about their students. Vinh expressed powerfully what he wanted teachers to know about him by reflecting on how superficial their knowledge was:

> They understand something, just not all Vietnamese culture. Like they just understand something *outside*. . . . But they cannot understand something inside our hearts.

Listen to Students.   Although school is a place where a lot of talk goes on, it is not often student talk. Student voices sometimes reveal the great challenges and even the deep pain young people feel when schools are unresponsive, cold places. One of the students participating in a project focusing on those "inside the school," namely students, teachers, staff, and parents, said, "This place hurts my spirit" (Poplin & Weeres, 1992, p. 11). Ironically, those who spend the most time in schools and classrooms are often given the least opportunity to talk. Yet, as we saw in the many examples above, students have important lessons to teach educators and we need to begin to listen to them more carefully. Suzanne Soo Hoo captured the fact that educators are losing a compelling opportunity to learn from students while working on a project where students became coresearchers and worked on the question, "What are the obstacles to learning?" a question that, according to Soo Hoo, "electrified the group" (1993, p. 386). Including students in addressing such important issues places the focus where it rightfully belongs, said Soo Hoo: "Somehow educators have forgotten the important connection between teachers and students. We listen to outside experts to inform us, and consequently, we overlook the treasure in our very own backyards: our students" (p. 390). As Mike, one of the coresearchers in her project, stated, "They think just because we're kids, we don't know anything" (p. 391).

When they are treated as if they do know something, students can become energized and motivated. For the ten young people in my study, the very act of speaking about their schooling experiences seemed to act as a catalyst for more critical thinking about them. For example, I was surprised when I met Marisol's mother and she told me that Marisol had done nothing but speak about our interviews. Most of the students in the study felt this enthusiasm and these feelings are typical of other young people in similar studies. As Laurie Olsen (1988) concluded in an extensive research project in California in which hundreds of immigrant students were interviewed, most of the students were gratified simply to have the opportunity to speak about their experiences. These findings have several implications for practice, including using oral histories, peer interviews, interactive journals, and other such strategies. Simply providing students with time to talk with one another, including group work, seems particularly helpful.

The feeling that adults do not listen to them has been echoed by many young people over the years. But listening alone is not sufficient if it is not accompanied by profound changes in what we expect our students to accomplish in school. Even more important than simply *listening* is *assisting* students to become agents of their own learning and to use what they learn in productive and critical ways. This is where social action comes in, and there have been a number of eloquent accounts of critical pedagogy in action (Peterson, 1991; Torres-Guzmán, 1992). I will quote at length from two such examples that provide inspiring stories of how listening to students can help us move beyond the written curriculum.

Iris Santos Rivera wrote a moving account of how a Freirian "problem-posing" approach was used with K–6 Chicano students in a summer educational program of the San Diego Public Schools in 1975 (Santos Rivera,

1983–1984). The program started by having the students play what she called the "Complain, Moan, and Groan Game." Using this exercise, in which students dialogued about and identified problems in the school and community, the young people were asked to identify problems to study. One group selected the school lunch program. This did not seem like a "real" problem to the teacher, who tried to steer the children toward another problem. Santos Rivera writes: "The teacher found it hard to believe in the problem's validity as an issue, as the basis for an action project, or as an integrating theme for education" (p. 5). She let the children talk about it for awhile, convinced that they would come to realize that this was not a serious issue. However, when she returned, they said to her, "Who is responsible for the lunches we get?" (p. 6). Thus began a summer-long odyssey in which the students wrote letters, made phone calls, traced their lunches from the catering truck through the school contracts office, figured out taxpayers' cost per lunch, made records of actual services received from the subcontractors, counted sandwiches and tested milk temperatures, and, finally, compared their findings with contract specifications, and found that there was a significant discrepancy. "We want to bring in the media," they told the teacher (p. 6). Both the local television station and the major networks responded to the press releases sent out by the students, who held a press conference to present the facts and answer reporters' questions. When a reporter asked who had told them all this, one nine-year old girl answered, "We found this stuff out. Nobody had to tell us anything. You know, you adults give yourselves too much credit" (p. 7). The postscript to this story is that state and federal laws had to be amended to change the kinds of lunches that students in California are served, and tapes from the students in this program were used in the state and federal hearings.

In a more recent example, Mary Ginley, a student in the doctoral program at the School of Education at the University of Massachusetts and a gifted teacher in the Longmeadow (Massachusetts) Public Schools, tries to help her second-graders develop critical skills by posing questions to them daily. Their responses are later discussed during class meeting time. Some of these questions are fairly straightforward ("Did you have a good weekend?"), while others encourage deeper thinking; the question posed on Columbus Day, "Was Columbus a hero?" was the culmination of much reading and dialogue that had previously taken place. Another activity she did with her students this year was to keep a daily record of sunrise and sunset. The students discovered to their surprise that December 21 was *not* the shortest day of the year. Using the daily almanac in the local newspaper, the students verified their finding and wrote letters to the editor. One, signed by Kaolin, read (spelling in original):

Dear Editor,
Acorting to our chart December 21 was not the shotest day of the year. But acorting to your paper it is. Are teacher says it happens evry year! What's going on?

As a result of this letter, the newspaper called in experts from the National Weather Service and a local planetarium. One of them said, "It's a fascinating question that [the pupils] have posed. . . . It's frustrating we don't have an adequate answer." (Kelly, 1994, p. 12). Katie, one of the students in Mary's class, compared her classmates to Galileo, who shook the scientific community by saying that the earth revolved around the sun rather than the other way around. Another, Ben, said, "You shouldn't always believe what you hear," and Lucy asserted, "Even if you're a grown-up, you can still learn from a second-grader!"

In the first part of this article, I posed the question, "Why listen to students?" I have attempted to answer this question using numerous comments that perceptive young people, both those from my study and others, have made concerning their education. In the final analysis, the question itself suggests that it is only by first listening *to* students that we will be able to learn to talk *with* them. If we believe that an important basis of education is dialogue and reflection about experience, then this is clearly the first step. Yolanda probably said it best when she commented, " 'Cause you learn a lot from the students. That's what a lot of teachers tell me. They learn more from their students than from where they go study."

CONCLUSION

I have often been struck by how little young people believe they deserve, especially those who do not come from economically privileged backgrounds. Although they may work hard at learning, they somehow believe that they do not deserve a chance to dream. This article is based on the notion that all of our students deserve to dream and that teachers and schools are in the best position for "creating a chance" to do so, as referred to in the title. This means developing conditions in schools that let students know that they have a right to envision other possibilities beyond those imposed by traditional barriers of race, gender, or social class. It means, even more importantly, that those traditional barriers can no longer be viewed as impediments to learning.

The students in my study also showed how crucial extracurricular activities were in providing needed outlets for their energy and for teaching them important leadership skills. For some, it was their place of worship (this was especially true for Avi, Manuel, and Rich); for others, it was hobbies (Linda loved to sing); and for others, sports were a primary support (Fern mentioned how she confronted new problems by comparing them to the sports in which she excelled: "I compare it to stuff, like, when I can't get science, or like in sewing, I'll look at that machine and I'll say, 'This is a basketball; I can overcome it' "). The schools' responsibility to provide some of these activities becomes paramount for students such as Marisol, whose involvement in the Teen Clinic acted almost like a buffer against negative peer pressure.

These students can all be characterized by an indomitable resilience and a steely determination to succeed. However, expecting all students, particularly those from subordinated communities, to be resilient in this way is an unfair burden, because privileged students do not need this quality, as the schools generally reflect their backgrounds, experiences, language, and culture. Privileged students learn that they are the "norm," and although they may believe this is inherently unfair (as is the case with Vanessa), they still benefit from it.

Nevertheless, the students in this research provide another important lesson about the strength of human nature in the face of adversity. Although they represented all kinds of families and economic and social situations, the students were almost uniformly upbeat about their future and their lives, sometimes in spite of what might seem overwhelming odds. The positive features that have contributed to their academic success, namely, caring teachers, affirming school climates, and loving families, have helped them face such odds. "I don't think there's anything stopping me," said Marisol, whose large family lived on public assistance because both parents were disabled. She added, "If I know I can do it, I should just keep on trying." The determination to keep trying was evident also in Fern, whose two teenage sisters were undergoing treatment for alcohol and drug abuse, but who nevertheless asserted, "I succeed in everything I do. If I don't get it right the first time, I always go back and try to do it again," adding, "I've always wanted to be president of the United States!" And it was evident as well in the case of Manuel, whose father cleaned downtown offices in Boston while his mother raised the remaining children at home, and who was the first of the eleven children to graduate from high school: "I can do whatever I want to do in life. Whatever I want to do, I know I could make it. I believe that strongly." And, finally, it was also clear in the case of Rich, whose mother, a single parent, was putting all three of her children through college at the same time. Rich had clearly learned a valuable lesson about self-reliance from her, as we can see in this striking image: "But let's not look at life as a piece of cake, because eventually it'll dry up, it'll deteriorate, it'll fall, it'll crumble, or somebody will come gnawing at it." Later he added, "As they say, self-respect is one gift that you give yourself."

Our students have a lot to teach us about how pedagogy, curriculum, ability grouping, and expectations of ability need to change so that greater numbers of young people can be reached. In 1971, Annie Stein expressed the wishes and hopes of students she talked with, and they differ little from those we have heard through the voices of students today: "The demands of high school youth are painfully reasonable. They want a better education, a more 'relevant' curriculum, some voice in the subject matter to be taught and in the running of the school, and some respect for their constitutional and human rights" (1971, p. 177). Although the stories and voices I have used in this article are primarily those of individual students, they can help us to imagine what it might take to transform entire schools. The responsibility to do so cannot be placed only on the shoulders of individual teachers who, in spite of the profound impact they can have on the lives of particular students, are part of a system that continues to be unresponsive to too many young people. In the final analysis, students are asking us to look critically not only at structural conditions, but also at individual attitudes and behaviors. This implies that we need to undertake a total transformation not only of our schools, but also of our hearts and minds.

REFERENCES

Abi-Nader, J. (1993). Meeting the needs of multicultural classrooms: Family values and the motivation of minority students. In M. J. O'Hair & S. Odell (Eds), *Diversity and teaching: Teacher education yearbook 1* (pp. 212–236). Fort Worth, TX: Harcourt Brace Jovanovich.

Banks, J. A. (1991). *Teaching strategies for ethnic studies* (6th ed.). Boston: Allyn & Bacon.

Bartolomé, L. (1994). Beyond the methods fetish: Toward a humanizing pedagogy. *Harvard Educational Review, 64,* 173–194.

Bempechat, J. (1992). *Fostering high achievement in African American children: Home, school, and public policy influences.* New York: ERIC Clearinghouse on Urban Education, Teachers College, Columbia University.

Bereiter, C., & Englemann, S. (1966). *Teaching disadvantaged children in the preschool.* Englewood Cliffs, NJ: Prentice Hall.

Clark, R. M. (1983). *Family life and school achievement: Why poor Black children succeed or fail.* Chicago: University of Chicago Press.

Commins, N. L. (1989). Language and affect: Bilingual students at home and at school. *Language Arts, 66,* 29–43.

Cummins, J. (1994). From coercive to collaborative relations of power in the teaching of literacy. In B. M. Ferdman, R-M. Weber, & A. G. Ramírez (Eds.), *Literacy across languages and cultures* (pp. 295–331). Albany: State University of New York Press.

Delpit, L. (1992). The politics of teaching literate discourse. *Theory into Practice, 31,* 285–295.

Díaz, E., Flores, B., Cousin, P. T., & Soo Hoo, S. (1992, April). *Teacher as sociocultural mediator.* Paper presented at the Annual Meeting of the AERA, San Francisco.

Donaldson, K. (1994). Through students' eyes. *Multicultural Education, 2*(2), 26–28.

Fine, Melinda. (1993). "You can't just say that the only ones who can speak are those who agree with your position": Political discourse in the classroom. *Harvard Educational Review, 63,* 412–433.

Fine, Michelle. (1991). *Framing dropouts: Notes on the politics of an urban public high school*. Albany: State University of New York Press.

Fordham, S., & Ogbu, J. (1986) Black students' school success: Coping with the "burden of acting White". *Urban Review, 18*, 176–206.

Frau-Ramos, M., & Nieto, S. (1993). "I was an outsider": Dropping out among Puerto Rican youths in Holyoke, Massachusetts. In R. Rivera & S. Nieto (Eds.), *The education of Latino students in Massachusetts: Research and policy considerations* (pp. 143–166). Boston: Gastón Institute.

Freire, P. (1970). *Pedagogy of the oppressed*. New York: Seabury Press.

Gibson, M. (1991). Minorities and schooling: Some implications. In M. A. Gibson & J. U. Ogbu (Eds.), *Minority status and schooling: A comparative study of immigrant and involuntary minorities* (pp. 357–381). New York: Garland.

Ginsburg, H. (1986). The myth of the deprived child: New thoughts on poor children. In U. Neisser (Ed.), *The school achievement of minority children: New perspectives*. Hillsdale, NJ: Lawrence Erlbaum.

Goodlad, J. I. (1984). *A place called school*. New York: McGraw-Hill.

Haberman, M. (1991). The pedagogy of poverty versus good teaching. *Phi Delta Kappan, 73*, 290–294.

Hallinan, M., & Teixeira, R. (1987). Opportunities and constraints: Black-White differences in the formation of interracial friendships. *Child Development, 58*, 1358–1371.

Hidalgo, N. M. (1991). *"Free time, school is like a free time": Social relations in City High School classes*. Unpublished doctoral dissertation, Harvard University.

Hollins, E. R., King, J. E., & Hayman, W. C. (Eds.). (1994). *Teaching diverse populations: Formulating a knowledge base*. Albany: State University of New York Press.

Kelly, R. (1994, January 11). Class searches for solstice. *Union News*, p. 12.

Kiang, P. N., & Lee, V. W-F. (1993). Exclusion or contribution? Education K-12 policy. In *The State of Asian Pacific America: Policy Issues to the Year 2020* (pp. 25–48). Los Angeles: LEAP Asian Pacific American Public Policy Institute and UCLA Asian American Studies Center.

Kohl, H. (1993). The myth of "Rosa Parks, the tired." *Multicultural Education, 1*(2), 6–10.

Kozol, J. (1967). *Death at an early age: The destruction of the hearts and minds of Negro children in the Boston Public Schools*. New York: Houghton Mifflin.

Lee, V. E., Winfield, L. F., & Wilson, T. C. (1991). Academic behaviors among high-achieving African-American students. *Education and Urban Society, 24*(1), 65–86.

Lucas, T., Henze, R., & Donato, R. (1990). Promoting the success of Latino language-minority students: An exploratory study of six high schools. *Harvard Educational Review, 60*, 315–340.

McNeil, L. M. (1986). *Contradictions of control: School structure and school knowledge*. New York: Routledge & Kegan Paul.

Mehan, H., & Villanueva, I. (1993). Untracking low achieving students: Academic and social consequences. In *Focus on Diversity* (Newsletter available from the National Center for Research on Cultural Diversity and Second Language Learning, 399 Kerr Hall, University of California, Santa Cruz, CA 95064).

Moll, L. (1992). Bilingual classroom studies and community analysis: Some recent trends. *Educational Researcher, 21*(2), 20–24.

Moll, L., & Díaz, S. (1993). Change as the goal of educational research. In E. Jacob & C. Jordan (Eds.), *Minority education: Anthropological perspectives* (pp. 67–79). Norwood, NJ: Ablex.

National Coalition of Advocates for Students. (1988). *New voices: Immigrant students in U.S. public schools*. Boston: Author.

Newmann, F. M. (1993). Beyond common sense in educational restructuring: The issues of content and linkage. *Educational Researcher, 22*(2), 4–13, 22.

Nieto, S. (1992). *Affirming diversity: The sociopolitical context of multicultural education.* White Plains, NY: Longman.

Nieto, S. (1994). Affirmation, solidarity, and critique: Moving beyond tolerance in multicultural education. *Multicultural Education, 1*(4), 9–12, 35–38.

Oakes, J. (1992). Can tracking research inform practice? *Educational Researcher, 21*(4), 12–21.

Olsen, L. (1988). *Crossing the schoolhouse border: Immigrant students and the California public schools.* San Francisco: California Tomorrow.

Peterson, R. E. (1991). Teaching how to read the world and change it: Critical pedagogy in the intermediate grades. In C. E. Walsh (Ed.), *Literacy as praxis: Culture, language, and pedagogy* (pp. 156–182). New Jersey: Ablex.

Phelan, P., Davidson, A. L., & Cao, H. T. (1992). Speaking up: Students' perspectives on school. *Phi Delta Kappan, 73*, 695–704.

Poplin, M., & Weeres, J. (1992). *Voices from the inside: A report on schooling from inside the classroom.* Claremont, CA: Claremont Graduate School, Institute for Education in Transformation.

Reissman, F. (1962). *The culturally deprived child.* New York: Harper & Row.

Reyes, M. de la Luz (1992). Challenging venerable assumptions: Literacy instruction for linguistically different students. *Harvard Educational Review, 62*, 427–446.

Ribadeneira, D. (1990, October 18). Study says teen-agers' racism rampant. *Boston Globe*, p. 31.

Rumbaut, R. G., & Ima, K. (1987). *The adaptation of Southeast Asian refugee youth: A comparative study.* San Diego: Office of Refugee Resettlement.

Santos Rivera, I. (1983–1984, October-January). Liberating education for little children. In *Alternativas* (Freirian newsletter from Río Piedras, Puerto Rico, no longer published).

Saravia-Shore, M., & Martínez, H. (1992). An ethnographic study of home/school role conflicts of second generation Puerto Rican adolescents. In M. Saravia-Shore & S. F. Arvizu (Eds.), *Cross-cultural literacy: Ethnographies of communication in multiethnic classrooms* (pp. 227–251). New York: Garland.

Shor, I. (1992). *Empowering education: Critical teaching for social change.* Chicago: University of Chicago Press.

Skutnabb-Kangas, T. (1988). Resource power and autonomy through discourse in conflict: A Finnish migrant school strike in Sweden. In T. Skutnabb-Kangas & J. Cummins (Eds.), *Minority education: From shame to struggle* (pp. 251–277). Clevedon, England: Multilingual Matters.

Sleeter, C. E. (1991). *Empowerment through multicultural education.* Albany: State University of New York Press.

Sleeter, C. E. (1994). White racism. *Multicultural Education, 1*(4), 5–8, 39.

Sleeter, C. E., & Grant, C. A. (1991). Mapping terrains of power: Student cultural knowledge vs. classroom knowledge. In C. E. Sleeter (Ed.), *Empowerment through multicultural education* (pp. 49–67). Albany: State University of New York Press.

Soo Hoo, S. (1993). Students as partners in research and restructuring schools. *Educational Forum, 57*, 386–393.

Stein, A. (1971). Strategies for failure. *Harvard Educational Review, 41*, 133–179.

Tatum, B. D. (1992). Talking about race, learning about racism: The application of racial identity development theory in the classroom. *Harvard Educational Review, 62*, 1–24.

Taylor, A. R. (1991). Social competence and the early school transition: Risk and protective factors for African-American children. *Education and Urban Society, 24*(1), 15–26.

Taylor, D., & Dorsey-Gaines, C. (1988). *Growing up literate: Learning from inner-city families.* Portsmouth, NH: Heinemann.

Torres-Guzmán, M. (1992). Stories of hope in the midst of despair: Culturally responsive education for Latino students in an alternative high school in New York City. In M. Saravia-Shore & S. F. Arvizu (Eds.), *Cross-cultural literacy: Ethnographies of communication in multiethnic classrooms* (pp. 477–490). New York: Garland.

Trueba, H. T. (1989). *Raising silent voices: Educating the linguistic minorities for the twenty-first century.* Cambridge, MA: Newbury House.

Wheelock, A. (1992). *Crossing the tracks: How "untracking" can save America's schools.* New York: New Press.

Zanger, V. V. (1993). Academic costs of social marginalization: An analysis of Latino students' perceptions at a Boston high school. In R. Rivera & S. Nieto (Eds.), *The education of Latino students in Massachusetts: Research and policy considerations* (pp. 167–187). Boston: Gastón Institute.

CRITICAL QUESTIONS

1. Think about a particular student whose case is discussed in this article. How would a teacher build on his or her experiences and background? Be specific.

2. Why do you think that Vanessa, the only European American student interviewed, had a hard time defining herself in ethnic or racial terms? Can you think of other examples where this might be the case?

3. If it is true that pride in culture and language is crucial for academic success, what does this mean for school policies and practices? Discuss some of the policies and practices you think schools should change to promote educational equity for all students.

4. Given what students had to say about curriculum and pedagogy, and about their experiences with discrimination, what implications are there for schools? What about implications for your classroom? How might you change your practice?

COMMUNITY-BASED ACTIVITIES AND ADVOCACY

Develop a case study of a young person to help you think more deeply about the issues in this chapter. Some specific guidelines to help you create the case study follow:

- Select a young person of the approximate age that you will be (or are currently) teaching. It would probably be best not to select a student who you know well or teach.
- Choose a young person from a background with which you are not very familiar. The activity should be a rich learning experience for

you, and this is most likely to occur when you interact with and do additional research about a person from a different background.

- As a class, develop and agree on a list of questions. What most interests you about young people? What do you most want to know? Think about identity, culture, school success, and the role of teachers and family in their lives.
- Decide how many times you will meet to interview the young people. It is generally better to meet for several short sessions of one hour or less than for one long session of one and a half or more hours. Dividing the questions by topic also makes sense.
- Make certain to meet the parents or guardians of the young people you plan to interview. Speak to them about the purpose and scope of the interviews and assure them of their child's confidentiality. Secure written and oral permission (on an audiotape), and let them know that they have the right to pull out at any time. Also tell them how you will be using the interview, and that you will share it with the family when it's completed.
- Get as much information from the family as you will need to develop the case study, but be sensitive to their privacy and feelings. Do not impose yourself on them, and be discreet.
- Select a comfortable, quiet, stress-free environment for the interviews. I would suggest meeting away from school, either in a community center, their home, the park, or a place where you can have a soda and relax.
- Try to make the interviews as comfortable as possible. Ask the young person for permission to audiotape, as that will give you the most accurate record of the interviews. Don't ask questions in a rushed way as if you're trying to get through an assignment; give your interviewee time to respond completely and then follow up with additional relevant questions. Ask the interviewee if he/she has any questions or concerns.
- Transcribing all the tapes is very time-consuming and labor-intensive, and it may not be realistic to expect complete transcriptions for a one-semester course. But you can still develop effective case studies. First, listen to the tapes several times. Then try to determine the conspicuous themes that keep cropping up. Once you have done this, you can transcribe those parts that seem to be the most intriguing or relevant for the student you interviewed.
- Do some research on the context in which the student lives: find out about his or her ethnic, racial and linguistic background and the history of their people in this country; look for information concerning the city or town in which they live; try to get some data on the school system they go to (number of students, types of programs, and so on).

Also ask interviewees if they would like to share writing samples such as poems, letters, or essays with you.

- Write up the case study. Begin with an introduction to the young person, including pertinent information about them, their family, community, cultural group, and schooling experience. Then let the young people speak for themselves by creating a narrative based on the themes you heard them address. Include any other information such as their writings or other material they may have given you.

Each case study is different, and there is no ideal model to follow. But these guidelines can help get you started on creating a convincing case study of a young person. The process may also help you develop useful insights about the lives of young people.

SUPPLEMENTARY RESOURCES FOR FURTHER REFLECTION AND STUDY

Igoa, Cristina (1995). *The inner world of the immigrant child*. New York: St. Martin's Press.

In this moving book about her experiences as a teacher of immigrant students, Igoa chronicles how she has developed her present teaching methodology to focus on literacy and the need for children to develop a sense of empowerment.

Phelan, Patricia, Davidson, Ann Locke, & Yu, Hanh Cao (1998). *Adolescents' worlds: Negotiating family, peers, and school*. New York: Teachers College Press.

The authors discuss their research with adolescents and the struggles these students have had concerning their identities and their sense of belonging in school and in their communities and families.

Poplin, Mary, & Weeres, Joseph (1992). *Voices from the inside: A report on schooling from inside the classroom*. Claremont, CA: The Institute for Education in Transformation, Claremont Graduate School.

Based on research in which the authors were engaged with numerous participants (teachers, administrators, students, families) in four representative public schools in southern California, this book chronicles the problems facing the schools in our rapidly changing society.

Writing for Real: Exploring and Affirming Students' Words and Worlds

INTRODUCTION

Students who do not speak English fluently can be found in all classrooms, not just in bilingual or ESL classrooms. In English-only classrooms, students who are not fluent in English are often given few opportunities to write because teachers harbor the false notion that the students first need to learn "the basics" before they can engage in meaningful writing. It is true that students need to be familiar with some conventions of writing, but young people eager to write may become reluctant to do so if teachers base their approach on the misguided idea that students cannot begin to write until they have reached a high level of English literacy. All students, except those who know absolutely no English, can use what English they do know to write about topics that are relevant to their lives.

The chapter that follows concerns what teachers can do to help language minority students feel comfortable in their writing, whether in English or in their native language. In it, I build on the previous article about "lessons from students" to suggest five guidelines teachers can use to approach writing with their language minority students.

From a keynote speech originally given at the Writing and Second Language Learning Institute, sponsored by the Western Massachusetts Writing Project and the Massachusetts Association for Bilingual Education, University of Massachusetts Campus Center, Amherst, Saturday, March 30, 1996.

What do we mean by "meaningful writing" for second language learners? How can we encourage our students who are learning English, and who are also learning a second culture, to become writers? Writing may pose an especially difficult challenge for some of our students because of the fact that their home cultures are neither represented nor affirmed in school curricula. I often think of what it meant for me, as a young girl learning English, to read and write in a world where my family and friends were invisible. As a child, I loved to read and write, although I thought that reading and writing were worlds apart from the world that I inhabited. The books I read were full of characters whose lives could not be more different from mine. In a sense, of course, that is as it should be, for reading is one of the primary ways that children expand their world. Nevertheless, it would have been comforting to sometimes see children whose names were like mine, who spoke Spanish at home, and who engaged in the same kinds of activities that my family did. For youngsters who happen to be from the majority culture, this is an every-day occurrence. For me, it was inconceivable that stories could be about my experiences.

As a young writer, I felt the same way. I remember, for example, that when I was in sixth grade I decided to write a novel. This was not a school project, mind you, although I was a very good student and I loved all the activities related to reading and writing in school. No, this was my *private* project, one that I told nobody about, not my sister or my parents, classmates, or teacher. As an eleven-year old, I had already learned the lesson that Richard Rodriguez (1982) years later would define as the unbroachable chasm between home and school: the *private* world where one used one's language and lived by one set of values, versus the *public* world of English and the formality and school lessons.

My project to write a novel was therefore mired in a fundamental dilemma: writing about what I knew best, me and my life, meant that what I wrote could not *really* be a novel. The way that I resolved the conflict was the true mark of an eleven-year old: I did indeed write about myself and my feelings and experiences, but I kept the novel hidden from everyone. This is, of course, just the thing that young girls do when keeping a diary. But as I recall, my book was not a diary but a story about a girl not too different from me, a story with a definite plot and characters and story line. Each day, I would steal into the bedroom I shared with my sister, close the door to make certain that neither she nor anyone else would find me, and I would write.

The novel grew to 150 pages, and it filled me with great satisfaction. Nevertheless, because I thought of it as a sham rather than as "writing for real," eventually I threw it away in the garbage. Perhaps it was simply an inevitable part of growing up and something that I might have done even if I were not a young Puerto Rican girl in a world of White characters in books. Who knows? What I do know, however, is that I have always regretted discarding it. Because I do not remember too much about it, other than that it was about a girl like me, I have on more than one occasion wondered how well written it was and how I expressed my ideas. Furthermore, I think my students as well as my own daughters might have enjoyed reading it.

I use this story as an illustration of how both educators and students lose a precious opportunity to learn and grow if students' voices are missing in their writing. It is also my way of rejecting Rodriguez' artificial separation between the *public* and the *private*, separations that do not exist to the same degree for those youngsters from the dominant culture. In this paper, I want to specifically discuss how using students' *words* and *worlds* (Freire, 1970) that is, their experiences, how they express those experiences (in whatever language they happen to use), and the social and cultural action embedded in their lives, can result in far richer and more "real" writing than does a focus on only academic deficiencies, social problems, or limited proficiency in English. The perspective I share is based on my work as a teacher of writing and reading in schools, and as a professor at the university level working with teachers and prospective teachers.

What follows is also based on my work in multicultural education. A central component of my understanding of multicultural education is that it needs to be understood within a *sociopolitical context*, that is, as connected to the social, cultural, and political realities in which students live (1996). Thus, rather than a frill or a fad, multicultural education needs to be viewed as fundamental to comprehensive school reform, including the reform of curriculum and pedagogy. What does this mean in practice? At a minimum, education that is multicultural must necessarily also be anti-racist and anti-bias; it must be serious about preparing students for their future as productive and critical citizens of a democratic society; it must permeate the educational environment; and it must be based on social justice. In what follows, I will briefly suggest five guidelines that teachers might use in teaching writing with a multicultural perspective, with specific attention to the writing of language minority students. I will be citing a number of examples and will also use an interesting article from the field of anthropology and nursing to further illuminate how our classrooms can learn from the teaching that takes place in other contexts.

GUIDELINES FOR APPROACHING THE TEACHING OF WRITING WITH A MULTICULTURAL PERSPECTIVE

If we understand multicultural education within the broad sociopolitical perspective suggested above, then it is clear that a transformation needs to occur in pedagogy, curriculum, other school policies and practices, the culture of the school in general, and indeed, in the very way that we view diversity. Let me suggest five guidelines that might help us transform what is done in classrooms and schools in the name of writing.

1. Avoid Simplistic And Formulaic Approaches To Diversity and To Writing

Diversity is often celebrated in token ways in classrooms and schools, resulting in what has been called a "holidays and heroes approach" (Banks, 1991); that is, an approach that focuses on culture as little more than static artifacts and as devoid of social and political import. Even well-intentioned lessons on important people and historic topics may end up perpetuating the myth that our society has been relatively conflict-free or that all our citizens now enjoy the full measure of freedom. Consequently, even impassioned heroes are, in the words of Kozol (1975), "tailored for school use." Kozol cites the celebration of Dr. Martin Luther King's birthday as a good example of such "tailoring." Those of us who work in schools know this to be the case. We need only walk down school halls during the month of January to see bulletin boards with ethereal pictures of Dr. King surrounded by clouds and with the words "I Have a Dream" followed by children's essays in which they interpret his dream. Most of these displays contain vapid and innocuous references to "brotherhood," but rarely do they mention injustice or racism or inequality.

I am not suggesting that we should not engage children in writing about the profound impact that Dr. King has had on our society and our history. What I am saying is that asking children to write about his dream if we give them only inaccurate and incomplete information about his life will result in writing that can best be described as pabulum. However, if we give them a more complete picture, including Dr. King's opposition to the Vietnam War and his criticism of unbridled capitalism, and if we include other writings besides the "I Have a Dream" speech, we are bound to receive more lively and exciting writing from them.

A related example is the story of Rosa Parks. In a brilliant essay in which he deconstructs the traditional story line of most of the children's books about Rosa Parks, Herb Kohl (1993) demonstrates that most of them render her a lifeless and passive subject rather than the vibrant civil rights activist that she was. Both examples remind us that if we want to celebrate "holidays and heroes," we need to do it much more critically than is currently the case in most classrooms.

2. Connect Writing To Students' Lives

A writing approach with a multicultural perspective does not see students as what I have called elsewhere "walking sets of deficiencies" (Nieto, 1994). We have all seen and heard these kinds of responses from teachers, professors, and others: "Poor kids! We can't possibly expect them to succeed because they don't have [fill in the blank: pencils; books at home; language; culture; fathers;" etc.]". Although it is true that many of our students are the victims of devastating life circumstances such as poverty, lack of health care, and even homelessness, we cannot use these as a rationale to expect any less of them. In addition, some of the characteristics that have been used as "evidence" that students are deficient (such as a lack of culture or language) need to be seriously reconsidered. For instance, if students do not speak English, that does not mean that they do not have language; if a child's culture is not that of the dominant cultural group, that does not mean that a child does not have a vibrant and meaningful culture. In sum, children's differences do not automatically condemn them to failure.

Instead of treating students' cultural and linguistic conditions as deficits, we need to think of them as talents and strengths that can be used in the service of their education. This approach is based on the most fundamental assumption made by all good teachers—that we all bring important experiences and insights to the educational enterprise. What could be more appropriate than connecting writing to students' lives? I certainly would have benefited from that perspective when I was writing my novel in sixth grade!

However, using students' experiences in their writing is not just voyeurism. It is true that many teachers now rely on having students write journals and personal narratives. Sometimes using these approaches may bring up difficult issues that teachers are unable to handle, issues such as confessions of abuse or thoughts of suicide. I would encourage teachers to use these approaches sparingly and judiciously, especially if the school in which they work provides limited access to counseling and other services.

I would argue that personal narratives and journals are not the only way to connect children's writing to their real lives. On the contrary, teachers can use some of the issues with which young people grapple every day. In the case of language minority students, teachers can encourage them to write about what it means to speak another language, about how they use that language in their homes, and on what the school can do to affirm their native language. Beginning where students are at, using experiences with which they are familiar, and then broadening those experiences is what is called for. This is a good example of incorporating what Luis Moll has called "community funds of knowledge" in the curriculum (Moll, 1992).

Another way to connect students' lives to the curriculum is to use a "family motif" in reading and writing. Joann Wilson-Keenan's second-grade classroom in Springfield, Massachusetts, in which both Jerri Willett and Judith Solsken collaborated, became a lively and exciting example of multiculturalism in action (Solsken et al., 1993). Here, parents and other family members were routinely brought into the classroom to share their own experiences with literacy. I was fortunate to be there one day when a mother, with toddler in tow, visited the classroom. Speaking haltingly at first, but with greater confidence as she went on, she told the children that she wrote poetry at night after her children had fallen asleep. When she read some of the poetry that she had brought, the second-graders were enraptured, not only because they had a poet among them, but because she was also the mother of one of their own. In this classroom, family and children's stories were interwoven with the curriculum; they were connected to students' real lives.

3. Focus On What Students Can Do, Not Only On What They Can Learn

In a related vein, education is not only about learning to read and write, but also learning how to *reflect* on one's learning and putting these skills to *use* in their day-to-day lives. Therefore, we need to think about how we can connect students' writing to what they can actually do individually and in their homes and communities and about their power and responsibility to change things.

A particularly insightful example of this need to use school skills in everyday life is found in an article concerning reading, writing, and democracy written by David Bloome in collaboration with his eleven-year old daughter Rachel and her friend Petra (1993). In telling the story of how Rachel and Petra organized a petition to allow students to leave the room during the reciting of the Pledge of Allegiance, Bloome raises important questions about the applicability of school learning to democracy. In organizing their petition and doing the necessary background research, Petra and Rachel received help from their highly educated parents: they reviewed case law and constitutional law, and they learned how to go about initiating a petition drive. But what happens to those children whose parents are not so highly educated? What about parents who do not even speak or perhaps cannot write the language of the society? How can they too become familiar with the tools of democracy? Teachers and schools have the responsibility to make democracy come alive in reading and writing for all children. After this experience with his daughter and her friend, Bloome concludes, "Part of what I learned from Rachel and Petra is that you cannot teach students everything about democracy and about using reading and writing for democracy—they must live it" (Bloome et al., p. 658). In the case of language minority students, this can happen, for example, when they are engaged in thinking and acting on how their languages are affirmed in the school setting and outside of it.

4. Believe And Act According To The Belief That All Students Are Smart And Deserve A Chance To Dream

Closely related to the second guideline above, this suggestion is based on the assumption that all students are capable of learning to high levels of achievement, and that their dreams can be given voice in the reading and writing they do. For instance, selecting literature that reinforces a belief that all students are worthy of the best we can give them is important. This means selecting high-quality, rigorous, and inclusive literature in which all children can see themselves as actors. It means providing them with writing experiences in which their particular talents and strengths can shine.

If we believe that all children are potential learners, this also means that we need to review classroom, school, and district policies and practices that assume that some children are smarter than others, or that some deserve more than others. Thus, for example, we need to critically analyze such policies as tracking, testing, and gifted and talented programs based only on academic abilities as revealed in standardized tests. All of these practices may result in watered-down curriculum, or in innovative pedagogical strategies for those students perceived to be "smart" and a steady diet of the "basics" for others. For language minority students, this is crucial because their inability to speak English may doom them to low-level instruction and low expectations. Luis Moll (1992) speaks of the "obsession" with learning English that is so prominent in many schools. Certainly learning English is necessary, but using whatever language students happen to speak is also essential and may in the long run help them learn English as well.

Ultimately, school policies and practices are the living embodiment of a society's underlying values and educational philosophy. That is to say, policies and practices in schools—whether curriculum, pedagogical strategies, assessment procedures, disciplinary policies, or grouping practices—do not emerge from thin air, but instead are tangible reminders of a school's beliefs, attitudes, and expectations of their students. In the case of language minority students, we need to reflect on how these policies and practices can impede "writing for real" for some students, while encouraging it for others.

5. Listen To Students

A final suggestion, and one that is essential in developing writing programs that are successful for language minority students, is to listen to what students themselves have to say. They have important insights about their lives, school, curriculum, and pedagogy. They also have important personal knowledge about the benefits, challenges, and obstacles to learning that are present in their schools, homes, and communities and in society at large. Their insights can help us provide a more relevant, exciting, and demanding education so that they at least have a chance to learn.

Listening to students can help teachers develop curriculum that is respectful and affirming of their experiences. Rather than begin with the assumption that language minority students have nothing to bring to their education, a more helpful approach is to seek out their suggestions to build a curriculum that is grounded in those experiences, but that will also transcend it.

At this point, it is instructive to look at the lessons learned from another context. In a highly perceptive article about the training of traditional Maya Indian midwives in the Yucatán, Brigitte Jordan (1989) drew on data from several years of ethnographic fieldwork and on participation in government-sponsored training courses for Indigenous midwives. She examined why these training courses had failed so badly, in spite of the fact that the teaching staff (doctors and nurses from regional hospitals and representatives from the Mexican Ministry of Health) were dedicated and concerned people. The same is true, of course, of many teachers. Because we often learn valuable lessons only when stepping out of our own context, Jordan's research is provided here as an example of why language minority students often fail to write. I will briefly review just five of the many problems that Jordan found with the training courses, and I encourage teachers to think about how some of them may be related to their own practices in schools.

1. *Imparting straight didactic material*

One of the major problems uncovered by Jordan was that the pedagogy of the training courses was unsuited to the students' lives and experiences. In what is uncannily similar behavior to that of disinterested language minority students in our own urban classrooms, Jordan describes what happens when classes begin:

> Any time one of these lectures begins, a series of significant behaviors on the part of the midwives can be observed . . . The midwives shift into their waiting-it-out posture: they sit impassively, gaze far away, feet dangling, obviously tuned out (p. 927).

2. *Emphasis on definitions*

Jordan also found that the formal lectures in the training courses reflected a preference for abstract principles, especially definitions, rather than useful skills. According to Jordan, hours of precious classroom time are spent on definitions. She provides an interesting example of this fixation on definitions:

Nurse to group: "What is a family?" This is a rhetorical question to which no answer is expected or offered, though nobody would doubt that midwives know what a family is. The nurse provides the answer "A family is a group of people who live under the same roof . . ." There is little response from the audience. Most continue to stare vacantly. Nurse looks expectantly at them, strongly conveying the message that the definition should be copied. She asks why they aren't writing. A number of reasons are given: "Forgot to bring a notebook." "Do not have a pencil." "Can't write" (p. 928).

3. Lack of appropriateness of course content

Probably the greatest indictment concerning the training courses is very relevant to our discussion here: there was little evidence throughout the classes that anyone had given serious thought to the relevance of the course content to the actual work that midwives did. Although the curriculum was modeled on the standard sequence of instruction in traditional medical education, the midwives' traditional methods of dealing with problems of infertility and unwanted pregnancy were primarily herbal and manipulative. No doubt the traditional medical personnel could have learned important insights from the midwives, but nowhere in the curriculum were the practices of the midwives to be found.

This is not meant to say that traditional midwives' practices are always correct. For example, most women in Yucatán, including midwives, believe that the most fertile time is immediately before and after menstruation. Thus, women tend to protect themselves most at times when they are least likely to become pregnant and least when they are most likely to become pregnant. The medical staff responsible for the training were not aware of this belief. Had they listened to their students, they might have used this belief as a crucial lesson to be included in the curriculum. Nevertheless, an important opportunity was missed to impart accurate information that could have been very helpful to the midwives. In any event, there was no time for discussing it in the curriculum.

4. Difficulties with universalizing visual literacy

In a fascinating discussion of the visual conventions used in different cultures, Jordan suggests that pictorial representations vary considerably across cultures. For example, she believes that Westerners may find it difficult to read the pictorial representations in Maya temple frescoes, while "midwives who participate in their own but not our tradition of representation may not translate a line drawing into its real-body equivalent." Thus, a disembodied uterus on the screen may be difficult for them to understand because it is not necessarily connected to the object they know intimately through their own practice. When midwives watched a slide show on conception, where an ovum is approached by several spermatozoa, they were polite but seemed unimpressed that this was how a baby starts. Jordan continued,

During a break, standing outside the hut away from the staff, I asked one of the midwives: "So what did you think about the slides we just saw?" She allowed that it was pretty interesting, especially the ball and the little sticks. "But," she said with an air of confidentiality, "here in Yucatán we do it differently. Our men have a white liquid that comes out of the penis, and that's how we make babies. Not with little sticks (palitos) like the Mexicans and gringos do" (p. 928).

5. *Inappropriateness of evaluation*

How does one evaluate the kind of learning that is for the most part irrelevant to the lives of students? In the case of the training course, a written objective test was given to the midwives at the end. Because of the need to demonstrate to funding agencies that these courses were indeed working, a high premium was placed of students' passing the tests. Thus, staff helped the midwives fill out the questionnaire and, not surprisingly, all the midwives passed. In the words of Jordan,

> The course was officially concluded with a ceremony during which certificates were awarded to the midwives, an occasion that was attended by all the dignitaries that could be mustered . . . That such tests do not measure what they are intended to measure does not need belaboring (p. 929).

What can Teachers of Language Minority Students Learn from this Story?

The major lesson that I would encourage teachers to think about is that curriculum and pedagogy can either reproduce the inequality with which students are confronted every day, or they can have transformative power for both individuals and institutions. In the case of language minority students, using their language and culture, encouraging them to tell their own stories, and engaging them in critical discussions about the issues which are most important to them—whether these be about racism, the importance of their language, or the central role of family—can all lead to a pedagogy that uses students as experts rather than as walking sets of deficiencies. I do not want to end this story, however, by blaming teachers, or by thinking of them as simply "walking sets of deficiencies" either. Jordan is clear on this point when she says:

> I would argue that underlying the medical staff's blindness to the cultural and material realities of people's lives is an imperialist view of the world which simply dismisses the local culture and its solutions. This attitude, of course, is no way is to be thought of as the personal deficiencies of staff members. Rather it is inherent in their socialization into the medical profes-

sion . . . I would suggest that if we want to understand where our pedagogy fails, we need to take seriously the knowledge that is handed down in the [culture of the midwives themselves].

In terms of the language minority students in our classrooms, and of the teachers who teach them, this means listening to students in order to understand where they are coming from. As Manuel, a Cape Verdean student and one of the young people interviewed for my book (Nieto, 1992) so aptly explained,

> What [teachers] need to do is try to know the student before they influence him. If you don't know a student there's no way to influence him. If you don't know his background, there's no way you are going to get in touch with him. There's no way you're going to influence him if you don't know where he's been (p. 175).

"Knowing where he's been" is a good place to begin. This implies that teachers need to also become students, learning as much as they can about the young people in their classrooms and communities, including something about their history and their culture, and even learning their language. It also means that students' cultures and native languages can be important sources of their learning. This approach challenges some of the most deeply-held values in our society: that students need to be stripped of their cultures and languages and other differences in order to be accepted and become acceptable; that learning means ingesting and regurgitating information; and that students' views are unimportant in creating a curriculum. It also challenges us as teachers to be courageous and engage in pedagogy and curriculum that challenge inequality, and that allow what might be thought of as dangerous discussions to take place because these can be riveting for students.

The same can be said of all students, not only those who happen to be speakers of other languages. I will conclude with two examples of how writing can reflect a critical and multicultural perspective. The first is a poem about racism that was written by Linda, a young woman who was about to graduate from high school when we interviewed her a number of years ago (Nieto, 1992). She identified herself as "Black American" and "White American" and resisted the rigid pigeonholes in which most biracial youngsters are placed. Her biracial status, however, did not shield her from racism. "I despise racism," she told us, and the following was one response to it that she shared with us (p. 41):

> Why do they hate me?
> I'll never know

Why not ride their buses
In the front row?
Why not share their fountains
Or look at their wives?
Why not eat where they do
Or share in their lives?
Can't walk with them
Can't talk with them unless I'm
a slave
But all that I wonder is who ever
gave them the right to tell me
What I can and can't do
Who I can and can't be
God made each one of us
Just like the other
The only difference is, I'm
darker in color.

The second example is even closer to home. It is a poem written over a dozen years ago by Tess Champoux, one of my daughter's best friends, when Tess was in fifth grade. Her teacher, Efraín Martínez, had given his students a writing assignment in which he had encouraged them to think about their favorite color, to reflect on why it was their favorite, and to give examples of why they loved it. Tess chose to write about the color brown, not a typical color that would have been selected by most fourth-graders. The "very best friend" to which she refers in her poem is my daughter, Marisa, who was eight years old at the time:

Brown is my teddy bear
Soft and furry.
Brown are the thoughts
That make me worry.
Brown is the freckle
On my sister's nose.
Brown is the dirt
On my hands and my toes.

Brown is the memory
Of my last dream.
Brown is the color
Of an old farmhouse beam.
Brown is the color
Of my very best friend.
Brown is the color
That will never end.

Both poems are examples of how writing can reflect the personal experiences of young people and at the same time move beyond those experiences. Language minority students deserve the same chance to explore their words and their worlds, to "write for real" so that their lives are respected and their horizons can be expanded.

REFERENCES

Banks, J. A. (1991). *Teaching strategies for ethnic studies*, 3rd. ed. Boston: Allyn & Bacon.

Bloome, D. with Bloomekatz, P, & Sander, P. (1993). Literacy, democracy, and the Pledge of Allegiance. *Language Arts, 70*(8), 655–658.

Freire, P. (1970). *Pedagogy of the oppressed*. New York: Seabury Press.

Jordan, B. (1989). Cosmopolitan obstetrics: Some insights from the training of traditional midwives. *Social Science and Medicine, 28*(9), 925–944.

Kohl, H. (1993). The myth of "Rosa the tired." *Multicultural Education, 1*(2), pp. 7–10.

Kozol, J. (1975). Great men and women (tailored for school use). *Learning Magazine* (December), pp. 16–20.

Moll, L. C. (1992). Bilingual classroom studies and community analysis: Some recent trends. *Educational Researcher, 21*(2), pp. 20–24.

Nieto, S. (1992). *Affirming diversity: The sociopolitical context of multicultural education*. White Plains, NY: Longman Publishers.

Nieto, S. (1994). Lessons from students on creating a chance to dream. *Harvard Educational Review, 64*(4), pp. 392–426.

Rodríguez, R. (1982). *Hunger of memory: The education of Richard Rodríguez*. Boston: David R Godine.

CRITICAL QUESTIONS

1. How can you connect writing to students' lives? Give specific examples of how you would approach this question in your classroom.

2. Why do you think I used the research by Jordan to make the point that teachers need to listen to students? What can the experience of Mayan midwives possibly have to do with young people of culturally and linguistically diverse backgrounds in U.S. schools?

3. How can you use writing to help expand students' worlds, even if the students are not fluent in English? Give some specific examples of the kinds of materials and approaches you might use.

COMMUNITY-BASED ADVOCACY

Ask students to collect—with the permission of the authors, of course—the writing of their relatives, from siblings to grandparents. Writings can include shopping lists, poems, letters, notes, and more. These may be in any language, but make sure that you have someone around who can translate them. Have students study what it is that their relatives write about and why. This activity can turn into an extensive project, with students focusing on the uses of writing for diverse purposes and audiences, and the richness of different genres. The project might conclude with some of the relatives visiting the classroom and reading their work. The book *Students as researchers of culture and language in their own communities* by Ann Egan-Robertson and David Bloome (see reference after chap. 1), is a valuable resource for this project.

SUPPLEMENTARY RESOURCES FOR FURTHER REFLECTION AND STUDY

Abi-Nader, Jeannette (1993). Meeting the needs of multicultural classrooms: Family values and the motivation of minority students. In Mary John O'Hair & Sandra J. Odell (Eds.), *Diversity and teaching: Teacher education yearbook I* (pp. 212–236). Fort Worth: Harcourt Brace Jovanovich College Publishers.

This article documents how a high school teacher's classroom practices embody cultural concepts to shape instruction and create a sense of belonging in a bilingual classroom of Latinos/as.

Bartolomé, Lilia I. (1994). Beyond the methods fetish: Toward a humanizing pedagogy. *Harvard Educational Review, 64 I*(2), 173–194.

Lilia Bartolomé takes a critical look at what she calls the "methods fetish," that is, the obsession with method as the panacea for educational problems. She suggests instead that teachers need to develop "political clarity" about teaching and about the students in their care, and a humanizing pedagogy to help them learn.

Christensen, Linda (1996). Whose standard? Teaching standard English. In Brenda Miller Power & Ruth Shagoury Hubbard (Eds.), *Language development: A reader for teachers.* Englewood Cliffs, NJ: Merrill.

A high school teacher, Christensen describes some of the ways she helps her students understand the power of their own language patterns while also learning standard English without humiliation.

Fránquiz, María E. & de la luz Reyes, María (1998). Creating inclusive learning communities through English language arts: From *chanclas* to *canicas*. *Language Arts, 75*(3), 211–220.

The authors describe classrooms where the students' native language—in this case, Spanish—is used to promote learning even when their teachers do not speak Spanish. They demonstrate that, by making a few accommodations in their teaching, all educators can affirm students' native languages as a valuable resource for learning.

Mercado, Carmen I. Caring as empowerment: School collaboration and community agency. *Urban Review, 25*(1), 79–104.

Based on ethnographic research she did with a classroom teacher and middle school students, the author's thesis is that young people are capable of becoming researchers of problems in their own communities. Through a series of compelling examples, Mercado demonstrates how students' worlds can become the focus for empowering education that also teaches them valuable skills.

Part III

IMPLICATIONS FOR THE PREPARATION OF CRITICAL TEACHERS

By now it should be clear that teachers need to develop close relationships with their students if they are to be effective with them. This means developing skills to become competent and caring mentors for a wide range of students of many backgrounds. But these skills are not acquired out of the blue; they need to be taught and nurtured. Teachers and prospective teachers, especially those who have not had extensive experience with students of diverse backgrounds, need to be guided in understanding human differences and they need to be shown how to best tap into the intelligence and capacity of all students. This is a life-long journey. The role of teacher preparation is crucial, although certainly it is just a beginning, in this journey.

In the three chapters that follow, the question of how to become effective with students of diverse backgrounds is addressed. Although the chapters are primarily addressed to teacher educators about their obligation to educate future generations of teachers, they also bring up weighty issues for teachers themselves. After reading these chapters, future and practicing teachers may understand more clearly the enormous responsibility that teacher educators have, and the kinds of demands they must juggle in preparing future teachers for the classrooms in which they will teach.

Chapter 7, "Diversity: What Do Teachers Need to Know?", suggests specific questions related to diversity and multiculturalism that teacher educators might address in their courses.

The following chapter, "Bring Bilingual Education Out of the Basement, and Other Imperatives for Teacher Education," recommends a number of conditions for teacher preparation that takes the education of language minority students seriously. The final chapter in this section, "Conflict and Tension, Growth and Change: The Politics of Teaching Multicultural Education Courses," recounts my experience in teaching a course in multicultural education several years ago. As frustrating as the experience was, it taught me many lessons and it may provoke some insights about teaching diverse populations for you as well.

Diversity: What Do Teachers Need to Know?

INTRODUCTION

I have always been critical of checklists for teachers, whether they concern supposed "traits and characteristics" of particular groups of students ("Native American students learn best when . . ."), or specific skills that teachers should develop ("All teachers should demonstrate expertise in . . ."). Life is too complex for simple-minded checklists, and I have been reminded too often that such lists do more harm than good. Why? Because they set in stone what might be *some* good ideas or insights for *some* people *some* of the time, and they make these insights or ideas universal and inflexible. Checklists also tend to perpetuate stereotypes, so that, for example, if Native American students are not quiet and observant, as the checklists say they must be, teachers may think they are deviant. Because of my distrust of such lists, I have worked hard to avoid using or developing them myself.

Despite my misgivings about checklists, I realize that teachers need some guidelines for working with students of diverse backgrounds. In the chapter that follows, rather than providing a checklist of abilities that prospective teachers need to develop, I have tried to provide guidelines by suggesting questions that need to be posed in teacher education programs. In order to do so, I revisit the policies and practices discussed in my definition of multicultural education (see chap. 1 of this volume), suggesting a number of questions for each. These questions can help you reflect on whether you are prepared to teach students of diverse backgrounds.

181

I hope that you will see from the questions I've posed throughout this chapter that there is no simple recipe for teacher preparation for diversity. But by thinking critically about the experiences you have had and will continue to have as you become immersed in the profession, you will understand some of the many dilemmas facing teacher education faculty as they attempt to prepare teachers for the new century.

From the time free and compulsory education became a fact of life in the 19th century, first in Massachusetts and then throughout the states, our society has had a social contract to educate all youngsters, not simply those who happen to be from economically privileged backgrounds or the cultural mainstream. In spite of this, too many students have traditionally been failed by our schools, and this is especially true of those from racially and culturally dominated and economically oppressed backgrounds. Research over the past half-century has documented a legacy of failure for students of all backgrounds, but particularly for those of Latino, African American, Native American, and poor White families and more recently for Asian and Pacific American immigrant students. Traditional explanations for this failure, especially beginning in the 1960s, have included theories of genetic inferiority, cultural deprivation, or family apathy to the benefits of education (Bereiter & Englemann, 1966; Jensen, 1969; Reisman, 1962).

Teacher education programs, reflecting the conventional wisdom that grew out of such theories, have been mired in assumptions about the necessity for assimilation and the role of schools as the standard bearers of a traditional and unchanging canon. In many teacher preparation programs, students of dominated cultures have been viewed as "walking sets of deficiencies" rather than as having cultures, languages, and experiences that could be helpful in their own learning and that could enrich the curriculum for all youngsters. Thus, although the blame for student failure has usually been placed squarely on the shoulders of students and their families, schools have been reluctant to face their own policies and practices as complicitous in creating a climate of failure. Colleges of education have been even slower to admit that their teacher education curriculum may be in need of reform.

How culture, ethnicity, language, and social class, among other differences, may influence student learning, and what teachers should learn about such differences in terms of school policies and practices, is the subject of this chapter. First, I will discuss what I mean by the terms *diversity* and *multicultural education*. I will then explore a number of school policies and practices and suggest questions that teacher educators can consider in order to change their own curriculum. In the process, I hope to challenge them to explore needed curricular, pedagogical, and structural changes that can transform professional preparation so it can better prepare future teachers to be effective, caring, and motivating for an increasingly diverse student body.

DEFINING DIVERSITY

The term *diversity* is one of those catchwords of the late 20th century that is often used but seldom defined. From preschool through graduate school, diversity is either extolled as a virtue from which all can benefit or blasted as a code word for quotas and declining standards. In educational circles, and more specifically in teacher education, diversity has recently been sanctioned through numerous calls for curriculum inclusion and certification. Whether one is for or against diversity, however, it is important to begin with a common understanding of this term and to explore what implications it might have for teacher education programs.

As used in this chapter, *diversity* will refer to the range of differences that encompass race, ethnicity, gender, social class, ability, and language, among others. It is frequently used interchangeably with *multicultural education*, which, although assumed to speak to only racial and ethnic differences, is actually used more broadly by most of its proponents (Banks & Banks, 1995; Bennett, 1990; Gollnick & Chinn, 1994; Nieto, 1996; Perry & Fraser, 1993; Sleeter & Grant, 1994). Although multicultural educators differ in their focus and in the weight they may give to each of these differences, there is little argument that diversity and multicultural education usually focus on the same thing. This chapter is based on an inclusive definition of diversity, but I will focus primarily on culture, language, and ethnicity and how these issues can be included in teacher education programs, with the hope that the discussion will have implications for the many other differences with which our students come to school.

Sometimes, however, *diversity* is used as a euphemism in an attempt to soften the blow of racism. Because it is a difficult and conflicted issue to discuss, especially among Americans of European descent, racism is too often quickly dismissed in teacher education courses in an effort to move on to more pleasant and less painful issues of difference. In such cases, diversity may assume a celebratory aspect, and multicultural fairs, festivals, and holidays are often the result. But racism needs to be confronted directly, and no softening of terms can help.

In this chapter, racism and other forms of *institutional discrimination* based on the privilege of race, gender, language, and social class, among others, will be of paramount importance in treating differences and their role in teacher education. It is typical for discussions of racism to focus on biases and negative perceptions of *individuals* toward those of other groups. Such prejudiced or racist individuals as Archie Bunker, the television character in *All in the Family*, come to mind. However, although the beliefs and behaviors of such individuals may be hurtful, there is far greater harm done by institutions such as schools, housing, health, and the criminal justice system through their policies and practices. In the discussion that follows, we will be concerned primarily with *institutional racism and other forms of institutional discrimination*; that is, harmful policies and practices within institutions aimed at certain groups of people by other groups of people. Whereas *racism* is specifically directed against racial groups, *discrimination* is a more general term and will be used here to mean the same kind of belief systems and behaviors, both personal and institutional, directed against individuals and groups based on their gender (sexism), ethnic group (ethnocentrism), social class (classism), language (linguicism),[1] or other perceived differences.

The major difference between individual and institutional discrimination is the wielding of *power*, because it is primarily through the power of the people who control institutions such as schools that oppressive policies and practices are reinforced and legitimized. Consequently, when we understand racism as a *systemic* problem and not simply as an individual dislike for a particular group of people, we can better understand the negative and destructive effects it can have. This is not meant to minimize the powerful effects of individual prejudice and discrimination, which can be personally painful, or to suggest that they occur only in one direction, for example, from Whites toward African Americans. There is no monopoly on prejudice and discrimination; they happen in all directions, and even within groups. However, interethnic hostility, personal prejudices, and individual biases, while negative and hurtful, simply do not have the long-range and life-limiting effects of *institutional racism* and *other forms of institutional discrimination*. Thus, because of the power of some groups over others, those groups with the most power in society are the ones that benefit from institutional discrimination, whether or not that is their intent. That is, males, Americans of European descent, the able-bodied, and English speakers are the beneficiaries of institutionally sexist, racist, or linguicist policies and practices.

In schools, testing practices may be racist and ethnocentric because students from dominated groups are stigmatized or labeled as a result of their performance on tests that favor the knowledge and experiences of the dominant group. What places some students at a disadvantage is not

---

[1] The term *linguicism*, coined by Tove Skutnabb-Kangas, refers to "ideologies and structures which are used to legitimate, effectuate and reproduce an unequal division of power and resources (both material and non-material) between groups which are defined on the basis of language" (Skutnabb-Kangas & Cummins, 1988, p. 13).

so much that particular teachers or even school systems may have prejudiced attitudes about them, but rather the negative impact of *particular institutions* on students from culturally dominated groups—in this case, the testing industry.

In addition to a focus on institutional discrimination in diversity, the *context* of education is also central. We cannot separate diversity from its sociopolitical context, just as we cannot understand the role diversity may play in our classrooms without considering how students are treated because *of the way their differences are perceived* rather than because of these differences per se. For instance, a student who speaks Haitian Creole and is economically poor may be viewed quite differently from one who speaks French and is economically and educationally privileged. Whether or not these two students are equally intelligent, capable of communicating in their native languages, or able to learn English competently are not the central issues. Rather, that one speaks a highly valued language whereas the other does not, and the economic disparities in their backgrounds, can create multiple cultural differences that are viewed not simply as differences but as deficits or strengths.

Given the differences in perceptions about student diversity—perceptions that are often based on elitist notions that have little to do with actual competence or intellectual capability—it is important to develop teacher education programs that look critically at the effect of school policies and practices on students. This exploration will help teacher educators and their students avoid what has been called the "holidays and heroes" approach to multicultural education (Banks, 1991) and instead will concentrate on how schools can create conditions that make it possible for all students to learn. What follows, then, is a definition of multicultural education that avoids the superficial trappings of simply adding foods, festivals, or ethnic tidbits to the curriculum.

DEFINING MULTICULTURAL EDUCATION: A PERSONAL, COLLECTIVE, AND INSTITUTIONAL ODYSSEY

Defining multicultural education is a matter of a personal, collective, and institutional exploration. A static or imposed definition is contrary to the development of a multicultural perspective because it assumes a "program in place" or a package that is unchanged by the particular conditions and histories of teacher education programs and the participants in those programs. It is nevertheless necessary to begin with a common basis for understanding multicultural education if we are to develop teacher education programs that are responsive to student diversity. In this section, I will review my own definition of multicultural education and suggest implications for teacher education in the hope that other teacher education faculty will consider how their campuses might define and incorporate a multicultural perspective into their curriculum and pedagogy.

There are two central questions for faculty in teacher education programs to think about in this regard. The first concerns whether diversity or multicultural education should be added to the program through infusion or through specific courses. Each campus will differ in location, size, student body, and history of experience with diversity, but it is probably safe to say that a combination of infusion of diversity concerns along with specific courses about diversity is the most appropriate course of action in bringing these issues to the attention of future teachers. Nevertheless, the balance between infusion and specific courses will vary depending on the context of the specific institution. For example, a specific course on multicultural education may be required at the same time that all other courses are changed to reflect awareness of multicultural concerns.

A second question concerns the kinds of experiences in diversity that are most appropriate for future teachers. Although there can be no list of experiences that will be relevant for all students, it makes sense to provide experiences in education courses, prepracticum and practicum experiences, and in courses and other experiences outside the school or college of education. Each college will vary according to the resources it has in faculty expertise and in the diversity of populations accessible to students. Extracurricular experiences and a wide range of courses in the liberal arts that focus on pluralism are also helpful in preparing future educators for teaching a diverse population.

The definition of multicultural education that drives each program may also vary because of context, experiences, and diversity of student body. The point, however, is to give time and attention to what multicultural education and diversity mean for a particular context. In arriving at my own definition of multicultural education, I began with the assumption that any worthwhile educational philosophy needs to be based on two central premises:

- To provide an equitable and high-quality education for all students.
- To provide an apprenticeship for active participation in democracy to prepare students for their roles as active and critical citizens.

Thus, my definition is as follows:

Multicultural education is a process of comprehensive and basic education for all students that challenges and rejects racism and other forms of discrimination in schools and society and accepts and affirms the pluralism (ethnic, racial, linguistic, religious,

economic, gender, among others) that students, their communities, and teachers repre-
sent. Multicultural education permeates the curriculum and instructional strategies
used in schools, as well as the interactions among teachers, students and parents, and
the very way that schools conceptualize the nature of teaching and learning. Because
it uses critical pedagogy as its underlying philosophy and focuses on knowledge, reflec-
tion, and action (praxis) as the basis for social change, multicultural education pro-
motes the democratic principles of social justice.

This definition is based on seven major characteristics that underscore
the sociopolitical context of education: multicultural education is *antiracist
education, basic education, important for all students, pervasive, education for all
students, a process,* and *critical pedagogy.* These characteristics will not be described fully here, but readers are encouraged to investigate them further
(see Nieto, 1996).

This definition, however, is not as important as the process I used to ar-
rive at it. I began by exploring interrelated school policies and practices
that either promote or hinder learning and the preparation of students
for active participation in a democracy. I will review these policies and
practices, suggesting pertinent questions for faculty to consider when going through their own process of defining multicultural education in order to build a solid knowledge base in diversity for teacher preparation.

SCHOOL POLICIES AND PRACTICES AND
IMPLICATIONS FOR TEACHER EDUCATION

There are a number of interrelated policies and practices that may influence student achievement and that should be examined by teacher educators in order to help determine how their own curriculum and pedagogy
can be transformed. These include institutional racism and other forms of
discrimination; expectations of student achievement; curriculum; pedagogy; tracking and ability grouping; testing; and student, teacher, and
parent involvement in education. In considering each of these, I will include some questions and concerns that teacher educators may want to explore further.

Institutional Racism and Other Forms of Discrimination

Teachers and schools are not exempt from the effects of institutional racism and other forms of discrimination present in our society. Try as we
might to shield children from the harmful effects of racism, we live in a society that is stratified by race, gender, and social class divisions, among
others, and these must be taken into consideration in revamping teacher
education programs. In addition, prospective teachers from the dominant
group often fail to acknowledge their own privilege and thus develop what

King (1991) has called *dysconscious racism*; that is, a limited and distorted view of racism based on a tacit acceptance of dominant White norms and privileges that fails to take into account basic structural inequities of society. As a result, White preservice students cannot see how some people benefit from racism while others inevitably lose simply because of their race. Most teacher preparation programs do little to confront this issue.

Some related questions that need to be considered by teacher educators include the following.

How many of us as teacher educators have grappled with our own biases? How do we prepare future teachers to confront racism in their classrooms? This is not a question of developing a "touchy-feely" curriculum or "sensitivity training," but instead concerns designing curriculum and experiences for future teachers that ask them to think about privileges that are earned simply by belonging to particular social groups in society and how this impacts on student learning.

For example, students might be encouraged to look for biases in teacher education texts and curriculum materials. They might be required to document critical incidents in their prepracticum experiences that signal biases in instruction or in their interactions with students. Teacher educators can encourage future teachers to express and confront their biases by developing small-group study circles to tackle difficult issues such as these.

Do we include examples of racism and other types of institutional discrimination in U.S. educational history, including the legacy of segregation, tracking, and exclusion? Our educational history has a long and complex legacy of two competing ideologies: one concerns the push to equalize education and afford all children from all families the benefits of free, compulsory, and high-quality education; the other is a history of exclusion, domination, and inequality evident in such practices as "separate but equal" schooling, unequal economic resources for education, and ability grouping. It is as important to teach future teachers this checkered history as it is to teach child development and methods courses because it helps them confront mythologized and partial views of our educational history and therefore moves the conventional explanation for student failure from an individual problem to that of a structural one.

Expectations of Student Achievement

An issue related to racism and other forms of discrimination concerns expectations of student achievement based on students' race, gender, social class, and other differences. Expectations are often deeply held convictions, but rarely are they directly articulated. This makes them more difficult to confront and discuss.

It is important not to blame just teachers for having low expectations of particular students, because teachers are members of an unequal society and they learn to internalize and hold negative views of students that are reinforced daily by media and other institutions. Blaming teachers alone fails to take into account the fact that they are often the ones who care most about their students and struggle valiantly to teach them. Teachers are not blameless in having low expectations, but they are certainly not alone or completely responsible. Thus, rather than *teacher expectations*, the focus in professional development programs needs to be on *negative expectations of student achievement* and how these may jeopardize the academic success of young people of particular backgrounds.

Some questions that can guide teacher educators in developing their programs include the following.

How do we work with future teachers to help them think about what they expect of students and how students' cultural and socioeconomic backgrounds might influence this?   Exposing students to the history of teacher expectancy effects is an important part of the teacher education curriculum. Although research on teacher expectations is not without its controversies and opinion is divided on how much of an impact teachers may have on the achievement of their students (Brophy, 1983; Eccles & Jussim, 1992; Goldenberg, 1992; Rosenthal, 1987; Rosenthal & Jacobson, 1968; Snow, 1969; Wineburg, 1987), prospective teachers need to be let in on such debates in order to be informed and aware of their own attitudes and prepared to make changes in their teaching practices and interactions with students.

When developing courses and other experiences in teacher education programs, faculty must consider how to help their students make unarticulated expectations more explicit so they can be more directly confronted. A focus on the pedagogy we use in courses (for example, using more small-group activities with less emphasis on lecture) can help make such discussions less uncomfortable for students. In addition, such strategies as journal writing can allow students the freedom to express attitudes and beliefs that they might be reluctant to express verbally. In turn, faculty can use such attitudes and beliefs as a basis for their curriculum—not pointing an accusatory finger at individual students but rather using such attitudes and beliefs to create learning experiences through which all students can learn to look critically at how their own attitudes and behaviors may impact negatively on the learning of some students.

What types of experiences do we give future teachers to have them look at interactions in classrooms, including their own, critically?   Teacher educators may want to focus some of their attention on the types of activities and assignments they give their students outside of class as well, so that students become more aware of how their unstated expectations may have unanticipated and negative consequences. These activities and assignments might include keeping field notes on their work with particular students, videotaping their teaching, and observing and working with their peers to help discuss how expectations, both positive and negative, may influence their teaching.

Curriculum

It is unfortunate that teachers sometimes view curriculum development as little more than a technical activity rather than as a dynamic and potentially empowering decision-making process. Part of the blame lies in teacher education programs that stress stale methods courses rather than challenge their students to think more creatively about what knowledge is of most worth. The fact that teachers have tremendous power in determining the curriculum is likewise not often addressed, and most beginning teachers enter schools ready to be handed a "curriculum-in-place" that they must "deliver." New teachers often appreciate the curriculum-as-product rather than curriculum-as-process approach because of their inexperience and need for guidance, but it soon becomes tiresome and unchallenging.

In contrast to this static view of curriculum, prospective teachers need to learn that curriculum can be powerful and that they have an important role in developing it. They need to be given experiences in which they design curriculum that is rigorous, informative, and engaging to students. Given the multicultural nature of our society, they also need to learn how to best use and reflect students' experiences, lives, and talents in the curriculum.

There is a distinct mismatch between the curriculum of the school and the lives of many children. For example, although students may learn about their cities and towns, they may never come across the types of real people who make their communities come to life. Add to this the fact that the joys, dilemmas, and conflicts of communities are seldom brought into the classroom in significant ways, and the result is that students report being bored because they see little in school that is of relevance to their lives (Grant & Sleeter, 1986; Poplin & Weeres, 1992). Alternatively, when students' strengths (such as native language proficiency or family skills) are unknown to teachers or not addressed in the curriculum (by using their native languages and other skills as valuable resources), schools lose the opportunity to make learning possible for these students (Commins, 1989; Moll, 1992).

Textbooks are an important part of the curriculum in most schools, and they, too, are implicated in teachers' understanding of the curriculum. In fact, if one were to ask teachers to describe their curriculum, many would point to their textbooks as the primary source of the knowledge and information presented to students. Yet textbooks, although more inclusive and representative of diversity than in the past, are still sadly lacking in appropriate content about differences and a critical perspective about the knowledge they do present (García, 1993; Sleeter & Grant, 1991). Not only do they still reinforce the dominance of European American perspectives and accomplishments but they usually present knowledge with such tremendous authority that the truths within their pages are rarely challenged.

How curriculum has traditionally been taught is therefore simply unacceptable for today's schools and classrooms. Some questions that teacher educators need to address in reforming their programs might include the following.

How can teacher preparation programs help future teachers develop a critical perspective about the curriculum?   Built into teacher education courses and other experiences for prospective teachers should be specific activities through which they learn to view curriculum as a decision-making process in which their own creativity and talents can be used. This means providing numerous situations in which teacher education students actually develop curriculum, try it out, and adapt and modify it to best reach their particular students.

In addition, teacher education courses should provide experiences in which future teachers can confront their own biases and limitations so that they understand that the curriculum is never neutral but always represents a point of view and a vested interest. This is best learned when prospective teachers are given opportunities to review textbooks and other instructional materials critically, both at the university and in their field placements.

What knowledge do future teachers need to possess in order to develop affirming, inclusive, and rigorous curricula?   One of the major dilemmas in multicultural education is that teachers cannot teach what they do not know, and most teachers have had little or no experience in knowledge that is outside the traditional canon. Undergraduate education and postbaccalaureate education in the field of education are ideal places in which to provide this type of knowledge and these perspectives to future teachers.

Teacher education programs cannot do it all. Close and collaborative arrangements with other departments and programs need to be developed to ensure that future teachers have a broad-based and comprehensive education in the arts, physical and biological sciences, and social sciences. For example, this means encouraging students to major in areas outside of education and urging them to take courses with content to which they have not been exposed previously, as well as courses that represent the traditional canon. Courses in anthropology and in African American, Latino, Asian, and women's studies, for example, provide alternative experiences because they concern perspectives frequently unknown to most students. An important function of teacher education is to encourage students to find ways to mesh the content they learn in different disciplines.

How can future teachers learn to accept the talents and skills students possess and incorporate them into the curriculum (rather than seeing students as a set of walking deficiencies)? A traditional response of teachers to accommodate for student differences is to water down the curriculum. Although this response may be due to their desire to equitably address differences, instead it can result in low expectations for some students and inequitable student outcomes. In addition, watered-down curriculum tends to be lifeless and dull, disengaging even more the students who need to be drawn into learning.

Prospective teachers can be guided to think critically about the conventional wisdom that students who are economically poor or who are from culturally and linguistically diverse families somehow lack the intellectual stamina to be productive learners. All good teachers know that learning begins where students are at, but because so many prospective teachers have not learned to recognize the particular skills of some students, they learn to view differences from a deficit perspective. That is, rather than seeing students who speak another language as, say, *Vietnamese-speaking* or *Spanish-speaking*, they think of them as *non–English-speaking*, and this in turn shapes how teachers think about what these students are capable of learning.

In both their teacher education courses and in their field placements, future teachers can be challenged to think about ways to develop curriculum that takes into account the skills and talents that students have as a basis for teaching them. In a study concerning the feelings and experiences of Latino students, a Dominican student called this building on their "already culture" (Zanger, 1993).

Pedagogy

It is unfortunate but true that teachers tend to teach as they themselves were taught. Given few alternative models, future teachers simply end up replicating stale and worn methods, and too many schools remain uninteresting and unchallenging places (Goodlad, 1984). This is particularly true of secondary schools, where subject matter controls pedagogy and teachers learn to believe that content is always more important than the form in which it is taught. Schools in economically disadvantaged communities are even more likely to rely on pedagogical strategies that focus on what Haberman (1991) has termed "the pedagogy of poverty"—that is, asking questions, giving directions, making assignments, and monitoring seatwork. Ironically, students who could benefit tremendously from creative, energetic, and challenging environments become even more bored by a pedagogy based on the assumption that children living in poverty cannot perform in such settings. Furthermore, classroom instruction at all levels is too often driven by standardized tests as gatekeepers to promotion and accreditation. Little wonder, then, that so many classrooms are characterized by the "chalk and talk" method of a century ago.

Although it is crucial that knowledge be made more accessible and engaging for students, this by itself is not what pedagogy is about. Pedagogy also concerns how teachers perceive the nature of learning and what they do to create conditions that motivate students to learn and become critical thinkers. For example, most classrooms still reflect the view that learning takes place best in a competitive and highly charged atmosphere, and techniques that stress individual achievement and extrinsic motivation are commonplace. Such policies as ability grouping, testing, and rote learning are the result.

Simply changing large-group instruction to small-group and cooperative groups is not the answer, however. Although cooperative learning is based on the premise that using the talents and skills of all students is important, it is too often accepted unproblematically by future teachers as the answer to all the problems in schools. Yet an examination of current school reform efforts found that, when done uncritically, small-group work can result in students becoming even more passive and dependent learners (McCaslin & Good, 1992). Viewing methods in a critical way is a potent reminder that methods should not become sacred cows, but instead must be understood as means to the end of learning (Bartolomé, 1994; Reyes, 1992).

Although future teachers should be encouraged to develop student-centered, empowering pedagogical strategies, they must also learn to view all pedagogical strategies as means, not as ends in themselves. Some questions to guide teacher educators include the following.

How can we get future teachers to increase their repertoire of pedagogical strategies and to avoid the limitations of "chalk talk"? The best way for teacher educators to challenge their students to develop other ways of teaching is to model the behavior in their own courses. The irony of using only a lecture format in courses that advocate student-centered learning cannot be lost on future teachers. If they are given few resources, they will go back to what is tried and familiar.

In addition, the placement of students in the field is crucial to the development of their pedagogical strategies and to how they think about student learning. It is not so important that future teachers learn the "jigsaw" approach to cooperative groups, for instance, but rather that they learn about the benefits and limitations of group work, among other strategies. For this to happen, they need to be placed with teachers who encourage them to be creative and take risks, and who themselves experiment with a wide variety of strategies.

What types of experiences do future teachers need to help them understand culturally responsive education?   Modifying instruction to be more culturally appropriate is an important skill for teachers who work with students of diverse backgrounds, yet few prospective teachers learn about cultural differences or the types of strategies that can help more students be successful learners. First, future teachers need to be informed about how culture may influence student learning. Although it is limiting and ultimately counterproductive to perceive culture as *predictive* of learning styles or preferences, it is nevertheless important for future teachers to understand that culture may influence (although it does not determine) how their students learn. This approach takes the burden of complete responsibility for learning from the student so that it is shared by teachers as well. That is, teachers need to develop strategies that will speak to the preferred working and learning styles of *all* students, not just of some students, as is usually the case.

Part of the teacher education curriculum can focus on the growing body of research concerning culture-specific educational accommodations (Hollins, King, & Hayman, 1994; Irvine, 1992; Jacob & Jordan, 1993). In addition, future teachers need to practice in a variety of settings so they understand that what has been traditionally viewed as deviant behavior may in fact be culturally influenced. This implies that future teachers will be placed with teachers of different backgrounds who use a variety of strategies and approaches with their students.

Tracking and Ability Grouping

Tracking, the placement of students in groups of similar ability, has been found to be one of the most inequitable practices in schools (Braddock, 1990; Ekstrom, 1992; Goodlad, 1984; Oakes, 1985). Until recently, it has also been quite undisputed and thought to be the most effective way to teach students of widely differing abilities. Yet it is clear from research on tracking that grouping decisions are often made on questionable grounds, and that those who most suffer the consequences of tracking are students who have had the least educational success in our schools, especially students from economically disadvantaged and culturally marginalized families. In fact, tracking decisions have generally reflected other inequities in society based on gender, race, and ethnicity. Thus, Latino, Native American, and African American children, and all children of low-income families, have been found to be at the lowest track levels, where they move slowly (if at all) out of those tracks, where they receive fewer resources and less innovative pedagogy and curriculum, and, as a result, where they develop poor self-esteem.

Some critical questions for teacher educators to consider about tracking would include the following.

What do future teachers need to understand about tracking and how can they learn from it? Prospective teachers should be given the opportunity to consider the debate on tracking in order to be aware of the research and to develop viable alternatives to it in their own classrooms. This means that tracking, rather than being taken for granted as the only way to group students, needs to be viewed critically as simply one option among several.

Simply rejecting tracking and accepting "detracking," however, is not the solution because it does nothing to prepare future teachers to plan their curriculum, organize their classrooms, or consider how to go about developing a learning environment in which all students can learn. In fact, if detracking is accepted without considering such issues as changes in pedagogy, materials, and curriculum, it may do more harm than good by exacerbating student failure and parent disapproval. Therefore, teacher educators also need to present future teachers with concrete suggestions for making detracking work, including skills in cooperative learning, alternative assessment, and empowering pedagogy (Estrin, 1993; Sapon-Shevin, 1992; Wheelock, 1992).

How can we work with future teachers so they understand that tracking is part and parcel of multicultural education and the diversity initiative? Multicultural education is often understood in a superficial way and results in such activities as celebrations of holidays and "ethnic months" in the curriculum. But prospective teachers should know that multicultural education is not just about bulletin boards with beautiful pictures of children from around the world, curricula that include references to many differences, or nice assembly programs. Multicultural education means looking critically at such practices as tracking because traditionally, marginalized students are the ones who suffer the greatest consequences of these decisions. Thus, it is necessary to make the issue of tracking an explicit part of the teacher education curriculum through relevant readings, specific assignments, and work in classrooms.

What skills must we give students so that they can develop viable alternatives to tracking? A review of the effects of tracking needs to be part of the teacher education curriculum in order to counter a simplistic view of multicultural education. Another strategy is to require students to consider diverse approaches to teaching, including peer tutoring, cross-age and cross-grade teaching, and team teaching.

Testing

The relationship of testing to tracking has often been symbiotic. Tests, especially intelligence tests, have been used as the basis for segregating and sorting students, and this is especially true for those whose cultures and languages differ from the mainstream. It has been estimated that about 100 million standardized tests are given yearly, an average of 2.5 tests per student per year (Medina & Neill, 1990). In addition, "high-stakes" testing—connecting the success of students, teachers, and schools to test scores—is a particularly negative form of the testing explosion.

Testing may affect other factors that get in the way of equal educational opportunity. For example, testing can have a negative effect on curriculum and pedagogy because teachers feel forced to "teach to the test" rather than create more innovative and challenging curricula for their students. In fact, a decline in the use of teaching and learning methods (such as student-centered discussions, essay writing, research projects, and laboratory work) has been found to result when standardized tests are required (Darling-Hammond, 1991).

Questions that may be helpful in reforming the way teacher education programs focus on testing include the following.

How do we work with students so that they develop a critical eye toward assessment? What do students need to know about tests and the testing industry? Prospective teachers need to know that much of the testing frenzy is a direct result of the educational reform movement of the 1980s and 1990s, and they need to develop an awareness of the results of assessment policies and how they impact on other school policies and practices. Prospective teachers need to learn what tests are for, how they are used, and the limits and benefits of testing.

What skills do future teachers need to develop so that they learn to assess all students in an equitable manner? The stated purposes of testing are frequently at odds with the ways in which they are used. This has led some researchers to suggest that all norm-based assessments should be abandoned, especially for linguistically and culturally diverse students (Figueroa & García, 1994). It is therefore important for future teachers to know what alternatives to norm-based assessments exist, and to be familiar and comfortable with developing and using these alternatives, including portfolios, performance tasks, and student exhibitions (Ascher, 1990; Estrin, 1993).

Student, Teacher, and Parent Involvement

Schools are not generally organized to encourage active student, parent, or teacher involvement. Although nominally represented in the governance, none of these groups has the kind of direct representation that would make their voices important in the very way that schools are organized and run. Teacher education programs perpetuate this loss of leadership and involvement by providing student teachers with few opportunities to develop the important skills they will need to work with parents or with their own students to develop appropriate and exciting learning environments.

Most new teachers also know very little about their rights and responsibilities as professionals. Teachers often feel as if they have no autonomy, and this curbs their enthusiasm and creativity (Lee, Bryk, & Smith, 1993). This should not be surprising when we consider that student teachers are given little sense of their own efficacy in the teaching-learning process. Teacher education courses and other experiences can make a difference in how teachers view their own involvement and that of others in their classrooms and in schools in general. Relevant questions about parent, student, and teacher involvement, and how to include these in the teacher education curriculum, might include the following.

How do we prepare future teachers to make decisions and see themselves as creative professionals rather than as technical workers? Instead of thinking of themselves as passive recipients of knowledge, future teachers can learn to see themselves as creative and powerful agents for change. In readings, class activities, and fieldwork, prospective teachers should be given opportunities to make decisions about curriculum, pedagogy, and student learning.

In the teacher education curriculum itself, provisions can be made for students to take a key role in their own learning by having them make decisions about the goals they have for their professional development, the kind of research in which they are interested, and the courses they need to take in order to meet their goals. This approach challenges a static and unchanging teacher education curriculum and instead demands flexibility in developing each student's curriculum based on his or her particular situation. Courses can also include information on the profession of teaching per se so that future educators become more aware of the complexity of their roles.

What experiences do we provide future teachers so that they understand the important role of parents in educational decision making and help them confront their fear, anxiety, or superiority concerning parents? Teacher education curriculum can include information about parent involvement and the effect it can have on student achievement and on what teachers and schools can learn from students and how this can affect the curriculum and pedagogy (Epstein & Dauber, 1989; Henderson, 1987). Their fieldwork can include observation of parent-teacher meetings and attendance at PTO and school board meetings. In their classrooms, they should be encouraged to contact and work with parents, not only when there are problems with particular students but as a general way of operating to improve student learning.

How do we help future teachers to involve their students in curriculum planning and to let go of their own power in the classroom? Rather than thinking of learning as a one-way process in which students learn and teachers teach, prospective educators should think of learning as a reciprocal process (Freire, 1970). Using students' ideas, experiences, and interests can also help future teachers think creatively about how the curriculum can be more engaging for their students (Nieto, 1994). Again, placement of students in prepracticum and practicum sites can go a long way in pairing them with teachers who believe that students can be effective in helping to plan the learning environment. In the final analysis, however, it will be through a transformation of the teacher education curriculum that future teachers can be assisted in developing the desire to work collaboratively with a wide range of students.

CONCLUSION

The foregoing discussion about diversity and the specific policies and practices that shape teacher education brings up a number of questions concerning the infusion of these issues in the teacher education curriculum and pedagogy. Given the tremendous variety of teacher education programs that currently exist, no set of changes will work for all. This discussion has not been aimed at providing a specific set of experiences, courses, or objectives for all programs. Curricular and institutional changes must be based on and consistent with the specific context of each program, including considerations of student profiles, the nature of the schools with which it collaborates, the experiences and expertise of the faculty, state guidelines and certification requirements, and, of course, the particular university or college in which the program is located.

The responsibilities of higher education in preparing teachers for the 21st century are awesome. Our society is faced with the daunting challenges of creatively facing the increasing diversity among the student body in elementary and secondary schools, and this diversity is a compelling reason for colleges of education to transform the process of preparing the next generation of teachers. Approaches that build on the experiences of teacher education students and that help them become better teachers of our diverse student populations in elementary and secondary schools are called for. The curriculum needs to be overhauled, of course, but even more important, our ideas about how teachers are prepared for the classroom need to undergo massive changes. Multicultural education and concerns about diversity are thus part of total school reform, not only for public elementary and secondary schools but for teacher education programs as well. Until faculty in teacher preparation programs develop the understanding that diversity means *all* of us, little change will occur in the learning environments and opportunities that are provided for the children in our schools.

REFERENCES

Ascher, C. (1990). *Testing students in urban schools: Current problems and new directions.* New York: ERIC Clearinghouse on Urban Education, Teachers College, Columbia University.

Banks, J. A. (1991). *Teaching strategies for multiethnic education* (5th ed.). Boston: Allyn & Bacon.

Banks, J. A., & Banks, C. M. (1993). *Multicultural education: Issues and perspectives.* Boston: Allyn & Bacon.

Banks, J. A., & Banks, C. A. M. (Eds.). (1995). *Handbook of research on multicultural education.* New York: Macmillan.

Bartolomé, L. (1994). Beyond the methods fetish: Toward a humanizing pedagogy. *Harvard Educational Review, 64*(2), 173–194.

Bennett, C. I. (1990). *Comprehensive multicultural education: Theory and practice* (2nd ed.). Boston: Allyn & Bacon.

Bereiter, C., & Englemann, S. (1966). *Teaching disadvantaged children in the preschool.* Englewood Cliffs, NJ: Prentice-Hall.

Braddock, J. J., II (1990, February). *Tracking: Implications for student race-ethnic subgroups.* Baltimore, MD: Johns Hopkins University, Center for Research on Effective Schooling for Disadvantaged Students, Report No. 1.

Brophy, J. E. (1983). Research on the self-fulfilling prophecy and teacher expectations. *Journal of Educational Psychology, 75,* 631–661.

Commins, N. L. (1989). Language and affect: Bilingual students at home and at school. *Language Arts, 66*(1), 29–43.

Darling-Hammond, L. (1991). The implications of testing policy for quality and equality. *Phi Delta Kappan, 73*(3), 220–225.

Eccles, J., & Jussim, L. (1992). Teacher expectations: Construction and reflection of student achievement. *Journal of Personality and Social Psychology, 63*(6), 947–961.

Ekstrom, R. B. (1992). Six urban school districts: Their middle-grade grouping policies and practices. In *On the right track: The consequences of mathematics course placement policies and practices in the middle grades* [Report to the Edna McConnell Clark Foundation]. New York: ETS and the National Urban League.

Epstein, J. L., & Dauber, S. L. (1989). Teacher attitudes and practices of parent involvement in inner-city elementary and middle schools [Report no. 33]. Baltimore Center for Research on Elementary and Middle Schools, John Hopkins University.

Estrin, E. T. (1993). *Alternative assessment: Issues in language, culture, & equity* [Knowledge Brief No. 11]. San Francisco: Far West Laboratory.

Figueroa, R. A., & García, E. (1994). Issues in testing students from culturally and linguistically diverse backgrounds. *Multicultural Education, 2*(1), 10–19.

Freire, P. (1970). *Pedagogy of the oppressed.* New York: Seabury Press.

García, J. (1993). The changing image of ethnic groups in textbooks. *Phi Delta Kappan, 75*(1), 29–35.

Goldenberg, C. (1992). The limits of expectations: A case for case knowledge about teacher expectancy effects. *American Educational Research Journal, 29*(3), 514–544.

Gollnick, D. M., & Chinn, P. C. (1994). *Multicultural education in a pluralistic society* (4th ed.). New York: Macmillan.

Goodlad, J. (1984). *A place called school.* New York: McGraw-Hill.

Grant, C. A., & Sleeter, C. E. (1986). *After the school bell rings.* Philadelphia: Falmer Press.

Haberman, M. (1991). The pedagogy of poverty versus good teaching. *Phi Delta Kappan, 73*(4), 290–294.

Henderson, A. T. (1987). *The evidence continues to grow: Parent involvement improves student achievement.* Columbia, MD: National Coalition of Citizens in Education.

Hollins, E. T., King, J. E., & Hayman, W. C. (Eds.). (1994). *Teaching diverse populations: Formulating a knowledge base.* Albany, NY: SUNY Press.

Irvine, J. J. (1992). Making teacher education culturally responsive. In M. E. Dilworth (Ed.), Diversity in teacher education: *Teacher education yearbook 1* (pp. 79–92). San Francisco: Jossey-Bass.

Jacob, E., & Jordan, C. (Eds.). (1993). *Minority education: Anthropological perspectives.* Norwood, NJ: Ablex.

Jensen, A. R. (1969). How much can we boost IQ and scholastic achievement? *Harvard Educational Review, 39,* 1–123.

King, J. E. (1991). Dysconscious racism: Ideology, identity, and the miseducation of teachers. *Journal of Negro Education, 60*(2), 133–146.

Lee, V. E., Bryk, A. A., & Smith, J. B. (1993). The organization of effective secondary schools. In L. Darling-Hammond (Ed.), *Review of research in education* (pp. 171–267). Washington, DC: American Educational Research Association.

McCaslin, M., & Good, T. L. (1992). Compliant cognition: The misalliance of management and instructional goals in current school reform. *Educational Researcher, 21*(3), 4–17.

Medina, N., & Neill, D. M. (1990). *Fallout from the testing explosion* (3rd ed.). Cambridge, MA: FairTest.

Moll, L. C. (1992). Bilingual classroom studies and community analysis: Some recent trends. *Educational Researcher, 21*(2), 20–24.

Nieto, S. (1994). Lessons from students on creating a chance to dream. *Harvard Educational Review, 64*(4), 392–426.

Nieto, S. (1996). *Affirming diversity: The sociopolitical context of multicultural education* (2d rev. ed.). White Plains, NY: Longman.

Oakes, J. (1985). *Keeping track: How schools structure inequality*. New Haven, CT: Yale University Press.

Oakes, J. (1992). Can tracking research inform practice? *Educational Researcher, 21*(4), 12–21.

Perry, T., & Fraser, J. W. (1993). *Freedom's plow: Teaching in the multicultural classroom*. New York: Routledge & Kegan Paul.

Poplin, M., & Weeres, J. (1992). *Voices from the inside: A report on schooling from inside the classroom*. Claremont, CA: The Institute for Education in Transformation, Claremont Graduate School.

Reisman, F. (1962). *The culturally deprived child*. New York: Harper & Row.

Reyes, M. (1992). Challenging venerable assumptions: Literacy instruction for linguistically different students. *Harvard Educational Review, 62*(4), 427–446.

Rosenthal, R. (1987). Pygmalion effects: Existence, magnitude, and social importance. *Educational Researcher, 16*(9), 37–44.

Rosenthal, R., & Jacobson, L. (1968). *Pygmalion in the classroom*. New York: Holt, Rinehart & Winston.

Sapon-Shevin, M. (1992). Ability differences in the classroom: Teaching and learning in inclusive classrooms. In D. A. Byrnes & G. Kiger, *Common bonds: Anti-bias teaching in a diverse society* (pp. 39–52). Wheaton, MD: Association for Childhood Education International.

Skutnabb-Kangas, T., & Cummins, J. (1988). Multilingualism and the education of minority children. In T. Skutnabb-Kangas & J. Cummins (Eds.), *Minority education: From shame to struggle* (pp. 9–44). Clevedon, England: Multilingual Matters.

Sleeter, C. E., & Grant, C. A. (1991). Race, class, gender and disability in current textbooks. In M. W. Apple & L. K. Christian-Smith (Eds.), *The politics of the textbook*. New York: Routledge & Chapman Hall.

Sleeter, C. E., & Grant, C. A. (1994). *Making choices for multicultural education: Five approaches to race, class, and gender* (2nd ed.). New York: Macmillan.

Snow, R. E. (1969). Unfinished Pygmalion. *Contemporary Psychology, 14*, 197–200.

Wheelock, A. (1992). *Crossing the tracks: How "untracking" can save America's schools*. New York: Free Press.

Wineburg, S. S. (1987). The self-fulfillment of the self-fulfilling prophecy: A critical appraisal. *Educational Researcher, 16*(9), 28–37.

Zanger, V. V. (1993). Academic costs of social marginalization: An analysis of the perceptions of Latino students at a Boston high school. In R. Rivera & S. Nieto, *The education of Latino students in Massachusetts: Issues, research, and policy implications* (pp. 170–190). Boston: The Mauricio Gastón Institute for Latino Community Development and Public Policy, University of Massachusetts.

CRITICAL QUESTIONS

1. One of the questions addressed to faculty in the preceding chapter was "What types of experiences do we give future teachers to have them look at interactions in classrooms, including their own, critically?" Have you had experiences to help you do this? If not, what can help you look at your own interactions with students critically?

2. In terms of assessment, one of the greatest challenges facing teachers at present is the growing focus on high-stakes testing. Educational environments throughout the country are increasingly characterized by the

message, unintended or not, to "teach to the test." What are the implications of this trend for students of culturally and linguistically diverse backgrounds? What are you doing to face this challenge? Have you discussed these issues in class?

3. Write a letter to one of your former professors and let her or him know what was most helpful about their course in preparing you for your profession. What other information might have helped you?

CLASSROOM/COMMUNITY-BASED ACTIVITIES AND ADVOCACY

1. Teacher certification is based on the assumption that all future teachers need to develop basic competencies and knowledge in their field. With a group of your classmates, develop teacher certification requirements based on the competencies and knowledge that *you* believe are essential for teachers to have if they are to be effective with students of diverse backgrounds. (Try to stay away from a simple checklist). Next, develop a series of courses or other teacher preparation experiences that might help prospective teachers develop the knowledge and competencies they need.

Are these courses and experiences similar to or different from the ones in which you've been involved? How are they different? What is missing in the teacher certification plan you've developed? Have you addressed teaching students of diverse backgrounds? You may consider writing a letter to your state department of education certification board with your suggestions for revising teacher certification requirements.

2. In *Lies My Teacher Told Me* (1995) (see reference following), James Loewen described the survey he did of 12 popular American history textbooks to determine how they dealt with race, the history of slavery, the Civil Rights movement, and so on. Among other things, he found that the topic of race relations is virtually missing in most of them, and they tend to credit the government, rather than ordinary citizens and young people, for progress during the Civil Rights movement.

Do a review of the history textbooks in use in your school. Look at how they present slavery and the Civil Rights movement. What about the women's movement and women's rights? What do they have to say about immigrants and immigration? about the education of language minority students and bilingual education? What is included in the texts? What is missing? What recommendations would you give your principal or district superintendent about your findings and what action would you suggest?

SUPPLEMENTARY RESOURCES FOR FURTHER REFLECTION AND STUDY

Cochran-Smith, Marilyn (1991). Learning to teach against the grain. *Harvard Educational Review, 61*, 279–310.

In this noteworthy article, the author argues that the most powerful way for student teachers to learn to "teach against the grain" is to work side-by-side with experienced teachers who are themselves struggling to be reformers in their own classrooms, schools, and communities.

Cummins, Jim (1996). *Negotiating identities: Education for empowerment in a diverse society.* Ontario, CA: California Association for Bilingual Education.

Jim Cummins argues that implementing true educational reform that has a goal of turning around deep-seated and long-term discrimination requires "*personal redefinitions* of the ways in which *individual educators* interact with the students and communities they serve" (p. 136).

Freire, Paulo (1998). *Teachers as cultural workers: Letters to those who dare teach.* Boulder, CO: Westview Press.

In this series of letters published shortly after his death, Paulo Freire speaks directly to teachers about the lessons learned from a lifetime of experience as a teacher and social activist.

Irvine, Jacqueline Jordan (Ed.) (1997). *Critical knowledge for diverse teachers and learners.* Washington, DC: American Association for Colleges of Teacher Education.

Written by scholars in teacher education, the chapters in this book include discussions about what is essential knowledge for teachers who work with diverse populations.

Loewen, J. W. (1995). *Lies my teacher told me: Everything your American history textbook got wrong.* New York: New Press.

In this critical review of a number of the most widely used U.S. history textbooks, Loewen demonstrates how much of what is taught is based on myths, inaccuracies, and one-sided perspectives.

Perrone, Vito (1991). *A letter to teachers: Reflections on schooling and the art of teaching.* San Francisco: Jossey-Bass Publishers.

The author reflects on his many years of teaching to share some of the knowledge he's learned and to suggest what teachers need to know to become better at their craft.

Bringing Bilingual Education Out of the Basement and Other Imperatives for Teacher Education

INTRODUCTION

Think about the bilingual program in your school or other schools that you know: Is it in the basement or next to the boiler room? Is it located in a closet or under the stairs? Is it in a temporary mobile unit? All of these are indications that the bilingual program (the same can often be said about the special education program) has a low position in the school and community. The "basement" is an apt metaphor for the place and status that bilingual education and other issues of concern for language minority students have in most schools.

In this chapter, I again address the issue of teacher education, this time with a lens on language minority students. In my answer to the question, "What do teachers and prospective teachers need to know about language minority students and why?", I suggest that there has often been a widespread assumption that language minority students are the responsibility of specialists such as ESL and bilingual teachers, and perhaps after leaving the program, of special education teachers. But we can no longer delude ourselves that this is the case. Language minority children and young people are found, or soon will be found, in almost every classroom around the country. As a result, all teachers of all backgrounds who teach in all schools need to be adequately prepared to teach them. Hence, I suggest that teachers need to develop competence in specific subject matters and, even more significantly, in the attitudes and values they have concerning young people of language minority backgrounds.

Schools and colleges of education by and large have failed to adequately prepare future and practicing teachers to teach language-minority students. Those teacher education programs that offer specializations in bilingual education and/or ESL, and even more so those that combine these strands, are well equipped to prepare teachers to face the challenges of the growing language-minority student population in our nation. But programs without such strands are frequently guided by the assumption that the job of schools of education is to train teachers to work in "regular"— that is, monolingual English—classrooms. They give little consideration to the fact that *all* classrooms in the future will have students whose first language is not English, even if they do not currently serve such students.

The number and variety of language-minority students have escalated tremendously in the past several years. For example, according to a 1996 report (Macías & Kelly, 1996), there were 3,184,696 students classified as having limited proficiency in English, almost a 5 percent increase in just one year. The same report indicated that students of limited English proficiency represent 7.3 percent of all public school students, and that far fewer than 50 percent of these students were enrolled in federal or state programs in bilingual education. As a result, over half of all students whose native language is other than English spend most or part of their day in monolingual English classrooms. This situation is reason enough to propose that all teachers, not only bilingual teachers, need to be prepared to work with language-minority students.

In this chapter, I suggest that, although schools and colleges of education need to teach specific skills and strategies for working with language-minority students, it is even more essential that teacher education programs help teachers to develop positive attitudes and beliefs toward these students. After all, questions of language are *pedagogical* as well as *ideological*. Ideologies reflect a deeply ingrained system of beliefs, and they generally include a political program for action. In terms of linguistic differences, ideologies reflect positive or negative values concerning specific languages and the people who speak them. In addition, ideologies either uphold or challenge established authority and existing policies. In the case of language diversity, ideologies can either engage human efforts behind pluralism and social equality, or they can support the status quo.

What is the responsibility of schools and colleges of education to prepare teachers to work with students who speak native languages other than English? What should *all* teachers know about language-minority students, and what kinds of skills do teachers need to be effective with these students? In the case of bilingual and ESL teachers, what distinct competencies do they need to develop? In what follows, I review the kinds of knowledge that schools and colleges of education need to develop in all their teacher candidates, whether these future teachers expect to work in bilingual settings or not. I will also mention a number of explicit areas of study that bilingual and ESL teachers need. But I will focus my attention on the values, beliefs, and attitudes that I believe should be at the core of teacher education programs. I propose three imperatives for teacher education programs as they prepare teachers for the new generation of Americans, many of whom are language-minority students. Specifically, I suggest that teacher education programs need to

1. take a stand on language diversity;
2. bring bilingual education out of the basement;
3. promote teaching as a lifelong journey of transformation.

WHAT SHOULD TEACHERS KNOW?

Students who are speakers of languages other than English are found in classrooms in all communities throughout the United States, from the most urban to the most rural and from the ethnically diverse to the seemingly homogeneous (Macías & Kelly, 1996). Yet most teacher education programs continue to behave as if language-minority students were found only in ESL or bilingual classrooms. As a result, teachers who have taken traditional courses in pedagogy and curriculum or who have had typical practicum experiences in English monolingual settings will not be prepared to teach the growing number of language-minority students who will end up in their classrooms. Even when language-minority students are primarily in ESL or bilingual settings, presuming that these students are the sole responsibility of ESL and bilingual teachers strengthens the perception that these youngsters should be in separate classrooms, halls, and even schools rather than integrated with their peers whenever pedagogically possible.

Because language-minority students are often physically isolated from their English-speaking peers, this separation adds to their alienation. The same is true of bilingual teachers, who in most schools are both physically and emotionally separated from other teachers. Bilingual teachers report feeling estranged, dismissed, or simply ignored by their peers and supervisors (Montero-Sieburth & Pérez, 1987). Consequently, the relationships among bilingual and "mainstream" teachers, and among students in bilingual and English-monolingual classrooms, are regularly fraught with misunderstanding. The emotional and physical separation experienced by bilingual and nonbilingual teachers does not lend itself to developing collegial relationships or opportunities to work collaboratively.

What might allow collaborative relationships between bilingual and nonbilingual teachers? One way to promote opportunities for them to work together is to start off all teachers with common knowledge concerning language diversity. All teachers, not only bilingual and ESL teachers, need to develop the following kinds of knowledge:

- familiarity with first- and second-language acquisition
- awareness of the sociocultural and sociopolitical context of education for language-minority students
- awareness of the history of immigration in the United States, with particular attention to language policies and practices throughout that history
- knowledge of the history and experiences of specific groups of people, especially those who are residents of the city, town, and state where they will be teaching
- ability to adapt curriculum for students whose first language is other than English
- competence in pedagogical approaches suitable for culturally and linguistically heterogeneous classrooms
- experience with teachers of diverse backgrounds and the ability to develop collaborative relationships with colleagues that promote the learning of language-minority students
- ability to communicate effectively with parents of diverse language, culture, and social-class backgrounds

In addition to these skills, all teacher candidates, regardless of the setting in which they will be working, should be strongly encouraged to learn a second language, particularly a language spoken by a substantial number of students in the community in which they teach or intend to teach. No matter how empathic teachers may be of the ordeal that students go through to learn English, nothing can bring it home in quite the same way as going through the process themselves. Bill Dunn, a doctoral student of mine who "came out of the closet" as a Spanish speaker a number of years ago, wrote eloquently about this experience in a journal he kept (Nieto, 1999). Bill teaches in a town with a student body that is about 75 percent Puerto Rican, and after twenty years in the system, he realized that he understood a good deal of Spanish. He decided to learn Spanish more systematically through activities such as taking a Spanish class at a community center, sitting in on bilingual classes in his school, and watching Spanish-language television shows. Although Bill had been a wonderful teacher before learning Spanish, the experience of placing himself in the vulnerable position of learner taught him many things: a heightened respect for students who were learning English; a clearer understanding of why his Spanish-speaking students, even those who were fluent in English, made particular mistakes in grammar and spelling; and a renewed admiration for the bilingual teachers in his school.

The skills and knowledge listed above are a common starting point for all teachers, but for those who are preparing to become bilingual and/or ESL teachers, the knowledge base needs to be expanded to include:

- fluency in at least one language in addition to English
- knowledge of the conceptual and theoretical basis for bilingual education
- knowledge of specific pedagogical strategies that promote language development
- ability to serve as cultural mediators between students and the school
- knowledge of various strategies for assessing students' language proficiency and academic progress

This list is not meant to be exhaustive, but rather to suggest that there are numerous specific strategies and approaches that teachers of language-minority backgrounds need to learn. But in spite of the importance of knowing particular strategies and approaches, I believe that the focus of teacher educators has to be elsewhere. Although bilingual education is about language and pedagogy, it is equally about power and ideology. That is, questions of *which* language to use, *when* and *how* to use it, and *why* it should be used are above all ideological questions. In the final analysis, native-language education brings up questions of whose language has legitimacy and power, and of how far our society is willing to allow differences to exist and even flourish. These questions go to the heart of what our schools are for, and what we value as a society. Consequently, I suggest that besides pedagogy and curriculum, schools and colleges of education need to help teachers develop critical perspectives about education. This means that the *values, beliefs*, and *attitudes* that underscore particular approaches also need to become the subject matter of their study and analysis.

THE IDEOLOGICAL UNDERPINNINGS
OF BILINGUAL EDUCATION

As we have previously discussed, ideology is a systematic set of principles usually linked with political action that either upholds or challenges the status quo. A generation ago, Paulo Freire's (1970) assertion that education is always political was greeted with denial or skepticism in many quarters in our society. The claim that education is political—that is, that it is fundamentally concerned with issues of power and dominance—flies in the face of education as understood in the United States, where we have always asserted that education is universal, equal, and fair. But the ideological basis of education is exposed through such blatant practices as vastly differentiated funding for rich and poor school districts (Kozol, 1991), and the detrimental effects of ability tracking and other sorting practices on students of diverse socioeconomic, racial, ethnic, and linguistic backgrounds (Oakes, 1985; Spring, 1989). The political nature of education has also been evident in the case of bilingual education, which has been under attack since its very inception (Nieto, 1992). Scholars of bilingual education have always known that it is political, and some books on the subject discuss openly its political nature and include reference to it in their titles (Arias & Casanova, 1993; Crawford, 1992).

But what does it mean to say that bilingual education is political? For one thing, it means that every discussion of bilingual education is based on a philosophical orientation concerning language diversity in our society and on the official status that languages other than English are to be given. It also means that all educational decisions about bilingual education—when and how to use which language, the nature of the program, who should teach in such programs, and the educational expectations of students who speak languages other than English—reflect a particular worldview. Prospective teachers need to understand that the mere existence of bilingual education affronts one of the most cherished ideals of our public schools, that is, the assimilation of students of nondominant backgrounds into the cultural mainstream. And because bilingual education challenges the assimilationist agenda of our schools and society, I believe that the greatest fear among its opponents is that *bilingual education might in fact work.* If this were not the case, why so much opposition to it?

Prospective teachers need to know that bilingual education developed in the 1960s as a result of the civil rights era; that linguistic democracy has been as crucial a civil rights issue for language-minority communities as desegregation has been for African American communities; and that language is a central value and birthright that many families treasure and seek to maintain. Prospective teachers also need to understand that the families of language-minority students want their children to become fluent speakers of English because they know that this knowledge will provide their children with their greatest opportunity for academic and economic success. Many of these families insist, however, that their children also maintain and use their first language.

The curriculum, as well as the quality and quantity of materials, available to students in bilingual programs, and decisions about when to move students from bilingual to nonbilingual classes are all political, and not merely pedagogical, decisions. Language-minority students in the United States are overwhelmingly poor and powerless, and their dominated status is related in no small way to how they are perceived and to the nature of the education they receive. For instance, because bilingual education is ordinarily a program for economically disadvantaged and oppressed communities, city and state boards of education are often unenthusiastic about spending money on a program they perceive as too expensive and "wasteful." But in middle-class neighborhoods, the costs associated with teaching children a second language are rarely challenged.

IMPERATIVES FOR TEACHER EDUCATION

If indeed all teachers will at some time or another be faced with teaching students whose first language is other than English, what is the responsibility of teacher educators and teacher preparation programs? Let me suggest three imperatives for teacher education: first, teacher educators and teacher preparation programs need to take a stand concerning the education of language-minority students; second, they need to bring bilingual education out of the basement, both literally and figuratively; and third, they need to prepare future teachers to think of teaching as a lifelong journey of transformation. I will comment briefly on the first two, and more thoroughly on the third of these imperatives.

Take a Stand on Language Diversity

Schools and colleges of education need to decide what they stand for concerning education in general, as well as in the specific case of language diversity and language-minority students. They can begin this process by asking a number of key questions, the answers to which they may assume are shared, but which very often are not:

• *What is the purpose of education? What are schools for?*
Other than to prepare lofty mission statements that have little to do with their day-to-day practice, it is rare for faculties of education to get together to discuss the very purposes of education: Is the purpose of schools to fit students into society? Is it to prepare students for specific jobs? Or is it to prepare students to become productive and critical citizens of a democratic society? Must schools replicate societal inequities? Should they seek to prepare a few good managers and many compliant workers? Or is the role of schools to prepare students for the challenges of a pluralistic

and rapidly changing society? Answers to these questions can determine the scope and quality of a teacher preparation program curriculum and the field experiences provided to students. If, for example, the faculty determines that the primary objective of education is to prepare students for our rapidly changing and pluralistic society, then attention to language diversity becomes a key component in their course offerings.

• *What do we do about language diversity?*

The issue of difference lies at the heart of the way that U.S. schools have defined their responsibility to educate young people. From the time that compulsory schooling in the United States began, the ideals of equality and fairness have struggled with the ideals of pluralism and diversity (Dewey, 1916; Spring, 1997; Weinberg, 1977). That is, the balance between *unum* and *pluribus* has always been contested. Many times, the zeal to assimilate and homogenize all students to one norm has won out; rarely has diversity been highlighted as a value in its own right.

In the case of language diversity, Luis Moll (1992) has pointed out the singular focus on the English language taken by many educators and society at large, suggesting that

> the obsession of speaking English reigns supreme—as if the children were somehow incapable of learning that language well, or as if the parents and teachers were unaware of the importance of English in U.S. society—and usually at the expense of other educational or academic matters. (pp. 20–21)

Historically, answers to the question of what to do about language diversity have ranged from grudging acceptance, to outlawing the use of languages other than English in instruction, to brutal policies, especially those directed at Mexican Americans and American Indians, that enforced the use of the English language at the exclusion of other languages (Crawford, 1992; Deyhle & Swisher, 1997; Donato, 1997). How schools of education answer these questions can help them either to focus on assimilation as a goal, or to think of ways to use language diversity as a resource.

Bring Bilingual Education Out of the Basement

The basement is a fitting metaphor for the status of bilingual education, both in elementary and secondary schools and in schools and colleges of education. Basements are dark, dank places where people store what they do not want to display in their homes. Bilingual programs are frequently found in basements next to the boiler room, in supply closets, or in trailers or hallways isolated from the rest of the school. Their very physical placement is a giveaway to their low status in schools and among the general public. But language-minority students will not disappear simply because they are hidden from sight. If it is true that the number of language-minority students will increase over the coming years, then all teachers need to learn how to best teach them. Further, all schools and colleges of education, no matter how remote they may be from the urban areas where most language-minority students live, have to prepare teachers who will specialize in teaching these students, because no geographic area will remain a monolingual enclave of English for long.

In schools and in teacher preparation programs, bilingual education needs to be moved out of the basement and onto the first floor. Figuratively speaking, at the university level, this means giving bilingual education and language diversity issues a place of prominence in the teacher education curriculum. Although there is a need to continue to offer specialized courses for bilingual and ESL teachers who will spend the bulk of their time with language-minority students, as a profession we can no longer afford to teach about bilingual education only to prospective bilingual teachers. Rather, all courses should be infused with content relating to language diversity, from those in secondary science methods to those in reading. Courses in educational foundations, history, and policy matters also should include reference to bilingual education. Pre-practicum and practicum placements, other field experiences, course assignments, and course readings also need to reflect support for language diversity. In addition, schools of education might rethink their requirements for admission, giving priority to those candidates who are fluent in at least one language other than English. In sum, language and language diversity issues would become part of the *normal experience* for all prospective teachers. In this way, it becomes clear that the responsibility for teaching language-minority students belongs to all teachers.

An approach that gives language diversity a high status in teacher preparation programs will invariably mean that teacher educators will face a good deal of resistance from some prospective teachers. It is by now a truism that most prospective teachers are White, middle-class, monolingual English-speaking women with little experience with people different from themselves, and that most of them believe—or at least hope—they will teach in largely White, middle-class communities (Aaronsohn, Carter, & Howell, 1995). Having to take courses that focus on students whom they may not want to teach, and that give weight to issues that they may want to dismiss, will certainly cause some tension. In fact, teaching courses that focus on diversity in any way usually results in conflict, and there is ample demonstration of this fact in the literature (Chávez Chávez & O'Donnell, 1998). But infusing the curriculum with content in language diversity may also result in expanding the vision and therefore enriching the perspectives of prospective teachers. In turn, their success and effectiveness with language-minority students may also be positively affected.

As is the case with teachers, most teacher educators are also White, middle-class, monolingual English speakers, and many have had little experience or training in language diversity issues. This means that teacher educators must themselves rethink how their courses need to be changed to reflect language diversity, and they need to be given the support and time to do so. Likewise, if we are serious about giving language diversity a positive status in the general teacher education program, we must recognize that the current teacher education faculty needs to be diversified. Consequently, another implication of bringing bilingual education out of the basement is that schools of education will have to recruit a more diverse faculty with specific training and experience in bilingual education, second-language acquisition, and the education of language-minority students.

Recruiting a diverse faculty does not in and of itself guarantee that the result will be a faculty that is more diverse in ideological perspective. For example, not all Latinos/as are supporters of bilingual education, nor should they be recruited for this reason. However, recruiting a faculty that is diverse in training and expertise, as well as in background and experience, will probably ensure a broader diversity of perspectives than is currently the case.

Promote Teaching as a Lifelong Journey of Transformation

Teacher educators have the lofty but frightening responsibility to prepare future teachers and other educational leaders. In terms of diversity, I believe that our major responsibility is twofold: to help teachers and prospective teachers affirm the linguistic, cultural, and experiential diversity of their students while at the same time opening up new vistas, opportunities, and challenges that expand their worlds. But because teaching is above all a matter of forming caring and supportive relationships, the process of affirming the diversity of students begins as a journey of the teachers. A journey always presupposes that the traveler will change along the way, and teaching is no exception. However, if we expect teachers to begin their own journey of transformation, teacher educators must be willing to join them because until we take stock of ourselves, until we question and challenge our own biases and values, nothing will change for our students.

Affirming the diversity of students is not just an individual journey, however. It is equally a collective and institutional journey that happens outside individual classrooms and college courses. How do teachers prepare for the journey, and what is the role of teacher educators? Let me suggest several central points to keep in mind as teachers and faculty begin this journey (these are discussed in much greater detail in Nieto, 1999).

Teachers Need to Face and Accept Their Own Identities.   As we have mentioned, most teachers in the United States are White, monolingual, middle-class females who are teaching a student body that is increasingly diverse in native language, race, ethnicity, and social class. Due to their own limited experiences with people of diverse backgrounds, including language-minority backgrounds, many teachers perceive of language diversity as a problem rather than an asset. This is probably due to the fact that they have internalized the message that their culture is the norm against which to measure all others. As a result, they seldom question their White-skin or English-language privilege (McIntosh, 1988). Schools and colleges of education need to provide prospective teachers with opportunities to reflect on all of these issues before teaching children from diverse backgrounds.

Because of the assimilationist nature of U.S. schooling, most people of European American background have accepted the "melting pot" as a true reflection of our society's experience with cultural pluralism. The immigration of Europeans is generally presented as the model by which all other groups should be measured, as if it represented the reality of others whose history, race, culture, and historical context differ greatly. Many teachers of European American descent, who are drawn primarily from working-class backgrounds, are quick to accept the myths about diversity, merit, success, and assimilation that they have learned along the way. In a compelling essay written over a quarter of a century ago, Mildred Dickeman (1973) explained how such myths operate:

> All mythologies serve to interpret reality in ways useful to the perpetuation of a society. In this case an ideology arose which interpreted the existence of ethnic diversity in America in ways supportive of the sociopolitical establishment. Probably the schools played an important role in the creation of this ideology. Certainly they came to serve as the major institutions for its propagation. (p. 8)

The myths to which Dickeman allude include the perception that people of nonmainstream backgrounds must completely "melt" in order to be successful; that individual effort is superior to community and collective identity and action; and that all it takes is hard work and perseverance to make it, with no attention paid to the structural barriers and institutional biases that get in the way of equality. If they believe these myths, it becomes easy for teachers to compare African American, Latino, American Indian, and Asian and Asian American students with the portrait of successful European immigrants they have accepted as the norm, and to blame students who do not achieve academically. Generally, the blame is couched in terms of the inferior culture or race of the students, or on passivity or lack of concern on the part of their parents.

One consequence of accepting these deficit views is that because only students of backgrounds visibly different from the mainstream are thought to have a culture, culture itself is defined as a problem. But teachers also have cultural identities, even though they have learned to forget or deny them. As cultural beings, they come into teaching with particular worldviews, values, and beliefs, and these influence all of their interactions with their students. For the most part, however, teachers of European American backgrounds are unaware that they even possess a culture, or that their culture influences them in any substantive way save for holiday celebrations or ethnic festivals they may still attend. All teachers of all backgrounds need to recognize, understand, and accept their own diversity and delve into their own identities before they can learn about and from their students. Specifically in the case of teachers of European American backgrounds, Dickeman suggests that they begin to uncover and recover their own histories:

> Coming as we do from a range of ethnic and cultural identities, and by the mere fact of recruitment primarily from the lower and lower middle classes, we have available to us, however forgotten, repressed or ignored, the experiences of self and family in the context of pressure for assimilation and upward mobility. . . . When teachers begin to recognize that their own ethnic heritages are valuable, that their own family histories are relevant to learning and teaching, the battle is half won. (p. 24)

Recovering their ethnic identities invariably leads European American teachers to a confrontation with their racial, linguistic, and social-class privilege (Howard, 1999; McIntosh, 1988), a painful but ultimately life-changing experience for many of them. For teacher preparation programs, this implies that opportunities and support need to be provided for teachers and prospective teachers to go through this process. These opportunities also need to be made available to teachers and future teachers from nondominant backgrounds. Although teacher educators often assume that prospective teachers of African American, Hispanic, and Asian American backgrounds are somehow automatically prepared to teach students of diverse backgrounds simply by virtue of their own backgrounds, this is not always true (Nieto, in press). That is, having an identity that differs from the mainstream—for example, being Chicana—does not necessarily guarantee sensitivity or knowledge about Vietnamese students. Likewise, being Chicana does not even mean that a teacher will be more knowledgeable about her Chicano students. Although it is generally true that teachers of nondominant backgrounds bring substantial skills, knowledge, and passion to their jobs, this is not always the case. Teacher preparation programs need to understand this, and they need to provide *all* prospective teachers, not just those of European American background, with the skills and attitudes to teach students of all backgrounds.

Teachers Need to Become Learners and Identify With Their Students. Without denying the need to teach students the cultural capital that they need to help them negotiate society, teachers also need to make a commitment to become *students of their students*. This implies at least two kinds of processes. First, teachers need to learn *about* their students, a change from the one-way learning that usually takes place in classrooms. For this to happen, teachers must become researchers of their students. Second, teachers need to create spaces in which they can learn *with* their students, and in which students are encouraged to learn about themselves and one another.

If we think of teaching and learning as reciprocal processes, as proposed by Paulo Freire (1970), then teachers need to become actively engaged in learning through their interactions with students. Developing a stance as learners is especially consequential if we think about the wide gulf that currently exists in the United States between the language backgrounds and other experiences of teachers and their students. Given this situation, the conventional approach has been to instruct students in the ways of White, middle-class, English-speaking America and, in the process, to rid them of as many of their differences as possible.

Learning about one's students is not simply a technical strategy, or a process of picking up a few cultural tidbits. It is impossible for teachers to become culturally or linguistically responsive simply by taking a course where these concerns are reduced to strategies. This does not mean that teaching is always an intuitive undertaking, although it certainly has this quality at times. But even more pivotal are the attitudes of teachers when they are in the position of learners. That is, teachers need to be open to their language-minority students' knowledge in order to find what can help them learn, and then change their teaching accordingly.

Defining the teacher as a learner is a radical departure from the prevailing notion of the educator as repository of all knowledge, a view that is firmly entrenched in society. Ira Shor (Shor & Freire, 1987) critiqued this conventional portrait of teachers vis-à-vis their students: "The students are not a flotilla of boats trying to reach the teacher who is finished and waiting on the shore. The teacher is also one of the boats" (p. 50). Yet in spite of how terrifying it may be for teachers to act as all-knowing sages, the conception of *teacher as knower* is a more familiar and, hence, less threatening one than *teacher as learner*. Once teachers admit that they do not know everything, they make themselves as vulnerable as their students. But it is precisely this attitude of learner on the part of teachers that is needed, first, to convey to linguistically diverse students that nobody is above learning; and second, to let students know that they also are knowers, and that what they know can be an important source of learning for others as well. It follows from this perspective that there needs to be a move away from the deficit model to a recognition of the cultural and linguistic knowledge and resources that students bring to their education. Teachers need to build on this knowledge as the foundation of their students' academic learning.

Teachers Need to Become Multilingual and Multicultural. Teachers can talk on and on about the value of cultural diversity, and about how beneficial it is to know a second language, but if they themselves do not attempt to learn another language, or if they remain monocultural in outlook, their words may sound hollow to their students. Even if their curriculum is outwardly supportive of students' linguistic and cultural diversity, if teachers do not demonstrate through their actions and behaviors that they truly value diversity, students can often tell.

Teachers who can call on their own identities of linguistic and cultural diversity usually have an easier time of identifying with their students of diverse backgrounds. But absent such connections with diversity, what is the responsibility of teacher preparation programs? I suggest that we need to find ways to engage future teachers in a process of becoming multicultural and multilingual, and I have already recommended a number of ways in which we can do so. I would just add that schools of education need to make their prospective teachers an offer they cannot refuse; that is, they need to make it worth their while to become multilingual and multicultural by having incentives that help future teachers view diversity as an asset. These incentives can include credit for learning another language; refusing to accept course work that does not reflect attention to diversity; and support for academic work that is tied to community service.

Becoming multilingual and multicultural is often an exhilarating experience, but it can also be uncomfortable and challenging because the process decenters students from their world. It necessarily means that students have to learn to step out of their comfortable perspectives and try to understand those of others. In the process, however, they usually gain far more than they give up: a broader view of reality, a more complex understanding of their students' lives, and a way to approach their students so that they can learn successfully.

Teachers Need to Learn to Confront Racism and Other Biases in Schools. If teachers simply follow the decreed curriculum as handed down from the central office, and if they go along with standard practices such as rigid ability tracking or high-stakes testing that result in unjust outcomes, they are unlikely ever to question the fairness of these practices. But when they begin to engage in a personal transformation through such actions as described above—that is, when they become learners with, of, and for their students and forge a deep identification with them; when they build on students' talents and strengths; and when they welcome and include the perspectives and experiences of their students and families in the classroom—then they cannot avoid locking horns with some very unpleasant realities inherent in the schooling process, realities such as racism, sexism, heterosexism, classism, and other biases. For instance, teachers begin to discover the biased but unstated ideologies behind some of the practices that they had previously overlooked. As a result, teachers have no alternative but to begin to question the inequitable nature of such practices. They become, in a word, critical educators. In this respect, helping prospective teachers become critical is a fundamental role of teacher education programs, and it means challenging not only the policies and practices of schools but also those of the very teacher education programs they are in.

A critical stance challenges the structure of schools at the elementary and secondary school levels so that teachers begin to question, among other school realities, the following:

- seemingly natural and neutral practices such as asking parents to speak English at home with their children (in fact, teachers who are supportive of language diversity begin to ask their students' parents to do just the opposite: to speak their native language at home, and to promote literacy in all forms in their native language whenever possible);
- the lack of high-level courses in students' native languages (critical teachers begin to ask, for example, whether schools have parallel and equal courses in science, math, social studies, and other subject areas in students' native languages);
- counseling services that automatically relegate students of some language backgrounds to nonacademic choices (critical teachers become aware of both subtle and overt messages that students are incapable of doing high-level academic work because they are not yet proficient in English, as if English proficiency were the primary barometer of intelligence).

At the teacher education level, a critical stance means that faculty and prospective teachers begin to question the following:

- the isolation of bilingual education as a separate strand in the teacher education program, and the separation between bilingual education and ESL (as if this separation made sense in the real world where students are struggling to become bilingual and where bilingualism is, in all other settings except for school, a highly valued skill);

- screening practices that make it impossible for a more diverse student body to become teachers (these include an overemphasis on grades with little attention paid to skills they might already have in language ability and cultural awareness; during interviews, a rigid conception of how the "ideal teacher" behaves, without acknowledging how cultural and social-class differences might influence their responses; a bias against prospective teachers who have an accent; and so on);
- how faculty are recruited and hired, and how these practices might mitigate against the possibility of retaining a faculty that is diverse in language and culture (for example, by failing to include competencies in culture and language in the job descriptions for nonbilingual positions, even though such competencies could be highly effective in those positions).

Facing and challenging racism and other biases is both an inspiring and a frightening prospect. It means upsetting business as usual, and this can be difficult even for committed and critical teachers. It is especially difficult for young teachers, who recognize that they have little power or influence among more seasoned school staffs. As a result, they often either lose hope or become solitary missionaries, and neither of these postures can accomplish any appreciable changes.

Help Future Teachers Learn to Develop a Community of Critical Friends. What I suggest instead is that we teach future teachers to become *critical colleagues*, that is, teachers who are capable of developing respectful but critical relationships with their peers. Working in isolation, no teacher can single-handedly effect the changes that are needed in an entire school, at least not in the long term. In fact, isolation builds walls, allowing teachers to focus on only their own students. In this way, it becomes far too easy to designate language-minority students as the responsibility of only the bilingual and ESL teachers. But developing a community of critical friends opens up teachers' classrooms—and their perspectives—so that they can acknowledge that the concerns of language-minority students are everyone's concerns, not just of one or two teachers in the school building.

Time and again, teachers in my classes have spoken about the need to develop a cadre of peers to help them and their school go through the process of transformation. But what is needed is not simply peers who support one another—essential as this may be—but also peers who debate, critique, and challenge one another to go beyond their current ideas and practices. This is especially useful in terms of bilingual education, a hotly contested issue seldom discussed in an in-depth way among teachers. Developing a community of critical friends is one way of facing difficult issues, and it is one more step in the journey of transformation.

Prospective teachers also need to build bridges to their students' families and to other members of the communities in which they work. Rather than viewing families and other community members as adversaries, prospective teachers need to develop skills in interacting effectively with them. Yet how many teachers have learned about these issues in their teacher education programs? Even in bilingual programs, where both parent involvement and communication with families are seen as central, there are few examples of actual exposure to these ideas. At the very least, teacher preparation programs need to provide courses, seminars, and practicum experiences so that prospective teachers learn to work with families.

In the end, teachers who work collaboratively with their peers and families in a spirit of solidarity will be better able to change schools to become more equitable and caring places for students of linguistically and culturally diverse backgrounds. Even personal transformation is best accomplished as a *collective* journey that leads to change in more than just one classroom. This means that prospective teachers need to learn to communicate and work with colleagues of varying perspectives; they need to learn to support and affirm one another, but also to question and confront one another to envision other possibilities.

That bilingual education works is a given in the chapters in this book. Rather than continue to endlessly debate its effectiveness, what are needed are strategies to improve it. What has *not* worked, on the other hand, are the approaches used by schools of education to prepare future teachers for the great diversity—linguistic, cultural, and socioeconomic, among others—that new teachers will face. These programs have a long way to go in preparing prospective teachers to respect and affirm the languages and identities of all the students who will inevitably be present in their classrooms in the coming years.

The three imperatives and numerous suggestions I have made in this chapter are only a beginning stage in the kinds of changes that are needed to help schools and universities shift from a focus on assimilation as their goal to an agenda of respect and affirmation for all students of all backgrounds. If teacher education faculties take these imperatives to heart, it means that they are willing to undergo a profound transformation in outlook, ideology, and curriculum. It also means that programs in general and faculty members in particular will welcome change, even though it may be a difficult prospect for many of us. But in the process of transformation, schools and colleges of education can become more hopeful places, because in the long run, we will be preparing better teachers for all students, including our bilingual and language-minority students. And the promise of social justice and equal educational opportunity for all students, an elusive dream in many places, will be closer to becoming a reality.

REFERENCES

Aaronsohn, E., Carter, C. J., & Howell, M. (1995). Preparing monocultural teachers for a multicultural world: Attitudes toward inner-city schools. *Equity and Excellence in Education, 28,* 5–9.

Arias, M. B., & Casanova, U. (Eds.). (1993). *Bilingual education: Politics, practice, research.* Chicago: University of Chicago Press.

Chávez Chávez, R., & O'Donnell, J. (Eds.). (1998). *Speaking the unpleasant: The politics of nonengagement in the multicultural education terrain.* Albany: State University of New York Press.

Crawford, J. (1992). *Hold your tongue: Bilingualism and the politics of "English Only."* Reading, MA: Addison-Wesley.

Dewey, J. (1916). *Democracy and education.* New York: Free Press.

Deyhle, D., & Swisher, K. (1997). Research in American Indian and Alaska Native education: From assimilation to self-determination. In M. W. Apple (Ed.), *Review of research in education* (vol. 22, pp. 113–194). Washington, DC: American Educational Research Association.

Dickeman, M. (1973). Teaching cultural pluralism. In J. A. Banks (Ed.), *Teaching ethnic studies: Concepts and strategies* (pp. 4–25). Washington, DC: National Council for the Social Studies.

Donato, R. (1997). *The other struggle for equal schools: Mexican Americans during the civil rights era.* Albany: State University of New York Press.

Freire, P. (1970). *Pedagogy of the oppressed.* New York: Seabury Press.

Howard, G. (1999). *We can't teach what we don't know: White teachers, multiracial schools.* New York: Teachers College Press.

Kozol, J. (1991). *Savage inequalities; Children in America's schools.* New York: Crown.

Macías, R. F., & Kelly, C. (1996). *Summary report of the survey of the states' limited English proficient students and available educational programs and services 1994–1995.* Washington, DC: United States Department of Education, Office of Grants and Contracts Services, George Washington University.

McIntosh, P. (1988). *White privilege and male privilege: A personal account of coming to see correspondences through work in women's studies* (Working Paper No. 189). Wellesley, MA: Wellesley College Center for Research on Women.

Moll, L. D. (1992). Bilingual classroom studies and community analysis: Some recent trends. *Educational Researcher, 21*(2), 20–24.

Montero-Sieburth, M., & Pérez, M. (1987). *Echar pa'lante,* moving onward: The dilemmas and strategies of a bilingual education. *Anthropology and Education Quarterly, 18,* 180–189.

Nieto, S. (1992). We speak in many tongues: Language diversity and multicultural education. In C. Díaz (Ed.), *Multicultural education for the 21st century* (pp. 112–136). Washington, DC: National Education Association.

Nieto, S. (1999). *The light in their eyes: Creating multicultural learning communities.* New York: Teachers College Press.

Nieto, S. (in press). Conflict and tension; growth and change: The politics of teaching multicultural education courses. In D. Macedo (Ed.), *Tongue-tying multiculturalism.* Boulder, CO: Roman & Littlefield.

Oakes, J. (1985). *Keeping track: How schools structure inequality.* New Haven, CT: Yale University Press.

Shor, I., & Freire, P. (1987). *A pedagogy for liberation: Dialogues on transforming education.* New York: Bergin & Garvey.

Spring, J. (1989). *The sorting machine revisited: National education policy since 1945.* New York: Longman.

Spring, J. (1997). *Deculturalization and the struggle for equality: A brief history of the education of dominated cultures in the United States* (2nd ed.). New York: McGraw-Hill.

Weinberg, M. (1977). *A chance to learn: A history of race and education in the U.S.* Cambridge, Eng.: Cambridge University Press.

CRITICAL QUESTIONS

1. How prepared do you feel to teach students of language minority backgrounds? Why?

2. One of the suggestions I make in this chapter is that teachers need to face and accept their own identities. I believe this is especially true for teachers of the dominant culture, that is, those who are White and English-speaking. This means challenging the "melting pot" as the sole explanation for the immigrant experience in our country. Re-read the quotes from Mildred Dickeman's article (p. 215–216), and write about what it would mean to "recover" *your* ethnic identity.

3. Another suggestion I make in the chapter is that teachers need to "become learners and identify with their students." Think of your own classroom and write about some of the ways in which you might be able to do this.

CLASSROOM ACTIVITY

I've stated in this article that when teachers engage in a process of transformation, they must face some difficult and unpleasant realities such as racism and other biases in the curriculum and other policies and practices. Some of these policies and practices may be based on the best intentions, but they end up perpetuating existing inequalities. With a group of your classmates, describe how language minority students are affected by particular policies and practices in the schools where you work. Develop some strategies for addressing these problems.

COMMUNITY-BASED ACTIVITIES AND ADVOCACY

Do you speak a language other than English? Have you ever tried to learn another language? You may want to read the story of Bill Dunn in my book *The light in their eyes* (Teachers College Press, 1999, pp. 146–152). As you will see, Bill decided to "come out of the closet as a Spanish speaker" when he realized that he understood most of what his Spanish-speaking students were saying! After being immersed in a community in which the Puerto Rican student population had grown from 5% to 70% in 20 years, Bill realized that he had picked up much more of the language than he thought, even though he had never studied it formally. Through an independent study project with me, Bill kept a journal documenting how he became a Spanish speaker, and he described how he learned first-hand what his student went through in learning English. In Bill's case, he took formal classes in Spanish, watched Spanish-language television, sat in on bilingual classes in his school, and so on.

As a semester-long project, try to learn another language. If you decide to do so, Bill Dunn's experience might be a good model for you to follow. For example, you can sit in on bilingual classes (if there are any in your school, or a neighboring school), read newspapers and watch TV in that language, take a formal course at a university, and so on. Keep a journal in which you document what it is like to learn another language, and describe what you've learned about your students and others who need to learn a second language. Make a presentation at the end of the semester to your classmates.

SUPPLEMENTARY RESOURCES FOR FURTHER REFLECTION AND STUDY

Beykont, Zeynep (Ed.) (2000). *Lifting every voice: Pedagogy and politics of bilingual education*, Cambridge, MA: Harvard Education Publishing Group.

Written by a mix of scholars, teachers, and activists, the chapters in this book provide insightful models for actual practice and pedagogy in bilingual classrooms and in teacher education.

Bigler, Ellen (1999). *American conversations: Puerto Ricans, White ethnics, and multicultural education*. Philadelphia: Temple University Press.

Bigler presents the case of the changing demographics of a small working-class city in New York State, and the conflicts between different points of view among the residents concerning the place of English and Spanish in the public schools.

Christian, Donna, Montone, Christopher, Lindholm, Kathryn J. & Carranza, Isolda (1997). *Profiles in two-way immersion education*. McHenry, IL: Delta Systems, 1997.

The authors provide a review and in-depth profile of a number of two-way bilingual programs, that is, programs in which language minority and language majority students learn through both English and another language.

James Crawford (1996). *Hold your tongue: Bilingualism and the politics of "English only."* Reading, MA: Addison-Wesley Publishing Co.

Crawford provides the most detailed and researched study of the "English-only" movement in the United States, with a historical perspective on its existence and a sharp analysis on why it continues.

Ovando, Carlos J., & Collier, Virginia P. (1998). *Bilingual and ESL classrooms: Teaching in multicultural contexts*. New York: McGraw-Hill, 2nd ed.

A comprehensive and up-to-date survey of bilingual education, this book reviews the history, legislation, and current research in the field, along with many suggestions for classroom practice.

Conflict and Tension, Growth and Change: The Politics of Teaching Multicultural Education Courses

INTRODUCTION

I have been teaching courses in multicultural education for many years, before it became a requirement and even before it was thought of as necessary in universities or schools. Although I love what I do, teaching these courses has not always been easy, as shown in this chapter. In fact, this particular course was probably the most difficult and contentious one I have ever taught. It ended up also being the most powerful and enduring lesson I have learned about teaching courses in multicultural education. Writing about the experience of teaching this particular group of graduate students years ago helped me to reflect on how tension and conflict are inevitable in teaching such courses, and about what it means to work creatively toward developing a sense of community in courses where diversity is a reality. As I discovered, "creating community" does not mean to develop an unproblematic environment in which differences are glossed over.

Teaching multicultural courses can also be compared with the many dilemmas of diversity with which classroom teachers must contend on a daily basis. As you read this chapter, think about your own situation as a teacher. Can you relate to some of the frustrations I experienced?

It is not easy to sustain the energy needed to teach courses that challenge the status quo, cause students—not to mention professors—anger and pain, and result in conflict, guilt, and anguish. Exploring issues of pluralism, diversity, and institutional oppression often has these effects. I have an intimate knowledge of this experience because I have been teaching courses in multicultural education since 1980. The introductory course I

227

teach, the subject of this chapter, is open to students in our graduate program in teacher education and curriculum studies, and to graduate students in other School of Education programs as well as those pursuing graduate degrees in disciplines throughout the university. The course is not a requirement in any program, but it is taken by a wide range of students: those with no experience with diversity but curious about the topic, those who consider it an important course to include on their transcript, or those who simply want to see what all the fuss concerning multiculturalism is about. It is a popular course, and every semester for years I have had to turn away scores of students because, in a class designed for 15, I could end up with 70. Yet no matter how many times I teach the course, it brings up for me many feelings, from anger and exasperation to satisfaction and jubilation. Given this roller coaster of emotions, nearly every semester I vow that this will be the last time I teach it.

My major frustration is that although the students only go through the experience once in their lives, I do it at least once a year, and often twice. By the middle of each semester, invariably I go home and announce that I will *not* do this again, that this work is too demanding, and that I'll just focus on easier content in the future. My husband usually just nods, knowing full well that by the end of the semester I will have changed my mind once more, again reaching the conclusion that the experience has been transformative and that nothing else could be as important as this kind of work.

One particular class stands out in my mind as being the most problematic, most troublesome, but in the end most exhilarating section of this course that I have ever taught. It was several years ago, and I was relieved and thankful to be looking forward to a needed and, I felt, well-deserved sabbatical in the near future.

In this chapter, I tell the story of that course in order to illustrate how some of the many conflicting and contradictory perspectives of students were expressed, negotiated, and, finally, used to create a community and to promote individual growth as well. First, I explain how the course challenges the general perception of multicultural teacher education as primarily or only necessary for students of European American backgrounds. After the description of the course, I discuss some of the lessons I have learned from this particular class and how my teaching has changed as a result.

MULTICULTURAL TEACHER EDUCATION: WHO NEEDS IT?

Given the changing demographics of the students in our public schools and of those responsible for teaching them, it is no surprise that most discussions of multicultural teacher education have emphasized the need for practicing and prospective teachers of European American backgrounds to be better prepared for the challenges of diversity they face in their class-rooms. It has been documented, for example, that there are currently about 2.3 million public school teachers; of these, fewer than 10% are members of what are traditionally called "minority groups," that is, African American, Latino, Asian, and American Indian communities (U.S. Bureau of the Census, 1993). In general, most teachers and prospective teachers are White, middle-class females and most have had little personal experi-ence or professional training in cross-cultural issues. Because it is expected that the percentage of students of color in our nation's schools will grow from some 30% in 1990 to 38% in 2010 (Hodgkinson, 1991), teacher prep-aration programs need to address this issue in their curriculum.

A growing number of studies in multicultural teacher education have generally documented the futility of superficial or "one-shot" treatments in educating White teachers about diversity (McDiarmid, 1990). The short-term effects of even more sustained and in-depth treatments have also been revealed (Sleeter, 1992). That is, because most teachers, but es-pecially those from European American backgrounds, have been sub-jected to a monocultural education themselves and because they have had few personal experiences with diversity, it takes more than either a series of workshops or even more long-range activities to prepare them to teach students who may be very different from themselves in backgrounds, val-ues, and experiences.

Another key lesson from research with prospective or practicing teach-ers of European American backgrounds is the negative attitudes and expectations they often have concerning students who are racially, ethni-cally, and socioeconomically different from them. For example, Aaron-sohn, Carter, and Howell (1995) investigated the attitudes of the partici-pants in three teacher education courses and found that their initial perceptions tended to be incredibly negative. For example, all but one of the practicing and prospective teachers assumed that their students' par-ents did not really care about their children's education. Even more dis-tressing, although most of them would probably end up teaching in cities and towns with culturally heterogeneous student populations, at first only 10% said they would be interested in teaching in such settings. Even this study, which is more optimistic than most, found that only about half of the teachers felt more comfortable around children of color after taking the class (Aaronsohn et al., 1995).

The very way that most Whites perceive of their own identity—either as "just American" without a critical analysis of what this means, or as not having any ethnicity at all compared to others who they perceive as being more easily ethnically and racially identified—has also been highlighted as a fundamental problem among many students (McIntosh, 1988; Ta-tum, 1992). This negation is especially troubling among preservice and practicing teachers because it allows them to deny or downplay the privileges they enjoy solely on the basis of their skin color (Bollin & Finkel, 1995; Howard, 1993; Pang, 1994; Sleeter, 1994). This perspective also allows them to buy into a view of the United States as a meritocracy where success is due solely to hard work and perseverance, rather than intimately connected to and influenced by deep-seated structural inequality based on racial, class, and gender differences. By accepting the meritocratic view of success in our society, teachers and prospective teachers conveniently sidestep uncomfortable discussions about racism, sexism, and other institutionalized barriers to mobility and achievement. They can proclaim that they do not see differences, that all their students are equal in their eyes, and that they themselves are in fact "color-blind."

The problem, of course, is that they are not. Racial differences and attitudes about them, although not "nice" to talk about in public conversations, figure prominently in teachers' attitudes and beliefs about why some students succeed and others do not; about their theories of intelligence; and about definitions of students from culturally and politically subordinated backgrounds primarily in terms of deficits. These teachers and prospective teachers, who have had precious little experience with people different from themselves, often display what King (1991) called *dysconscious racism*, that is, a limited and distorted view of racism that fails to take into account how inequality is created and perpetuated by the very structures of schools and society that these teachers generally believe promote equality.

It comes as no surprise, then, that one of the major problems consistently cited in the literature in multicultural teacher education has rightly been the lack of preparation of teachers of European American backgrounds to teach ethnically and racially diverse populations. In a study of excellent teachers of diverse student populations, for instance, Olsen and Mullen (1990) found that 30 of the 36 teachers identified were themselves members of culturally subordinated groups, and the other six had consciously placed themselves in the position of experiencing firsthand the diversity they would later encounter. Another major concern has been how to recruit a more diverse student body into teacher education programs to better reflect the growing diversity in the schools. Suggestions include restructuring teacher education programs (Brown, 1992; Garibaldi, 1992); making teacher education culturally responsive (Irvine, 1992; Ladson-Billings, 1994); engaging prospective teachers in ethnographic and other field work in the kinds of schools and communities in which they will teach (Trueba & Wright, 1992); multiculturalizing the entire higher education curriculum (Schoem, Frankel, Zúñiga, & Lewis, 1993); and, in an effort to diversify the profile of the nation's teachers, aggressively recruiting and retaining teachers from underrepresented groups (Arends, Clemson, & Henkelman, 1992; James, 1993).

All of the foregoing suggestions are logical responses to the fundamental problem of the great number of teachers who are neither prepared nor particularly interested in addressing the challenges of teaching students from culturally and socially dominated communities. In this chapter, I contend that this approach, as important and necessary as it may be, is insufficient because it fails to recognize that students from backgrounds other than European American are *also* largely unprepared to teach students from groups other than their own. That is, we cannot assume that, simply because of their own marginal status in society, African American, Latino, Asian, and American Indian prospective and practicing teachers and others different from the majority can teach students from other backgrounds. Although it is true that their unique experiences and perspectives as members of culturally subordinated groups may indeed help them to understand marginality per se, it does not necessarily give them an added advantage in confronting actual differences in the classroom and helping them address these differences effectively.

My own experiences in diverse classrooms, from elementary through graduate school, have taught me that teachers from one particular ethnic or racial group cannot be expected to automatically understand or appreciate their students of other racial, ethnic, or linguistic backgrounds. This is so for at least two reasons. First, all cultures have created their own stereotypes and misconceptions about other groups. Second, these stereotypes tend to be reinforced by a monocultural Eurocentric curriculum and by the dominant group stereotypes and negative beliefs of subordinated groups. Consequently, over the years, I have seen cases in which Latino teachers harbored racist attitudes about their African American students, some even suggesting that it is better to keep Latino students in bilingual classes in order to shield them from their African American peers; I have heard some African American teachers voice vehement objections to bilingual education, not only because of what they considered the unnecessary diversion of funds for those programs but also because of their insistence that in the United States there is no room for instruction in any language other than English; and I have heard teachers of all backgrounds stand by while their female students were harassed by male students, or turn a deaf ear when one of their students was taunted by sneers of "faggot" by other students. In short, I have seen teachers, themselves from socially and culturally dominated groups, behave toward some of their students in the same ways they decry when other teachers behave toward children from their background.

I have learned as well that even teachers from the same ethnic or racial group as their students do not have a "built-in" capacity to be excellent teachers of those students. As a neophyte teacher in a junior high school in New York City in a mostly African American community undergoing profound changes during the heyday of community control, I was impressed by the love and respect that parents and students had for most of the handful of African American teachers in the school. Clearly, their shared culture was an important point of reference and a source of pride in their relationships with students and parents. I was stunned, then, when activists in the community demanded the ouster of, along with several notoriously ineffective and racist White teachers, one of the few African American teachers. He was, they said, arrogant and authoritarian, treating students in insensitive and demeaning ways. "He's even worse than some of those White teachers," one person told me, "because he should know better."

Several years later, I taught at a bilingual school where well over three fourths of the students and one half of the teachers were of Puerto Rican or other Latino backgrounds. Here, among the many committed and inspiring Latino teachers, there were a small number who believed the worst stereotypes about their students, for example that they were, in the jargon of the day, "culturally deprived" because they lived in poverty and had not had the privileges that greater financial stability would have given them. Although it was true that many of the students lived in difficult circumstances and were academically underprepared, these teachers had low expectations of their students simply because they lived in poverty. Consequently, they had little respect for what these young people were capable of learning or what their parents could contribute to their education. In both cases, the insensitive teachers were a small minority, but these were eye-opening experiences for me because they underscored that culturally sensitive teaching could not be guaranteed by simply being a member of a particular cultural group.

In citing these examples, I am not suggesting that teachers alone are to blame for such behaviors. Situations such as these need to be understood in the larger sociopolitical context of how difference is perceived, constructed and played out in our society. All of us learn early the lessons of the status of light versus dark skin, thin versus full noses and lips, English-language fluency versus heavily accented English, heterosexual versus gay orientation, Christianity versus Jewry and Islam, and able-bodiedness versus disability, among others. Suffering from one of these stigmas is often enough to teach us to regard the others in negative ways; it somehow helps us to feel more powerful when we can look down on others who do not share in one of the few privileges to which we tenaciously cling. The result may be that some individuals from culturally subordinated groups feel a sense of symbolic superiority over others who are even more marginalized.

The mere ignorance of otherness should be mentioned as well. That is, being Mexican American does not necessarily mean knowing about Cambodians, just as being African American does not mean one knows about

Puerto Ricans. Because most of us are products of a monocultural education, there are few ways to learn about others different from ourselves other than through direct experience, determined effort and hard work, or through self-initiated experiences such as immersion in a particular community or a stint in the Peace Corps (Olsen & Mullen, 1990).

Consequently, there is almost an unstated assumption that teachers from culturally subordinated groups do not need multicultural teacher education, as least not as much as others do, because their own backgrounds have taught them how to be effective teachers of all students. The private complaints and grumblings in conversations among our own groups about racist or insensitive attitudes and behaviors on the part of teachers from other cultural and racial groups belie this assumption. The feeling that multicultural education is primarily necessary for White teachers is based on the faulty reasoning that all ethnic and racial groups different from the majority are in fact not very different from one another. Yet nothing could be further from the truth. All ethnic and racial groups differ from one another on many dimensions, and within the more general groupings of Latinos, Asians, and American Indians there are often dramatic differences. Even within specific ethnic groups, say Japanese Americans, there are differences of social class, language or languages spoken, geographic location, and the number of generations one's family has lived in the United States.

Just as multicultural education at the elementary and high school levels is not just for African American students—an all-too-common assumption—but for all students (Nieto, 1996), multicultural teacher education too is not simply for Whites, but for all preservice and practicing teachers. Because they enter teacher education programs with different perspectives and experiences, teachers of all backgrounds may learn different lessons from teacher education with a multicultural perspective, but they can all benefit from it. An effective program of multicultural teacher education helps all participants shed their cultural blinders, develop an awareness and respect for differences with which they may be unfamiliar, and prepare them for teaching students of all backgrounds with knowledge and care.

If, as stated by Banks (1993), a major goal of multicultural education is to reform the school and other educational institutions so that students from diverse backgrounds will at least have a chance at educational equality, then schools and colleges of education need to be included in this reform. In turn, teacher education must be based on the assumption that all teachers have something to learn, regardless of whether they are completely ignorant of diversity or intimately connected with some aspect of it through their own life experience.

In what follows I describe a course in which there was tremendous student diversity of all kinds. In this sense, the course was quite different from others in multicultural education, which generally include mostly

White students with a smattering of students of color. Having a great deal of diversity in a course of this kind is rare, but I have been privileged to teach many such classes. They can provide a living laboratory in which all students can learn firsthand about all kinds of differences with which they may be unfamiliar. Although all my classes tend to be quite diverse, this particular course was unusual in the extent of its diversity. I was looking forward to what I thought would be a model of consensus and harmony.

Far from a model of consensus, the course was instead mired in conflict and competition from the first, and this was in part due to the very diversity that should have led to its coalescence. Why this occurred, the kinds of tensions that resulted, and how they were eventually resolved is the subject of the narrative that follows.

THE COURSE

The graduate course "Introduction to Multicultural Education" was developed and first taught by Professor Bob Suzuki in the Fall 1975 semester in the School of Education at the University of Massachusetts, Amherst. In fact, this was the very first course I took as a new doctoral student and it was memorable for me not only because of this but also because it spoke profoundly to many of my own personal and professional concerns and questions. Professor Suzuki became one of my mentors and a great influence in how I think about multicultural education. A renowned scholar in the field, he gave the course its soul. Despite all the changes I have made in the course over the years, it has retained his imprint: a particularly critical way of looking at what was then a nascent field of inquiry. It was a powerful course that first semester, and it has continued to be so every semester since then.

The extensive course syllabus includes a description, outline, format, and grading information. It also provides an in-depth description of the course requirements: a reflective journal, a research paper preceded by an oral presentation in class about the topic, and a book critique. One of the primary reasons for asking students to keep a journal is that it can serve as a sounding board for those who may be reluctant to express themselves in class. Given the nature of its content, the course often brings up anger, resentment, alienation, and other emotions that might not otherwise be expressed. The syllabus also includes an extensive list of topics along with relevant resources from which students can select to write a research paper. They have the opportunity to work alone or in a group on their oral presentation and research paper.

The topics for the research paper and oral presentation are often controversial in nature. They have changed over the years, reflecting the particular political climate of the day, but no matter what the topic, I have made an attempt to always include issues that will get students to reflect critically and, in their classrooms, to "teach against the grain" (Cochran-Smith, 1991). That particular semester, the topics selected by students included the "English-Only" movement, the pros and cons of I.Q. testing, bias and stereotyping in children's literature, multicultural education and social change, cultural differences in learning styles, and the myth of the "model minority," among many others.

The syllabus ends with an extensive bibliography, organized according to each of the four themes, which are:

1. Analysis of pluralism in the United States;
2. Reinterpretation of United States history and culture, including the study of Nativism and perspectives of people of color, women, and the immigrant experience;
3. Sociocultural and sociopolitical influences on learning, including racism and other biases in schools, and teacher expectations; and
4. The philosophy and pedagogy of multicultural education, with particular attention to developing a sound conceptual framework and connecting multicultural education to social change.

The Participants

As usual, the course was filled beyond capacity, mostly due to my reluctance to exclude many of the students who wanted to enroll. I was especially excited about the great diversity among those who asked to be admitted so I wanted to make certain that they were not excluded. The class could have climbed to 50 but I kept it to 27, still too large for the kinds of activities I had in mind and the environment of trust and comfort I believe is crucial in these classes. On that first Wednesday in September, the participants squeezed into a "temporary" classroom about a block away from t'·· School of Education building. The "temporary," which has now been in the same spot for over 10 years, was the university's answer to overcrowding in the main building. It was too hot in the first few weeks of class, too cold in the last days when the temperature outside dipped well into the teens. But the glorious fall colors in the early part of the semester and the beautiful landscape of snow-covered fields and trees in the winter made it a less uninviting place than it might have been otherwise.

The classroom itself was too small for the number of course participants, especially for how I usually teach my classes (circle for large-group discussions, semi-circle for viewing videos and films, and lots of small-group work in different sections of the room). The small size of the classroom made the circle look lopsided, with rings around the edges. Invariably there were some students who could not fit in the main circle and needed to sit in a second row.

Although they were all graduate students, the course participants represented a broad range of differences in race, ethnicity, national origin, language, age, sexual orientation, teaching experience, knowledge of multiculturalism, socioeconomic status, and political perspective. Among the students were two African American males, one who worked in a professional position at the University and another who had recently been released from prison; an American Indian male whose goal was to study history or perhaps law, but who had decided to first get a master's in education; a Tibetan who as a child had escaped by foot from his country to India and who had been educated in a Tibetan school there; a South African man who had been educated under the oppressive system of apartheid and for whom questioning or disagreeing with a teacher was at first unthinkable; a young woman from Taiwan who was genuinely perplexed by the power of the emotions expressed in class; three island-born middle-class Puerto Ricans, one an administrator for bilingual education in a nearby school system, another a recent graduate of the University of Puerto Rico who had attended private schools until she went on to post-secondary education, and a third who had recently returned from studying for a masters degree in political theory from Latin America; an Israeli who had emigrated to the United States and wanted to teach ESL to inner-city youths; a Cape Verdean woman with many years of teaching experience in her native country beginning her first semester in a doctoral program; a young Japanese woman who was fluent both in the English language and in U.S. mainstream culture; a White lesbian who was working in a battered women's shelter and whose dream it was to become a classroom teacher; a number of students self-identified as "ethnic" (Italian, Jewish, Irish) and others who considered themselves "just Americans"; three young White women who had recently completed an undergraduate degree in education and who were intimidated by some of the more experienced students and by the level of discourse, which was not only quite complex but also at times deeply troubling.

In terms of teaching and other work experiences, there was a college professor of sociology, a day-care center teacher, a number of elementary school teachers, several full-time doctoral students, a chairman of an English department at a nearby high school, and various post-B.A. candidates for ESL teaching certificates. The students came not only from every corner of the globe, but from every corner of the United States. Some had grown up in poverty, others with relative wealth. Their ages ranged from early twenties to mid-fifties, and their teaching experience from 0 to over 20 years. This group was, in sum, a multiculturalist's dream.

The dream, however, did not last long.

Claiming Hegemony

Almost from the beginning, there was conflict in the classroom. The conflict was due not just to the resistance and anger of several White students, but also to the feeling on the part of some students from culturally subordinated backgrounds that their particular difference should have precedence in our considerations of diversity. It was almost as if these students had finally found a place in the university where they belonged. Here, their difference could be discussed, researched, made public. After what for some had been years of trying to hide or downplay their diversity, here was a place where differences were accepted and affirmed.

The problem was that some students, having found a place where they could feel comfortable, wanted to make it their exclusive niche. They were the latter-day Puritans, casting out others who disagreed with their creed, in a sad repetition of what previously they had suffered. It was, of course, a logical consequence of their rejection that led some students to see this class as a redemption, as a place where they would finally have a voice, and I welcomed their voices. However, some of these individuals' insistence on "Me! Me! Me!" became untenable, as they drowned out the voices of others. The course could be described as a cacophony of disparate voices claiming hegemony. In fact, I often felt like a symphony conductor in that class, waving my baton from one side of the classroom to the other, trying to create consensus where there was none.

The class was permeated by rage, and this rage sometimes was translated into clamors for dominance. For example, an African American student insisted that race should be our dominant theme; one of the Puerto Rican students contended that colonialism was at the core of U.S. history; and a number of the women focused on patriarchy as the primary social problem in all societies. Many of the White students squirmed uneasily in their seats or exploded with exasperation whenever the topics of racism and institutional oppression came up, whereas the international students were by and large lost in discussions that focused so heavily on U.S.-based experiences and perspectives.

A number of students stand out in my mind as giving this class its particular character. There was Ron, an African American man in his late twenties who had just been released from prison after a conviction for robbery motivated by the need for money to support his drug addiction.[1] Ron had just graduated *cum laude* from a prison education program while on day-time release to attend classes, and after having served his sentence, he applied to and was accepted in the graduate program. The multicultural

---

[1]To protect the confidentiality of the course participants, all names used in this chapter are fictitious.

education class was his first graduate course. According to a newspaper article written about him several months before, he was to be the first convicted felon from the program to complete an undergraduate degree at the University of Massachusetts. The article described the dramatic change in his life, from crime and drugs to education:

> For [Ron], it was the beginning of a journey, one filled with as many frustrations as accomplishments: the taunting of jealous prison guards, the difficulty of tackling overwhelming reading assignments while others watched television. And later he would face adjusting from a regimented lockup to a bustling campus—and having to leave it each day at 5 p.m. to return to prison.

Ron was an angry man, and he had every reason to be. Growing up in a working-class family in an inner-city neighborhood, Ron's father died when he was 10. By the time he was a teenager, his life was, according to the article, "a blur of police chases, robbery charges, and short jail terms." The short jail terms of his adolescence became longer jail terms for more serious crimes when he was in his twenties. Ron seemed convinced that life for African American males in America's inner cities was worse than for any other group in society, and it was sometimes difficult for him to hide his anger in class. During one of the first confrontations in class, he turned to Peter, a White student, and said angrily, "You don't wear the face, man!"

Peter, a young man in his mid-twenties, was sincere in his search for meaning in our discussions of pluralism and the need for multicultural education. He was studying to be an ESL teacher and he had experience tutoring African American youngsters as well as advising undergraduate students in a school-based tutoring program that focused on working with a culturally diverse high school student body. Originally from the South, on the first day of class he introduced himself as the great-grandson of slave owners. During the course of the semester, Peter had a number of clashes with Ron and with other students of color in the class. Although he was interested in and committed to issues of cultural and linguistic diversity, some members of the class felt that his level of awareness of racism was minimal. His girlfriend, also in the class, was Yoshiko, a young Japanese woman who was pursuing a graduate degree in sociology.

Yoshiko spent several years in the United States. She seemed to find our class a refreshing respite from what she considered the overly theoretical and abstract courses in sociology that she was taking, courses that had little to do with the day-to-day lives of real people in communities. The level of sophistication with which she understood pluralism in our society was in direct contrast to most of the international students who often seemed baffled by the animosity and anger demonstrated by some of the course participants. Yoshiko, however, also was impatient with the amount of time and attention given to racism and other institutional forms of oppression.

Dianne was a lesbian who "came out" to the class several sessions into the semester much to the chagrin and embarrassment of some class participants who felt this was an issue best left untouched. She lived with her partner and taught children at a shelter for battered women. Wanting to become a classroom teacher, she returned to get her masters degree as a way to get back in the educational field. She felt she had a lot to learn about the kinds of issues she had not herself experienced. Consequently, Dianne was very serious about the multicultural quest on which she was embarking, and she took every opportunity to read and learn about children of various backgrounds.

The conflicts among these and the other students in the course were palpable almost as soon as one set foot in the classroom. Facilitating the discussions was no easy matter either inside the classroom or out. Besides waving my baton, I also had to practice the skills of negotiation and affirmation that I had tried to hone over the years. Sometimes they worked, and sometimes they did not. I remember one day when Ron chafed at the suggestion that the oppression faced by African Americans could be compared to that faced by lesbians and gays (an issue he still feels strongly about, as evident in his feedback to me, at the end of this chapter). Another day, Peter and James, an African American staff member at the University, almost came to blows over their differing opinions about what stood in the way of the advancement of Blacks.

Outside the classroom there was tension as well, and this usually manifested itself in my office. I do not know how many times that semester I sat with crying, angry, hurt, or guilt-ridden students, but it was far more than is usual in a semester. On one occasion, a young White woman wrung her hands in agony as she cried, feeling the weight of the entire burden for racism on her shoulders. Needless to say, this was not an objective of the class, and I tried to convince her of this. Although guilt can be a spur to action, a steady diet of guilt can do little to change the way things are. Another day, Ron came to apologize for letting his anger get the best of him in class and I suggested he speak with other students about it. However, it seemed to me that as long as anger did not directly humiliate or hurt others, there was no need for anybody to apologize. About one third into the semester, Peter came in to see me because he was losing patience with the class. We had a long talk about White guilt, about his exasperation with others in the course, and about his feelings about himself. One of his comments on that day was especially compelling: "I'm a nice guy," he said. Despite my caution to students about separating institutional racism from individual prejudice and from "being a nice guy," he seemed overwhelmed by what was happening in class. He decided, he said, to drop the course.

However, Peter came back the following day and he remained in the class for the duration of the semester. In fact, I do not believe anybody dropped out of that class, as difficult as it was. Every week, I braced myself as I walked in, waiting for the next controversy to erupt as a result of students' oral presentations. What would it be? Another critique of Eurocentrism? (I could almost hear some students groan). An attack on children's book classics as racist and sexist? An insistence on romanticizing the history of oppressed groups? And so it went, from week to week, with one unrelenting issue after another. Many of these issues were absolutely essential to confront, but the way in which they were sometimes discussed resulted in silencing some of the more reticent students.

Despite the conflict in the class, I could tell as the semester wore on that some cross-cultural friendships were tentatively forming: during the break, I would see the Puerto Rican intellectual speaking with an experienced White classroom teacher, the South African discussing apartheid with the Taiwanese student, the Tibetan explaining Buddhism to an older White woman interested in Eastern philosophy. There were other changes too. Ron decided to do his research paper on women in prison, a slight but significant departure from his consuming attention to his own experience. Yoshiko delved into the myth of the "model minority," a myth she had heard for the first time when she came to this country. She simply could not believe that people actually thought this was true (in fact, she thought it was a joke when she first heard it), so her research from the perspective of a member of the "model minority" itself was intriguing. Dianne shifted her topic from the history of lesbians to the perspectives of some American Indian Nations concerning lesbianism. The class began to coalesce, uneasy alliances at first, but gradually stronger connections began to be made.

It was not until about three quarters through the semester that a specific incident occurred to bring the participants together in the realization that by sharing space, greater power may be created (Kreisberg, 1992).

Sharing Space

The turning point in this class began on the day that Dianne presented the results of her investigation into Native American views of lesbians. It was not so much her topic itself that captured the students' attention, but the fact that she had brought her mother to class. As Dianne began her presentation, some students listened intently, whereas others took notes. With careful attention to detail, she talked about the difficulty of finding appropriate resources and about taking what little information she got and trying to expand on it. She was left, she said, with many unanswered questions but with a commitment to find out more. When she finished, she introduced her mother and asked her to say a few words about why she had come to class.

Mrs. Butterfield, a homemaker and retired teacher in her early seventies, said that she wanted to meet the students that Dianne had talked so much about. Everyone became silent, watching her attentively as she talked about her experiences as a mother, and specifically what it was like being the mother of a lesbian. She spoke of her initial rejection when Dianne first told her, and of her tremendous disappointment of not being able to look forward to having grandchildren. (As of this writing, Dianne and her partner have a daughter.) She was a devout church-goer, she said, but she could not even dream of speaking openly about Dianne's lesbianism in her church, or for that matter, in any setting outside of this class. In the midst of this very personal and private story she surprised everyone by injecting unexpected humor into her monologue by saying, "You know, I wouldn't mind so much that they're lesbians. I just wish they weren't Democrats!" This welcome moment of comic relief resulted in thunderous laughter. Finally, Mrs. Butterfield described how much she had grown to love Dianne's partner, and how she now embraced and cherished her as a member of the family. At the end of her 15-minute talk, you could hear the proverbial pin drop; everyone, it seemed, was at a loss for words. Everyone, that is, except Ron. He turned to her and said with a deep-felt respect, "You must be very proud of your daughter, Mrs. Butterfield."

That was the moment in which the class changed. Ron had said exactly what was needed at that moment, and it was an especially moving comment coming from him. Until then, Ron had a fierce devotion to his own experience, and that experience had been a great teacher for him and for many others in the class. But it was when he extended his experience to embrace Dianne's that he was able to create solidarity. Some of the students in the class wept openly, and all were moved by what we recognized as a moment of transcendence. Nothing further could be said, and we took a needed break.

The object of this story is not to create a sentimental or romantic view of the power of multicultural education courses because, no matter what their impact, they can never erase the conflict that is a natural component of such courses. Nevertheless, they can be powerful in promoting empathy and caring that go beyond one's particular experiences. Dianne's mother was the catalyst that brought conflicting ideologies, anger, and guilt to the fore to create a true community. Ron's modeling of a respectful and compassionate reaction to Dianne's mother was a reminder that we can sometimes get "stuck" in self- or group-centeredness. Something happened in the course after that. There seemed to be more listening, less rage, more introspection, less self-centeredness. There seemed to be a shared understanding that the process of learning about oneself, an absolutely essential process in multicultural education, needs to lead to learning about and with others.

For some students of European American backgrounds, what they had perceived as the onslaught of finger-pointing and blame led to a far greater understanding of their own responsibility for creating change. Several years earlier, a young undergraduate student who had been profoundly affected by a similar course had speculated on the responsibility that comes from knowledge. In her last journal entry she wrote, "Now I can never not know again." This message seems to have been learned by many of the students in this class as well.

For the students from marginalized cultural groups, there was also an awakening and it had to do with recognizing that, although their experiences were hidden from and denied in the mainstream discourse, they too were limited. After this incident, there seemed to be a genuine interest on the part of most of the course participants to learn about others. On a concrete level, other changes took place: Ron and Dianne met for coffee before class on a number of occasions; Peter went to visit James in his office on campus and they had a long talk about some of their disagreements, and in the end they became friends.

The last day of class was a sad one in many ways. Many people felt as if they were saying good-bye to old friends. It can probably be compared to the solidarity that develops when people experience a common disaster, an airplane crash or a fire. Having experienced the crisis, they could now trust one another. Of course, this was not true for everybody; some would never become friends due to their dramatic ideological differences. But some of the friendships have continued. However, for me, "sharing space" in that class became a metaphor for learning to share the ideological space that people inhabit.

LESSONS LEARNED

The story of this class, however, is not a fairytale. It did not end with everyone "living happily ever after." On the contrary, some conflicts and dilemmas were never resolved: Anger remained constant for a small number of course participants, perspectives that differed dramatically continued to differ, and I am more than certain that a few of the teachers and administrators who took the course did not change their thinking, curriculum, or pedagogy in any substantive way.

There were some profound changes, however, and I know that a number of people walked away from the course with new insights that helped them transform their teaching and how they think about education in general. I am one of them, and I want to focus briefly on some of the lessons I learned from teaching this course.

The Limits of Identity, Personal Status, and Experience

First, the course taught me about the folly of believing that understanding one kind of bias will automatically prepare students to understand others. The transfer is far easier, to be certain, but it is not automatic. This means that instructors need to be aware that all of us, students and professors alike, bring to our education a particular life experience that, although important and worthy of attention, is also limited. In the words of the writer Chaim Potok (Hock, 1995) we all need to learn "to rebel against the monolithic worlds" inside ourselves. Yet there are tendencies within multicultural education itself that discourage cross-group empathy and connection to others of different backgrounds. Consequently, we need to build into our courses experiences that will foster both knowledge and empathy about the variety of differences that teachers of young people will encounter in their classrooms.

Knowledge and Feelings Cannot Be Separated

Second, no matter how we may resist it, teaching courses in diversity carries with it a moral responsibility to help students work through conflicting and powerful emotions. Of course, we should see ourselves first as academics and as such we need to promote critical and thoughtful analyses of the many issues and concerns that are at the core of multicultural education. But because these issues and concerns also challenge deeply held views and feelings, to leave these unattended is to abrogate part of our responsibility as educators. I am not advocating that these courses become what have been derisively called "touchy-feely" courses, or that they engage in group therapy. A professor at a conference at which I spoke recently contended that courses in diversity were "a type of therapy" for marginalized students. This is a common view. I suggested to him instead that many *mainstream* courses are exercises in "therapy," although the therapy they provide is generally for students from dominant groups in society because they create false illusions and artificial self-esteem by inflating the achievement of those already in power, often at the expense of others whose community's achievements go unheeded.

Change Takes Time

Third, teaching this course taught me to be patient with the process of change. In an age of fast food and instant answers, we can too easily forget that real change takes a great deal of reflection and experimentation. Change, if it is to go beyond superficiality, needs time to simmer. I no more could expect the students to apply overnight what they had learned in this course than I could expect a dramatic change in reading scores a month after beginning a new reading program. Over the years since I taught this particular section, I have come across a number of the former participants who have told me of changes they made in their curriculum or pedagogy, of how their views of students had changed, or how their dissertations had benefited as a result of the course. One of the former students in the course is now a teacher of multicultural education; several others have become professors of ESL or secondary teacher education, and they have brought their multicultural perspective to bear on these areas; others have remained or have become public school administrators, and I know that some of the policies and practices in their schools have been reformed partially as a result of this course. In fact, I ran into Peter at a conference about 5 years after teaching this course, and he told me that the course had been a formative experience for him, one that he thought about very often in his work as an ESL teacher.

Need to Reform Higher Education and Teacher Education

One course cannot do it all. For all the changes cited here, I could probably find examples of former course participants who continue their teaching or research without wanting to look back on issues that had made the semester a difficult and painful one. The fourth lesson I took from this course, therefore, was the necessity to reform higher education in general, and teacher education in particular. This cannot be managed by simply adding a course or two in diversity to the curriculum. Reform of higher education in general would help alleviate what occurred in this particular graduate course: because it was the only course in which they could discuss perplexing but often silenced issues of oppression and privilege, it became almost a battleground of competing interests. *All* students need more courses that they can call their own. Just as students in the majority have a curriculum that more closely represents them, their history and legacy, and their values, all of our students need the same opportunity.

At the same time, all students need more courses in which they become a "minority." I often advise male students to take courses in women's studies, and non-African Americans to take African American studies. These are often eye-opening experiences in which they become, for one brief semester, the "other," with all the discomfort and alienation that it may imply. Yet they are often surprised at the generally positive reception they get in these courses, and they are forced to reflect on how students from marginalized groups do not always get the same reception in mainstream courses. In addition, they learn to look at reality from a different perspective, and invariably they benefit from the experience.

The reasons for multiculturalizing the entire teacher education program are also clear. A course or two in multicultural education, although important and even necessary, can get lost in the curriculum. It can give preservice and practicing teachers the impression that they only "do" multicultural education in those courses, just as they "do" reading in reading courses and social studies in social studies courses. All courses benefit from a multicultural perspective, especially a perspective that goes beyond the superficial "food and festivals" approach to consider issues of privilege and structural inequality. Unless diversity includes an examination of the sociopolitical context of school policies and practices and becomes a central concern of the entire teacher education program, it will continue to be marginalized and isolated from the mainstream of professional development. As such, it can be easily dismissed.

The Need to Challenge Hegemonic Policies and Practices in Teaching and Learning

The course also reinforced the importance of having all of us—students, teachers, and professors—learn to challenge hegemonic policies and practices in the classroom. Developing, in the words of Cummins (1994), "collaborative versus coercive relations of power" with students and with our students' communities is one important way to achieve this. Rather than the authoritarian wielding of power, either on the part of professors or of students, collaborative relations of power means working together to create learning experiences that can both challenge and support all learners. Using a critical eye to analyze our own taken-for-granted viewpoints and practices is crucial for all of us, no matter what our backgrounds may be.

For instance, some students felt silenced in the course, as sometimes happens in courses of this kind. (Of course, we could point to the fact that students from dominated backgrounds often feel the same way in "mainstream" courses, but the purpose in this course was not to replicate marginality but rather to help do away with it.) If silencing was indeed the result, then it seemed to me that one of the primary objectives of the course—to provide a safe place to consider and speak openly and critically about difficult issues—was not being met. This is an issue I have faced repeatedly over the years, and I believe this course helped me formulate a response to "silencing" more than any other that I have taught. Although speaking freely cannot take the form of personal vendettas, or cannot be used to cause pain or disrespect of others, or used as a soapbox to malign or disparage any group of people, I also make it clear to students that there can be no "politically correct" or unchallenged perspectives. This sounds much easier in theory than it is in practice. It often proves to be a complex balancing act between providing equal access to all, or hurting

personal feelings by making statements that are outright racist, hetero-
sexist, and so on. However, this class made me much more aware of the issue and in subsequent courses I have spoken more directly with students
about the problem and how we can confront it.

Another case in point in this course was the discussion we had of racism
as a system of "privilege and penalty" (McIntosh, 1988; Weinberg, 1990).
This is an approach that I find particularly appropriate because it helps
people see that status and resources are often doled out according to attributes such as race and gender, although such privileges may be unwar-
ranted. In addition, those who receive such privileges are often unaware of
how they benefit from their White skin, maleness, or other high-status attributes. In contrast, racism can be described in ways that are overly contentious and destructive. In relation to this discussion, a statement that
generated a great deal of conflict was that all Whites are racist if they benefit from a society that is racist. The reactions were swift and angry, and this
idea still strikes a chord of dissent (see Peter and Yoshiko's statements at
the conclusion of this chapter). I have found that this approach is generally ineffective. That is, people who are in fact racist or biased may simply
dismiss the entire topic of racism, while those who are sincerely working
against racism may feel disheartened and disempowered by it. This discussion once again brought into clear focus how different life experiences
shape different views. It is precisely because of this that such ideas need to
be presented to foster dialogue rather than provoke guilt and anger. The
important point is not that discussions of racism should be suppressed, but
in fact just the opposite: They need to be broached directly and honestly,
but in a way that creates a sense of community rather than pointing fingers
and closing down communication.

CONCLUSION

Every class I teach brings with it unexpected challenges and surprises. No
course, however, has touched me as deeply as this one because it reflected
so clearly many of the dilemmas and joys of multicultural education itself,
including resistance, transformation, and community. I wanted to create
consensus in this class, and it never happened. Far more important, I
learned that consensus need not, and probably should not, be the result of
courses such as these. Rather, creating community, with all the messiness
this term implies and with continued struggle and conflict, is probably the
most we can hope for.

If a community is created in which all voices are respected, it seems to
me that this is itself a noble first step. What I mean by *community* here, however, is not only that all voices are respected, but that a deeper sense of

bonding and caring can develop despite the very real differences that exist. That is, the course participants seemed to recognize their differences and the tensions that they caused, but they were able to form a caring loyalty to one another despite this. Creating a community also means that deep ideological and philosophical differences do not disappear. For example, Ron never accepted the idea that sexual orientation is as oppressive as racism, although he demonstrated profound respect and admiration for Dianne's mother in her role as a mother. I would have wanted Ron to make more of a theoretical connection here, but that did not happen. Needless to say, there were probably numerous other examples of the lack of change among the participants. But this does not mean that the course was a failure. On the contrary, I believe it was successful precisely because it promoted a sense of community that had not existed before. In fact, Ron's comment to Mrs. Butterfield remains a compelling example of creating the kinds of communities we all deserve.

PERSPECTIVES FROM FOUR PARTICIPANTS

Before writing the story of this multicultural education course, I decided to locate Ron, Dianne, Peter, and Yoshiko. I wanted to contact them to ask if they would assist me with what were at times hazy recollections of the course as well as to give me feedback on my interpretations of the events. Although it had been years since I had seen any of them, I was fortunate to eventually find them all. I found Ron by calling the phone number he had listed as his several years before, which turned out to be his mother's. Ron, now married and with a daughter, is currently an HIV educator in the city in which he grew up. I had seen Peter at a conference several months before beginning to write, and because we had exchanged addresses, I had no trouble contacting him. Peter and Yoshiko are now married to one another, and both are ESL teachers in another state. I was unable to find Dianne for over a year when I first began chronicling this course, and I had reluctantly given up trying to find her when we ran into one another at a conference where I was speaking. Dianne is teaching in a treatment facility for troubled boys in a large urban area.

After I wrote a preliminary draft of the chapter, I sent a copy to each of them and encouraged them to write a response. I include some of their reactions for a number of reasons. First, I am keenly aware that the story of the course as related here is necessarily my story, based on my position in the class and my particular experiences and perspectives. I wanted some of the others who had participated to share their viewpoints as well. Second, although the course had a deep impact on some of the participants, it was different for each person. Finally, I include their recollections and thoughts because they point out not that consensus was reached, but that because the issues were laid bare and confronted directly, there was at least a forum for discussion and learning that might not have otherwise happened.

Here are the recollections of Yoshiko, Peter, Ron, and Dianne.

Yoshiko

This class was indeed one of the few places where those of us from nonmainstream backgrounds could "unload" things that had accumulated inside us over the course of our lives. This unloading, however, should be done only so long as it enriches the context within which important issues regarding not only coexistence but also cooperation of different groups in our society are discussed. Although it was eye-opening for me to listen to the first-person account of experiences unique to the groups I had little or no exposure to before taking this class, it soon started to annoy me that some individuals, intentionally or unintentionally, had taken the class primarily as their political platforms, to the extent that they were so angry or forceful that others (especially mainstream students who didn't carry any "minority" labels with them) felt as if they should not speak up at all.

Reflecting on my experiences in this class, my hope is that those who take multicultural education courses come out knowing that, although members of certain groups might have been more likely to act in certain ways than others in the past, they cannot and should not be too sure about how a person of a certain group they meet in the future would act and feel about things in life. This is because I have met quite a few people (many of them educators) who seem to think that their multicultural or diversity courses have armed them with all the knowledge needed to treat people of various groups in ways that are "proper" for those groups. Knowledge of and experience with different groups' history, customs, sociopolitical situations, and so forth certainly are helpful on many occasions in interpersonal relationships. However, we must not label individuals with that knowledge before we get to know them as individuals. Multicultural education courses should not teach a new kind of labeling, and students taking the courses must become aware that they are all responsible, through the ways they act, for making or breaking multicultural unity that could come into their classroom.

Peter

If this class had been a play, I'm sure it would have been performed to packed houses . . . and encouraged audience participation!

Some of the things I enjoyed and valued about this experience were the mix of people and levels of experience, and the chance to communicate with others whose life experiences were different and similar to my own. I also disliked some things about it. For instance, I still do not accept the definition of racism that "if you are White in America, you have benefited, and are therefore racist." This guilt-laden definition is great for provoking response, but in my opinion is simplistic, divisive, and more importantly, could completely discourage adherents from seeking change. The definition itself is racist, or at least too "pat."

Furthermore, if some in the group are not speaking up, a politically correct mood can develop, and that can border on an anti-intellectual atmosphere. Accurate statements, and open dialogue need to occur for the multicultural class to be truly meaningful. Anger cannot displace truth. The tragic and ongoing legacy of oppression and racism does not need to be embellished with inaccurate statements, and continued blame and finger-pointing will not necessarily change the future.

In conclusion, if I was talking with some of the class participants, I might say, "I'm way past telling you 'I understand how you feel' when you describe your experiences in this racist society. But have you gone beyond the 'all White Americans are . . .' stage, or are you still there? Do you know that there are many levels of difficulty and discrimination in people's lives?" Lastly, I want to say that I will always believe actions speak louder than words, and I hope that the participants in this class have let their professional actions for positive change speak louder than their words. That, at least, is my goal, and this class played an important role in affirming that goal.

Ron

Many times when relating about unsavory experiences to Whites, I find they tend to undermine the content that's being presented due to a lack of understanding, or out of guilt of their own, or just as a blatant disregard for people of color. One of the reasons Peter and I had confrontations is that he was able to make weak points with others who wouldn't stand up to him. I feel that because Peter was stood up to by me, this has made him a more understanding person of other people's plight, and therefore he can begin to realize the full impact that racism tends to carry.

The confrontation between Peter and James surprised me and kind of changed my view of James' being more White than Black. (The reason for James's behavior could've been he was a university employee, and showing his Blackness might not have been "politically correct.") Peter needed to be put on the spot. He was never really confronted with or forced to face the real deal about how ugly racism is in his protected little world. Maybe something got the attention of Peter and other students, which was long overdue. But when I went to apologize to you in your office, it was because I felt I was putting the heat on you as a teacher, and my actions were not a nice way to say thank you, especially after allowing me to enter the class late.

I still believe that the weight of comparing race and sexual orientation will never be the same. A person could continue to be gay or lesbian; however, I could or never would change the color of my skin. Gays and lesbians could go into the closet and no one would know. My reason for speaking directly to Dianne's mother was I know how my mother felt about me and the things I had done while in my active drug addiction. "There's no love like a mother's love" and this was proven once again that day in that class. I was and always will be about what is right and not wrong when it comes to people. We need to understand each other and accept people and their differences. More importantly, this is the reason that courses like [this] should be mandatory on the undergraduate and graduate levels.

Dianne

When reading this chapter, I could not totally remember the intensity, anxiety, and conflict of the course. However, when I re-read the journal I kept as a class require-ment, it all came back to me. Those feelings were a prevalent theme in my writing throughout that semester. The journal writing was a beneficial tool because I often wrote what I didn't or couldn't verbalize. The reason for that was my own self-confidence, which was evolving at the time. And although the class itself was a safe space due much to your facilitation and role modeling, being an educator, I was concerned about the professional ramifications. One other point regarding my jour-nal: I noticed in the entries before the class in which my mother spoke, there was much mention of anxiety. Afterward, there wasn't. In hindsight, that's telling.

What did I learn by taking this class? This class gave me answers, arguments, or responses to "What is multicultural education?" I gained the ability to clarify my philosophy. I could explain more clearly why multicultural education is not Chanu-kah, Martin Luther King Day, or Black History Month, but a whole interwoven curriculum. As a criticism, I often hear that history is being watered down. No, it's being expanded *to include different perspectives. History is more than the study of "White men and wars." Historical accuracy is always important, but so too are the perspectives of other groups in history as well as contemporary views of society.*

I vividly remember the simple equation "prejudice + [abuse of] power = rac-ism," with which I agree. I know there were some very heated discussions in class about racism. Basically, I think Whites are racist, but to different degrees, obvi-ously. By being White (or male, Christian, heterosexual, etc.), people have some in-herent privileges. But none of us need to live in the past; we must take responsibility for our own thoughts and actions and move forward and change, to whatever de-gree we can.

My mother lives in a nursing home now. She had a massive stroke a couple of years ago. At 79, she still has that sense of humor that keeps the staff, and me, laughing. I didn't realize her talk would have such an effect on the class. When I was deciding what to do my research paper on, I thought of interviewing my mother on tape or perhaps bringing her in as a guest speaker. I wrote in my journal, "It's important to me that people know how wonderful my mother is. Also talking about mothers [in class] can legitimize lesbianism!" At age 29, I was still looking for pub-lic support, affirmation, and acceptance. Maybe her speaking in public allowed her to be more open as well—like the time she confronted people at a senior citizen party for making disparaging remarks about gays. With her love for me, and with time and new, accurate information, my mother's transformation took place. It was a slow process but one that we all can go through if we choose to.

NOTE

This chapter is an expanded version of an earlier one I wrote for the book *Speaking the unpleasant: The politics of non-engagement in the multicultural education terrain* by R. Chávez Chávez & J. O'Donnell (Eds.) (1998), Albany: State University of New York Press.

ACKNOWLEDGMENTS

I am deeply appreciative of the feedback, critical reflections, and comments that I received from Ron, Yoshiko, Peter, and Dianne. Their insights taught me new and important lessons once again, years after I first taught this class. I also wish to thank Irv Seidman, Larry Blum, and Paula Elliott for critical responses and helpful suggestions on an earlier draft of this chapter.

REFERENCES

Aaronsohn, E., Carter, C. J., & Howell, M. (1995). Preparing monocultural teachers for a multicultural world: Attitudes toward inner-city schools. *Equity and Excellence in Education, 28*(1), 5–9.

Arends, I., Clemson, S., & Henkelman, J. (1992). Tapping nontraditional sources of minority teaching talent. In M. E. Dilworth (Ed.). *Diversity in teacher education: New expectations* (pp. 160–180). San Francisco: Jossey-Bass.

Banks, J. A. (1993). Multicultural education: Historical development, dimensions, and practice. In Darling-Hammond, L. (Ed.). *Review of research in education, 19th Yearbooks* (pp. 3–49). Washington, DC: American Educational Research Association.

Bollin, G. G., & Finkel, J. (1995). White racial identity as a barrier to understanding diversity: A study of preservice teachers. *Equity and Excellence, 28*(1), 25–30.

Brown, C. E. (1992). Restructuring for a new America. In M. E. Dilworth (Ed.). *Diversity in teacher education: New expectations* (pp. 1–22). San Francisco: Jossey-Bass.

Cochran-Smith, M. (1991). Learning to teach against the grain. *Harvard Educational Review, 61*(3), 279–310.

Cummins, J. (1994). From coercive to collaborative relations of power in the teaching of literacy. In Ferdman, B. M., Weber, R., & Ramirez, A. (Eds.). *Literacy across languages and cultures* (pp. 295–331). Albany, NY: SUNY.

Garibaldi, A. M. (1992). In M. E. Dilworth (Ed.). *Diversity in teacher education: New expectations* (pp. 23–39). San Francisco: Jossey-Bass.

Hock, Z. M. (1995). Authority and multiculturalism: Reflections by Chaim Potok. *The Council Chronicle* (newsletter of the National Council of Teachers of English), *4*(7), 7.

Hodgkinson, H. (1991). Reform versus reality. *Phi Delta Kappan, 73*(1), 9–16.

Howard, G. (1993). Whites in multicultural education: Rethinking our role. *Phi Delta Kappan, 75*(1), 36–41.

Irvine, J. J. (1992). Making teacher education culturally responsive. In M. E. Dilworth (Ed.). *Diversity in teacher education: New expectations* (pp. 79–92). San Francisco: Jossey-Bass.

James, J. R. (1993). *Recruiting people of color for teacher education.* Bloomington, IN: Phi Delta Kappa.

King, J. E. (1991). Dysconscious racism: Ideology, identity, and the miseducation of teachers. *Journal of Negro Education, 60*(2), 133–146.

Kreisberg, S. (1992). *Transforming power: Domination, empowerment, and education.* Albany, NY: SUNY.

Ladson-Billings, G. (1994). *The dreamkeepers: Successful teachers of African American children.* San Francisco: Jossey-Bass.

McDiarmid, W. W. (1990). *What to do about differences? A study of multicultural education for teacher trainees in the Los Angeles Unified School District.* East Lansing, MI: National Center for Research on Teacher Education.

McIntosh, P. (1988). *White privilege and male privilege: A personal account of coming to see correspondences through work in women's studies.* Working paper no. 189. Wellesley, MA: Wellesley College Center for Research on Women.

Nieto, S. (1996). *Affirming diversity: The sociopolitical context of multicultural education* (2nd ed.). White Plains, NY: Longman.

Olsen, L., & Mullen, N. A. (1990). *Embracing diversity: Teachers' voices from California's classrooms.* San Francisco: California Tomorrow.

Pang, V. O. (1994). Why do we need this class? Multicultural education for teachers. *Phi Delta Kappan, 76*(4), 289–292.

Schoem, D., Frankel, L., Zúñiga, X., & Lewis, E. A. (1993). *Multicultural teaching at the university.* Westport, CT: Praeger.

Sleeter, C. E. (1992). *Keepers of the American dream: A study of staff development and multicultural education.* London: The Falmer Press.

Sleeter, C. E. (1994). White racism. *Multicultural Education, 1*(4), 5–8, 39.

Tatum, B. D. (1992). Talking about race, learning about racism: The application of racial identity development theory in the classroom. *Harvard Educational Review, 62*(1), 1–24.

Trueba, H. T., & Wright, P. G. (1992). On ethnographic studies and multicultural education. In M. Saravia-Shore & S. F. Arvizu (Eds.). *Cross-cultural literacy: Ethnographies of communication in multiethnic classrooms* (pp. 299–337). New York: Garland.

United States Bureau of the Census (1993, July). *Monthly News.*

Weinberg, M. (1991). *Racism in the United States: A comprehensive classified bibliography.* Westport, CT: Greenwood Press.

CRITICAL QUESTIONS

1. How do the course or courses you've taken in multicultural education compare with the one I've described? How have they been similar? Different?

2. What lessons can be learned from the experience I've described in this chapter for your own classroom? How?

3. React to the perspectives from the four students in the course included at the end of the article by writing each of them a letter.

CLASSROOM ACTIVITIES

Think about the diversity of perspectives among the students in your classroom. That is, what are the ideologies, values, and beliefs among your students and their families that might lead to the same kinds of conflict and tension I've described in this chapter? Develop some strategies that teachers can use to both face and ameliorate these differences.

COMMUNITY-BASED ADVOCACY

Imagine that, given your experience in and support for multicultural education, the principal of your school has approached you to coteach a professional development seminar on this topic to your fellow teachers. Given what you read in the previous chapter, what would you want to keep in mind in developing the seminar? What would you include in the course? With a fellow teacher, prepare a tentative syllabus.

SUPPLEMENTARY RESOURCES FOR FURTHER REFLECTION AND STUDY

Benton, Janet E. & Daniel, Patricia L. (1996). Learning to talk about taboo topics: A first step in examining cultural diversity with preservice teachers. *Equity and Excellence in Education,* *29*(3), 8–17.

> The authors, instructors of teacher education at two different universities, discuss the reluctance of their students to address issues of cultural diversity, and they present strategies to create a safe environment for doing so.

Chávez Chávez, Rudolfo, & O'Donnell, James O. (1998). *Speaking the unpleasant: The politics of non-engagement in the multicultural education terrain.* Albany: State University of New York Press.

> The chapters in this book address the challenges faced by professors who teach courses in multicultural education, and the steps they have taken to address these challenges.

Oakes, Jeannie and Lipton, Martin (1999). *Teaching to change the world.* Boston: McGraw-Hill.

> The authors approach teaching as a transformative project and they provide a solid foundation for prospective teachers to approach their work as change agents.

Part IV

PRAXIS IN THE CLASSROOM

Having a genuine awareness of diversity implies thinking deeply about classroom practice. But practice must also move beyond the proverbial "What shall I do on Monday morning?" A concern with practice should concentrate on the dispositions of teachers and schools to address linguistic and cultural diversity in meaningful ways through pedagogy, curriculum, outreach to families, disciplinary policies, and many other classroom-based and school-based practical considerations.

In the chapters that follow, I speak specifically to questions of practice. In the first, "Moving Beyond Tolerance in Multicultural Education," I provide a model of various levels of multicultural education, with *tolerance* as a basic first step toward understanding and honoring diversity, with implications for actual classrooms and schools. In Chapter 11, the final chapter in the book, I ask the question "What Does it Mean to Affirm Diversity?" Here, I provide more of a philosophical, rather than a strictly practical, answer to the question of diversity in classroom practice. I do so with the firm conviction that what both new and practicing teachers need *is not* a kit of predetermined strategies, but an attitude of mindfulness and care with which to approach the young people they teach. In this final chapter, I suggest five realities that educators need to understand if they are to create affirming schools for all students.

Affirmation, Solidarity, and Critique: Moving Beyond Tolerance in Multicultural Education

INTRODUCTION

Tolerance is a word commonly used when speaking about appropriate responses to difference. In fact, practicing tolerance is what many educators espouse as the ultimate sign of a civil and respectful society. In this chapter, I challenge this belief and suggest that tolerance actually represents a low level of support for differences. I submit instead that tolerance does little to encourage true diversity or to help schools develop a multicultural perspective.

If all we expect of our students is tolerance, can we ever hope that they will reach the point where they understand, respect, and affirm differences? That is the question this chapter seeks to answer. By describing scenarios of various levels of support for diversity in a number of school settings, I propose an answer to this question by discussing both the conceptualization and the concrete implementation of a multicultural education that moves beyond tolerance.

Tolerance: the capacity for or the practice of recognizing and respecting the beliefs or practices of others.
—The American Heritage Dictionary,
as quoted in Teaching Tolerance, Spring, 1993.

"We want our students to develop *tolerance* of others," says a teacher when asked what multicultural education means to her. "The greatest gift we can give our students is a *tolerance* for differences," is how a principal explains it. A school's mission statement might be more explicit: "Students at the Jefferson School will develop critical habits of the mind, a capacity for creativity and risk-taking, and *tolerance* for those different from themselves." In fact, if we were to listen to pronouncements at school board meetings, or conversations in teachers' rooms, or if we perused school handbooks, we would probably discover that when mentioned at all, multicultural education is associated more often with the term tolerance than with any other.

My purpose in this article is to challenge readers, and indeed the very way that multicultural education is practiced in schools in general, to move beyond tolerance in both conceptualization and implementation. It is my belief that a movement beyond tolerance is absolutely necessary if multicultural education is to become more than a superficial "bandaid" or a "feel-good" additive to our school curricula. I will argue that tolerance is actually a low level of multicultural support, reflecting as it does an acceptance of the *status quo* with but slight accommodations to difference. I will review and expand upon a model of multicultural education that I have developed elsewhere (*Affirming Diversity: The Sociopolitical Context of Multicultural Education*) in order to explore what multicultural education might actually look like in a school's policies and practices.

LEVELS OF MULTICULTURAL EDUCATION SUPPORT

Multicultural education is not a unitary concept. On the contrary, it can be thought of as a range of options across a wide spectrum that includes such diverse strategies as bilingual/bicultural programs, ethnic studies courses, Afrocentric curricula, or simply the addition of a few "Holidays and Heroes" to the standard curriculum (See James A. Banks, *Teaching Strategies for Ethnic Studies*, Allyn & Bacon, 1991), just to name a few. Although all of these may contribute to multicultural education, they represent incomplete conceptualizations and operationalizations of this complex educational reform movement. Unfortunately, however, multicultural education is often approached as if there were a prescribed script.

The most common understanding of multicultural education is that it consists largely of additive content rather than of structural changes in content and process. It is not unusual, then, to hear teachers say that they are "doing" multicultural education this year, or, as in one case that I heard, that they could not "do it" in the Spring because they had too many other things to "do." In spite of the fact that scholars and writers in multicultural education have been remarkably consistent over the years about

the complexity of approaches in the field (see, especially, the analysis by
C. E. Sleeter & C. A. Grant, "An Analysis of Multicultural Education in the
United States," *Harvard Educational Review*, November, 1987), it has often
been interpreted in either a simplistic or a monolithic way. It is because of
this situation that I have attempted to develop a model that clarifies how
various levels of multicultural education support may actually be apparent
in schools.

Developing categories or models is always an inherently problematic
venture, and I therefore present the following model with some hesitancy.
Whenever we classify and categorize reality, we run the risk that it will be
viewed as static and arbitrary, rather than as messy, complex, and contradictory, which we know it to be. Notwithstanding the value that theoretical
models may have, they tend to represent information as if it were fixed
and absolute. Yet we know too well that nothing happens exactly as portrayed in models and charts, much less social interactions among real people in settings such as schools. In spite of this, models or categories can be
useful because they help make concrete situations more understandable
and manageable. I therefore present the following model with both reluctance and hope: reluctance because it may improperly be viewed as set in
stone, but hope because it may challenge teachers, administrators, and educators in general to rethink what it means to develop a multicultural perspective in their schools.

The levels in this model should be viewed as necessarily dynamic, with
penetrable borders. They should be understood as "interactive," in the
words of Peggy McIntosh (see her *Interactive Phases of Curricular Re-vision:
A Feminist Perspective*, Wellesley College Center for Research on Women,
1983). Thus, although these levels represent "ideal" categories that are in-
ternally consistent and therefore set, the model is not meant to suggest
that schools are really like this. Probably no school would be a purely
"monocultural" or "tolerant" school, given the stated characteristics under
each of these categories. However, these categories are used in an effort to
illustrate how support for diversity is manifested in schools in a variety of
ways. Because multicultural education is primarily a set of beliefs and a
philosophy, rather than a set program or fixed content, this model can assist us in determining how particular school policies and practices need to
change in order to embrace the diversity of our students and their communities.

The four levels to be considered are: **tolerance**; **acceptance**; **respect**;
and, finally, **affirmation, solidarity, and critique**. Before going on to consider how multicultural education is manifested in schools that profess
these philosophical orientations, it is first helpful to explore the antithesis
of multicultural education, namely, **monocultural education**, because
without this analysis we have nothing with which to compare it.

In the scenarios that follow, we go into five schools that epitomize different levels of multicultural education. All are schools with growing cultural diversity in their student populations; differences include staff backgrounds, attitudes, and preparation, as well as curriculum and pedagogy. In our visits, we see how the curriculum, interactions among students, teachers, and parents, and other examples of attention to diversity are either apparent or lacking. We see how students of different backgrounds might respond to the policies and practices around them. (In another paper entitled "Creating Possibilities: Educating Latino Students in Massachusetts," in *The Education of Latino Students in Massachusetts: Policy and Research Implications*, published by the Gaston Institute for Latino Policy and Development in Boston, which I co-edited with R. Rivera, I developed scenarios of schools that would provide different levels of support specifically for Latino students.)

MONOCULTURAL EDUCATION

Monocultural education describes a situation in which school structures, policies, curricula, instructional materials, and even pedagogical strategies are primarily representative of only the dominant culture. In most United States schools, it can be defined as "the way things are."

We will begin our tour in a "monocultural school" that we'll call the George Washington Middle School. When we walk in, we see a sign that says "NO UNAUTHORIZED PERSONS ARE ALLOWED IN THE SCHOOL. ALL VISITORS MUST REPORT DIRECTLY TO THE PRINCIPAL'S OFFICE." The principal, assistant principal, and counselor are all European-American males, although the school's population is quite diverse, with large numbers of African-American, Puerto Rican, Arab-American, Central American, Korean, and Vietnamese students. As we walk down the hall, we see a number of bulletin boards. On one, the coming Christmas holiday is commemorated; on another, the P.T.O.'s bake sale is announced; and on a third, the four basic food groups are listed, with reference to only those foods generally considered to be "American."

The school is organized into 45-minutes periods of such courses as U.S. history, English, math, science, music appreciation, art, and physical education. In the U.S. history class, students learn of the proud exploits, usually through wars and conquest, of primarily European-American males. They learn virtually nothing about the contributions, perspectives, or talents of women or those outside the cultural mainstream. U.S. slavery is mentioned briefly in relation to the Civil War, but African Americans are missing thereafter. In English class, the students have begun their immersion in the "canon," reading works almost entirely written by European and European-American males, although a smattering of women and African American (but no Asian, Latino, or American Indian) authors are included in the newest anthology. In music appreciation class, students are exposed to what is called "classical music," that is, European classical music, but the "classical" music of societies in Asia, Africa, and Latin America is nowhere to be found. In art classes, students may learn about the art work of famous European and European-American artists, and occasionally about the "crafts" and "artifacts" of other cultures and societies mostly from the Third World.

Teachers at the George Washington Middle School are primarily European-American women who have had little formal training in multicultural approaches or perspectives. They are proud of the fact that they are "color-blind," that is, that they see no differences among their students, treating them all the same. Of course, this does not extend to tracking, which they generally perceive to be in the interest of teaching all students to the best of their abilities. Ability grouping is a standard practice at the George Washington Middle School. There are four distinct levels of ability, from "talented and gifted" to "remedial." I.Q. tests are used to determine student placement and intellectually superior students are placed in "Talented and Gifted" programs, and in advanced levels of math, science, English, and social studies. Only these top students have the option of taking a foreign language. The top levels consist of overwhelmingly European-American and Asian-American students, but the school rationalizes that this is due to either the native intelligence of these students, or to the fact that they have a great deal more intellectual stimulation and encouragement in their homes. Thus, teachers have learned to expect excellent work from their top students, but little of students in their low-level classes, who they often see as lazy and disruptive.

Students who speak a language other than English as their native language are either placed in regular classrooms where they will learn to "sink or swim" or in "NE" (non-English) classes, where they are drilled in English all day and where they will remain until they learn English sufficiently well to perform in the regular classroom. In addition, parents are urged to speak to their children only in English at home. Their native language, whether Spanish, Vietnamese, or Korean, is perceived as a handicap to their learning, and as soon as they forget it, they can get on with the real job of learning.

Although incidents of racism have occurred in the George Washington Middle School, they have been taken care of quietly and privately. For example, when racial slurs have been used, students have been admonished not to say them. When fights between children of different ethnic groups take place, the assistant principal has insisted that race or ethnicity has nothing to do with them; "kids will be kids" is the way he describes these incidents.

What exists in the George Washington Middle School is a monocultural environment with scant reference to the experiences of others from largely subordinated cultural groups. Little attention is paid to student diversity, and the school curriculum is generally presented as separate from the community in which it is located. In addition, "dangerous" topics such as racism, sexism, and homophobia are seldom discussed, and reality is represented as finished and static. In summary, the George Washington School is a depressingly familiar scenario because it reflects what goes on in most schools in American society.

TOLERANCE

How might a school characterized by "tolerance" be different from a monocultural school? It is important here to mention the difference between the *denotation* and the *connotation* of words. According to the dictionary definition given at the beginning of this chapter, tolerance is hardly a value that one could argue with. After all, what is wrong with "recognizing and respecting the beliefs or practices of others"? On the contrary, this is a quintessential part of developing a multicultural perspective. (*Teaching Tolerance*, a journal developed by the Southern Anti-Poverty Law Project, has no doubt been developed with this perspective in mind, and my critique here of tolerance is in no way meant to criticize this wonderful classroom and teacher resource.)

Nevertheless, the connotation of words is something else entirely. When we think of what **tolerance** means in practice, we have images of a grudging but somewhat distasteful acceptance. To *tolerate* differences means that they are endured, not necessarily embraced. In fact, this level of support for multicultural education stands on shaky ground because what is tolerated today can too easily be rejected tomorrow. A few examples will help illustrate this point.

Our "tolerant" school is the Brotherhood Middle School. Here, differences are understood to be the inevitable burden of a culturally pluralistic society. A level up from a "color-blind" monocultural school, the "tolerant" school accepts differences but only if they can be modified. Thus, they are accepted, but because the ultimate goal is assimilation, differences in language and culture are replaced as quickly as possible. This ideology is reflected in the physical environment, the attitudes of staff, and the curriculum to which students are exposed.

When we enter the Brotherhood School, there are large signs in English welcoming visitors, although there are no staff on hand who can communicate with the families of the growing Cambodian student population. One prominently-placed bulletin board proudly portrays the winning essays of this year's writing contest with the theme of "Why I am proud to be an American." The winners, a European-American sixth grader and a Vietnamese seventh grader, write in their essays about the many opportunities given to all people in our country, no matter what their race, ethnicity, or gender. Another bulletin board boasts the story of Rosa Parks, portrayed as a woman who was too tired to give up her seat on the bus, thus serving as a catalyst for the modern civil rights movement. (The Fall 1993 issue of *Multicultural Education* includes a powerful example of how people such as Rosa Parks have been de-contextualized to better fit in with the U.S. mainstream conception of individual rather than collective struggle, thus adding little to children's understanding of institutionalized discrimination in our society; see "The Myth of 'Rosa Parks the Tired' " by Herbert Kohl, pages 6–10, in which Kohl reports that based on his research most stories used in American schools present Rosa Parks simply as "Rosa Parks the Tired.")

Nevertheless, a number of important structural changes are taking place at the Brotherhood School. An experiment has recently begun in which the sixth and seventh graders are in "family" groupings, and these are labeled by family names such as the Jones family, the Smith family, and the Porter family. Students remain together as a family in their major subjects (English, social studies, math, and science) and there is no ability tracking in these classes. Because their teachers have a chance to meet and plan together daily, they are more readily able to develop integrated curricula. In fact, once in a while, they even combine classes so that they can team-teach and their students remain at a task for an hour and a half rather than the usual three quarters of an hour. The students seem to like this arrangement, and have done some interesting work in their study of Washington, D.C. For instance, they used geometry to learn how the city was designed, and have written to their congressional representatives to ask how bills become laws. Parents are involved in fund-raising for an upcoming trip to the capital, where students plan to interview a number of their local legislators.

The curriculum at the Brotherhood School has begun to reflect some of the changes that a multicultural society demands. Students are encouraged to study a foreign language (except, of course, for those who already speak one; they are expected to learn English and in the process, they usually forget their native language). In addition, a number of classes have added activities on women, African Americans, and American Indians. Last year, for instance, Martin Luther King Day was celebrated by having all students watch a video of the "I Have a Dream" speech.

The majority of changes in the curriculum have occurred in the social studies and English departments, but the music teacher has also begun to add a more international flavor to her repertoire, and the art classes recently went to an exhibit of the work of Romare Bearden. This year, a "multicultural teacher" has been added to the staff. She meets with all students in the school, seeing each group once a week for one period. Thus far, she has taught students about Chinese New Year, *Kwanzaa, Ramadan,* and *Dia de los Reyes*. She is getting ready for the big multicultural event of the year, Black History Month. She hopes to work with other teachers to bring in guest speakers, show films about the civil rights movement, and have an art contest in which students draw what the world would be like if Dr. King's dream of equality became a reality.

Students who speak a language other than English at the Brotherhood School are placed in special E.S.L. classes, where they are taught English as quickly, but sensitively, as possible. For instance, while they are encouraged to speak to one another in English, they are allowed to use their native language, but only as a last resort. The feeling is that if they use it more often, it will become a "crutch." In any event, the E.S.L. teachers are not required to speak a language other than English; in fact, being bilingual is even considered a handicap because students might expect them to use their other language.

The principal of the Brotherhood School has made it clear that racism will not be tolerated here. Name-calling and the use of overtly racist and sexist textbooks and other materials are discouraged. Recently, some teachers attended a workshop on strategies for dealing with discrimination in the classroom. Some of those who attended expect to make some changes in how they treat students from different backgrounds.

Most teachers at the Brotherhood School have had little professional preparation to deal with the growing diversity of the student body. They like and genuinely want to help their students, but have made few changes in their curricular or instructional practices. For them, "being sensitive" to their students is what multicultural education should be about, not overhauling the curriculum. Thus, they acknowledge student differences in language, race, gender, and social class, but still cannot quite figure out why some students are more successful than others. Although they would like to think not, they wonder if genetics or poor parental attitudes about education have something to do with it. If not, what can explain these great discrepancies?

ACCEPTANCE

Acceptance is the next level of supporting diversity. It implies that differences are acknowledged and their importance is neither denied nor belittled. It is at this level that we see substantial movement toward multicultural education. A look at how some of the school's policies and practices might change is indicative of this movement.

The name of our school is the Rainbow Middle School. As we enter, we see signs in English as well as in Spanish, and Haitian Creole, the major languages besides English spoken by students and their families. The principal of the Rainbow School is Dr. Belinda Clayton, the first African-American principal ever appointed. She has designated her school as a "multicultural building," and has promoted a number of professional development opportunities for teachers that focus on diversity. These include seminars on diverse learning styles, bias-free assessment, and bilingual education. In addition, she has hired not only Spanish- and Haitian Creole-speaking teachers for the bilingual classrooms, but has also diversified the staff in the "regular" program.

Bulletin boards outside the principal's office display the pictures of the "Students of the Month." This month's winners are Rodney Thomas, a sixth-grader who has excelled in art, Neleida Cortés, a seventh-grade student in the bilingual program, and Melissa Newton, an eight-grader in the special education program. All three were given a special luncheon by the principal and their homeroom teachers. Another bulletin board focuses on "Festivals of Light" and features information about *Chanukah*, *Kwanzaa*, and Christmas, with examples of *Las Posadas* in Mexico and Saint Lucia's Day in Sweden.

The curriculum at the Rainbow Middle School has undergone some changes to reflect the growing diversity of the student body. English classes include more choices of African American, Irish, Jewish, and Latino literature written in English. Some science and math teachers have begun to make reference to famous scientists and mathematicians from a variety of backgrounds. In one career-studies class, a number of parents have been invited to speak about their job and the training they had to receive in order to get those positions. All students are encouraged to study a foreign language, and choices have been expanded to include Spanish, French, German, and Mandarin Chinese.

Tracking has been eliminated in all but the very top levels at the Rainbow School. All students have the opportunity to learn algebra, although some are still counseled out of this option because their teachers believe it will be too difficult for them. The untracked classes seem to be a hit with the students, and preliminary results have shown a slight improvement among all students. Some attempts have been made to provide flexible scheduling, with one day a week devoted entirely to "learning blocks" where students work on a special project. One group recently engaged in an in-depth study of the elderly in their community. They learned about services available to them, and they touched on poverty and lack of health care for many older Americans. As a result of this study, the group has added a community service component to the class; this involves going to the local Senior Center during their weekly learning block to read with the elderly residents.

Haitian and Spanish-speaking students are tested and, if found to be more proficient in their native language, are placed in transitional bilingual education programs. Because of lack of space in the school, the bilingual programs are located in the basement, near the boiler room. Here, students are taught the basic curriculum in their native language while learning English as a second language during one period of the day with an ESL specialist. Most ESL teachers are also fluent in a language other than English, helping them understand the process of acquiring a second language. The bilingual program calls for students to be "mainstreamed" (placed in what is called a "regular classroom") as quickly as possible, with a limit of three years on the outside. In the meantime, they are segregated from their peers for most of the day, but have some classes with English-speaking students, including physical education, art, and music. As they proceed through the program and become more fluent in English, they are "exited" out for some classes, beginning with math and social studies. While in the bilingual program, students' native cultures are sometimes used as the basis of the curriculum, and they learn about the history of their people. There is, for instance, a history course on the Caribbean that is offered to both groups in their native languages. Nevertheless, neither Haitian and Latino students in the bilingual program nor students of other backgrounds have access to these courses.

Incidents of racism and other forms of discrimination are beginning to be faced at the Rainbow Middle School. Principal Clayton deals with these carefully, calling in the offending students as well as their parents, and she makes certain that students understand the severe consequences for name-calling or scapegoating others. Last year, one entire day was devoted to "diversity" and regular classes were canceled while students attended workshops focusing on discrimination, the importance of being sensitive to others, and the influence on U.S. history of many different immigrants. They have also hosted a "Multicultural Fair" and published a cookbook with recipes donated by many different parents.

The Rainbow Middle School is making steady progress in accepting the great diversity of its students. They have decided that perhaps assimilation should not be the goal, and have eschewed the old idea of the "melting pot." In its place, they have the "salad bowl" metaphor, in which all students bring something special that need not be reconstituted or done away with.

RESPECT

Respect is the next level of multicultural education support. It implies admiration and high esteem for diversity. When differences are respected, they are used as the basis for much of what goes on in schools. Our next scenario describes what this might look like.

The Sojourner Truth Middle School is located in a mid-size town with a changing population. There is a fairly large African-American population with a growing number of students of Cape Verdean and Vietnamese background, and the school staff reflects these changes, including teachers, counselors, and special educators of diverse backgrounds. There is, for example, a Vietnamese speech pathologist, and his presence has helped to alleviate the concerns of some teachers that the special needs of the Vietnamese children were not being addressed. He has found that while some students do indeed have speech problems, others do not, but teachers' unfamiliarity with the Vietnamese language made it difficult to know this.

When we enter the Sojourner Truth Middle School, we are greeted by a parent volunteer. She gives us printed material in all the languages represented in the school, and invites us to the parents' lounge for coffee, tea, and danish. We are then encouraged to walk around and explore the school. Bulletin boards boast of students' accomplishments in the Spanish Spelling Bee, the local *Jeopardy* Championship, and the W.E.B. DuBois Club of African-American history. It is clear from the children's pictures that there is wide participation of many students in all of these activities. The halls are abuzz with activity as students go from one class to another, and most seem eager and excited by school.

Professional development is an important principle at the Sojourner Truth Middle School. Teachers, counselors, and other staff are encouraged to take courses at the local university and to keep up with the literature in their field. To make this more feasible, the staff gets released time weekly to get together. As a consequence, the curriculum has been through tremendous changes. Teachers have formed committees to develop their curriculum. The English department decided to use its time to have reading and discussion groups with some of the newly available multicultural literature with which they were unfamiliar. As a result, they have revamped the curriculum into such overarching themes as *coming of age, immigration, change and continuity,* and *individual and collective responsibility.* They have found that it is easier to select literature to reflect themes such as these, and the literature is by its very nature multicultural. For instance, for the theme *individual and collective responsibility* they have chosen stories of varying difficulty, including *The Diary of Anne Frank, Bridge to Terabithia* (by Katherine Paterson), *Morning Girl* (by Michael Dorris), and *Let the Circle be Unbroken* (by Mildred D. Taylor), among others. The English teachers have in turn invited the history, art, and science departments to join them in developing some integrated units with these themes. Teachers from the art and music departments have agreed to work with them, and have included lessons on Vietnamese dance, Guatemalan weaving, Jewish Klezmer music, and American Indian story telling as examples of individual and collective responsibility in different communities.

Other changes are apparent in the curriculum as well, for it has become more antiracist and honest. When studying World War II, students learn about the heroic role played by the United States, and also about the Holocaust, in which not only six million Jews, but millions of others, including Gypsies, gays and lesbians, and many dissenters of diverse backgrounds, were exterminated. They also learn, for the first time, about the internment of over a hundred thousand Japanese and Japanese Americans on our own soil.

It has become "safe" to talk about such issues as the crucial role of labor in U.S. history and the part played by African Americans in freeing themselves from bondage, both subjects thought too "sensitive" to be included previously. This is one reason why the school was renamed for a woman known for her integrity and courage.

The Sojourner Truth Middle School has done away with all ability grouping. When one goes into a classroom, it is hard to believe that students of all abilities are learning together because the instruction level seems to be so high. Upon closer inspection, it becomes apparent that there are high expectations for all students. Different abilities are accommodated by having some students take more time than others, providing cooperative groups in which students change roles and responsibilities, and through ongoing dialogue among all students.

Students who speak a language other than English are given the option of being in a "maintenance bilingual program," that is, a program based on using their native language throughout their schooling, not just for three years. Changing the policy that only students who could not function in English were eligible for bilingual programs, this school has made the program available to those who speak English in addition to their native language. Parents and other community members who speak these languages are invited in to classes routinely to talk about their lives, jobs, or families, or to tell stories or share experiences. Students in the bilingual program are not, however, segregated from their peers all day, but join them for a number of academic classes.

Teachers and other staff members at this middle school have noticed that incidents of name-calling and interethnic hostility have diminished greatly since the revised curriculum was put into place. Perhaps more students see themselves in the curriculum and feel less angry about their invisibility; perhaps more teachers have developed an awareness and appreciation for their students' diversity while learning about it; perhaps the more diverse staff is the answer; or maybe it's because the community feels more welcome into the school. Whatever it is, the Sojourner Truth Middle School has developed an environment in which staff and students are both expanding their ways of looking at the world.

AFFIRMATION, SOLIDARITY, AND CRITIQUE

Affirmation, solidarity, and critique is based on the premise that the most powerful learning results when students work and struggle with one another, even if it is sometimes difficult and challenging. It begins with the assumption that the many differences that students and their families represent are embraced and accepted as legitimate vehicles for learning, and that these are then extended. What makes this level different from the others is that conflict is not avoided, but rather accepted as an inevitable part of learning. Because multicultural education at this level is concerned with equity and social justice, and because the basic values of different groups are often diametrically opposed, conflict is bound to occur.

Affirmation, solidarity, and critique is also based on understanding that culture is not a fixed or unchangeable artifact, and is therefore subject to critique. Passively accepting the status quo of any culture is thus inconsistent with this level of multicultural education; simply substituting one myth for another contradicts its basic assumptions because no group is inherently superior or more heroic than any other. As eloquently expressed by Mary Kalantzis and Bill Cope in their 1990 work *The Experience of Multicultural Education in Australia: Six Case Studies*, "Multicultural education, to be effective, needs to be more active. It needs to consider not just the pleasure of diversity but more fundamental issues that arise as different groups negotiate community and the basic issues of material life in the same space—a process that equally might generate conflict and pain."

Multicultural education without critique may result in cultures remaining at the romantic or exotic stage. If students are to transcend their own cultural experience in order to understand the differences of others, they need to go through a process of reflection and critique of their cultures and those of others. This process of critique, however, begins with a solid core of solidarity with others who are different from themselves. When based on true respect, critique is not only necessary but in fact healthy.

The Arturo Schomburg Middle School is located in a mid-size city with a very mixed population of Puerto Ricans, Salvadoreans, American Indians, Polish Americans, Irish Americans, Chinese Americans, Philippinos, and African Americans. The school was named for a Black Puerto Rican scholar who devoted his life to exploring the role of Africans in the Americas, in the process challenging the myth he had been told as a child in Puerto Rico that Africans had "no culture."

The school's logo, visible above the front door, is a huge tapestry made by the students, and it symbolizes a different model of multicultural education from that of either the "melting pot" or the "salad bowl." According to a publication of the National Association of State Boards of Education

(*The American Tapestry: Educating a Nation*), "A tapestry is a hand-woven textile. When examined from the back, it may simply appear to be a motley group of threads. But when reversed, the threads work together to depict a picture of structure and beauty" (p. 1). According to Adelaide Sanford, one of the study group members who wrote this publication, a tapestry also symbolizes, through its knots, broken threads, and seeming jumble of colors and patterns on the back, the tensions, conflicts, and dilemmas that a society needs to work out. This spirit of both collaboration and struggle is evident in the school.

When we enter the Schomburg Middle School, the first thing we notice is a banner proclaiming the school's motto: LEARN, REFLECT, QUESTION, AND WORK TO MAKE THE WORLD A BETTER PLACE. This is the message that reverberates throughout the school. Participation is another evident theme, and the main hall contains numerous pictures of students in classrooms, community service settings, and extracurricular activities. Although housed in a traditional school building, the school has been transformed into a place where all children feel safe and are encouraged to learn to the highest levels of achievement. While there are typical classrooms of the kind that are immediately recognizable to us, the school also houses centers that focus on specific areas of learning. There is, for instance, a studio where students can be found practicing traditional Philippino dance and music, as well as European ballet, and modern American dance, among others. Outside, there is a large garden that is planted, cared for, and harvested by the students and faculty. The vegetables are used by the cafeteria staff in preparing meals and they have noticed a marked improvement in the eating habits of the children since the menu was changed to reflect a healthier and more ethnically diverse menu.

We are welcomed into the school by staff people who invite us to explore the many different classrooms and other learning centers. Those parents who are available during the day can be found assisting in classrooms, in the Parent's Room working on art projects or computer classes, or attending workshops by other parents or teachers on topics ranging from cross-cultural child-rearing to ESL. The bulletin boards are ablaze with color and include a variety of languages, displaying student work from critical essays on what it means to be an American to art projects that celebrate the talents of many of the students. Learning is going on everywhere, whether in classrooms or in small-group collaborative projects in halls.

What might the classrooms look like in this school? For one, they are characterized by tremendous diversity. Tracking and special education, as we know them, have been eliminated at the Schomburg Middle School. Students with special needs are taught along with all others, although they are sometimes separated for small-group instruction with students not classified as having special needs. All children are considered "talented" and special classes are occasionally organized for those who excel in dance, mathematics, poetry, or science. No interested students are excluded from any of these offerings. Furthermore, all students take algebra and geometry, and special coaching sessions are available before, after, and during school hours for these and other subjects.

Classes are flexible, with an interdisciplinary curriculum and team-teaching, resulting in sessions that sometimes last as long as three hours. The physical environment in classrooms is varied: some are organized with round work tables, others have traditional desks, and still others have scant furniture to allow for more movement. Class size also varies from small groups to large, depending on the topic at hand. Needless to say, scheduling at this school is a tremendous and continuing challenge, but faculty and students are committed to this more flexible arrangement and willing to allow for the daily problems that it may cause.

There are no "foreign languages" at the Schomburg Middle school, nor is there, strictly speaking, a bilingual program. Rather, the entire school is multilingual, and all students learn at least a second language in addition to their native language. This means that students are not segregated by language, but instead work in bilingual settings where two languages are used for instruction. At present, the major languages used are English, Spanish, and Tagalog, representing the most common languages spoken by this school's community. It is not unusual to see students speaking these languages in classrooms, the hallways, or the playgrounds, even among those for whom English is a native language.

Students at the Schomburg Middle School seem engaged, engrossed, and excited about learning. They have been involved in a number of innovative long-range projects that have resulted from the interdisciplinary curriculum. For instance, working with a Chinese-American artist in residence, they wrote, directed, and produced a play focusing on the "Know-Nothing" Movement in U.S. history that resulted in, among other things, the Chinese Exclusion Act of 1882. In preparation for the play, they read a great deal and did extensive research. For example, they contacted the Library of Congress for information on primary sources and reviewed newspapers and magazines from the period to get a sense of the climate that led to Nativism. They also designed and sewed all the costumes and sets. In addition, they interviewed recent immigrants of many backgrounds, and found that they had a range of experiences from positive to negative in their new country. On the day of the play, hundreds of parents and other community members attended. Students also held a debate on the pros and cons of continued immigration, and received up-to-date information concerning immigration laws from their congressional representative.

The curriculum at the Schomburg Middle School is dramatically different from the George Washington School, the first school we visited. Teachers take very seriously their responsibility of *teaching complexity*. Thus, students have learned that there are many sides to every story, and that in order to make informed decisions, they need as much information as they can get. Whether in English, science, art, or any other class, students have been encouraged to be critical of every book, newspaper, curriculum, or piece of information by asking questions such as: *Who wrote the book? Who's missing in this story? Why?* Using questions such as these as a basis, they are learning that every story has a point of view and that every point of view is at best partial and at worst distorted. They are also learning that their own backgrounds, rich and important as they may be, have limitations that can lead to parochial perceptions. Most of all, even at this age, students are learning that every topic is fraught with difficulties and they are wrestling with issues as diverse as homelessness, solar warming, and how the gender expectations of different cultures might limit opportunities for girls. Here, nothing is taboo as a topic of discussion as long as it is approached with respect and in a climate of caring.

What this means for teachers is that they have had to become learners along with their students. They approach each subject with curiosity and an open mind, and during the school day they have time to study, meet with colleagues, and plan their curriculum accordingly. Professional development here means not only attending courses at a nearby university, but collaborating with colleagues in study groups that last anywhere from half a day to several months. These provide a forum in which teachers can carefully study relevant topics or vexing problems. Some of these study groups have focused on topics such as Reconstruction and the history of the Philippines, to educational issues such as cooperative learning and diverse cognitive styles.

Especially noteworthy at this school is that *multicultural education* is not separated from *education*; that is, all education is by its very nature multicultural. English classes use literature written by a wide variety of people from countries where English is spoken. This has resulted in these classes becoming not only multicultural, but international as well. Science classes do not focus on contributions made by members of specific ethnic groups, but have in fact been transformed to consider how science itself is conceptualized, valued, and practiced by those who have traditionally been outside the scientific mainstream. Issues such as AIDS education, healing in different cultures, and scientific racism have all been the subject of study.

One of the major differences between this school and the others we visited has to do with its governance structure. There is a Schomburg School Congress consisting of students, faculty, parents, and other community members, and it has wide decision-making powers, from selecting the principal to determining reasonable and equitable disciplinary policies and practices. Students are elected by their classmates and, although at the beginning these were little more than popularity contests, in recent months it has been clear that students are beginning to take this responsibility seriously. This is probably because *they* are being taken seriously by the adults in the group. For instance, when students in one class decided that they wanted to plan a class trip to a neighboring city to coincide with their study of toxic wastes and the environment, they were advised to do some preliminary planning: what would be the educational objectives of such a trip? how long would it take? how much would it cost? After some research and planning, they presented their ideas to the Congress and a fund-raising plan that included students, parents, and community agencies was started.

The Schomburg School is a learning center that is undergoing important changes every day. As teachers discover the rich talents that all students bring to school, they develop high expectation for them all. The climate that exists in this school is one of possibility, because students' experiences are used to build on their learning and expand their horizons. Students in turn are realizing that while their experiences are important and unique, they are only one experience of many. A new definition of "American" is being forged at this school, one that includes everybody. Above all, learning here is exciting, engrossing, inclusive, and evolving.

CONCLUSION

One might well ask how realistic these scenarios are, particularly the last one. Could a school such as this really exist? Isn't this just wishful thinking? What about the reality of bond issues rejected by voters?, of teachers woefully unprepared to deal with the diversity in their classrooms?, of universities that do little more than offer stale "Mickey Mouse" courses?, of schools with no pencils, paper, and chalk, much less computers and video cameras?, of rampant violence in streets, homes, and schools?, of drugs and crime?, of parents who are barely struggling to keep their families together and can spare precious little time to devote to volunteering at school?

These are all legitimate concerns that our society needs to face, and they remind us that schools need to be understood within their sociopolitical contexts. That is, our schools exist in a society in which social and economic stratification are facts of life, where competition is taught over caring, and where the early sorting that takes place in educational settings often lasts a lifetime. Developing schools with a multicultural perspective is not easy; if it were, they would be everywhere. But schools with a true commitment to diversity, equity, and high levels of learning are difficult to achieve precisely because the problems they face are pervasive and seemingly impossible to solve. Although the many problems they face are certainly daunting, schools as currently organized are simply not up to the challenge. In the final analysis, if we believe that all students deserve to learn at the very highest levels, then we need a vision of education that will help achieve this end.

The scenarios above, however, are not simply figments of my imagination. As your read through the scenarios, you probably noticed bits and pieces of your own school here and there. However, because the "monocultural school" is the one with which we are most familiar, and unfortunately even comfortable, the other scenarios might seem far-fetched or unrealistic. Although they are *ideal* in the sense that they are not true pictures of specific schools, these scenarios nevertheless describe *possibilities* because they all exist to some degree in our schools today. These are not pie-in-the-sky visions, but components of what goes on in schools every day. As such, they provide building blocks for how we might go about transforming schools. In fact, were we to design schools based on the ideals that our society has always espoused, they would no doubt come close to the last scenario.

It is not, however, a monolithic model or one that can develop overnight. The participants in each school need to develop their own vision so that step by step, with incremental changes, schools become more multicultural, and thus more inclusive and more exciting places for learning. If we believe that young people deserve to be prepared with skills for living ethical and productive lives in an increasingly diverse and complex world, then we need to transform schools so that they not only teach what have been called "the basics," but also provide an apprenticeship in democracy and social justice. It is unfair to expect our young people to develop an awareness and respect for democracy if they have not experienced it, and it is equally unrealistic to expect them to be able to function in a pluralistic society if all we give them are skills for a monocultural future. This is our challenge in the years ahead: to conquer the fear of change and imagine how we might create exciting possibilities for all students in all schools.

CRITICAL QUESTIONS

1. Do you agree with the assertion that "tolerance" is a low level of support for multicultural education? Why or why not? Explain your reasons.

2. Using the levels described in the scenarios in this article, where would you place your school? Why? Give some examples.

3. If you were to design a school that promoted diversity as you believe it should be promoted, what would it look like? Write a description of it.

4. Do you think the scenarios I've described are realistic? If not, what would make them more so?

CLASSROOM ACTIVITY

Think about your classroom and what you can do within your own four walls to make it more responsive to higher levels of multicultural education. Make a list of changes you can begin to implement. Next to each, describe what resources you need, how you can get them, and a reasonable timeline for implementation. Begin implementing *one* of the ideas you have and report back to the other participants in the course about your progress.

Review some of your other ideas, and follow the same process as above. At the end of the semester, figure out how many of these ideas you've put into practice. Have they had an impact on the climate of your classroom? on student enthusiasm and learning? on family involvement? on your own ideas about diversity?

COMMUNITY-BASED ADVOCACY

If there is a site-based management team in your school, consider becoming a member of it. Develop alliances with other teachers or parents who have expressed support for diversity. Bring up with the group some of the changes you considered for your own classroom and suggest how they might be implemented at the school level. Think about starting small, with incremental changes. Document your success with these changes, and reflect on why things have or have not worked. How might you change your approach in the future?

SUPPLEMENTARY RESOURCES FOR FURTHER REFLECTION AND STUDY

Allen, Andrew M. A. (1997). Creating space for discussions about social justice and equity in an elementary classroom. *Language Arts, 74*(7), 518–524.

In this article, the author discusses how he uses his second graders' sense of fairness as a foundation for constructing an anti-racist/anti-bias curriculum in his classroom.

Ballenger, Cynthia (1999). *Teaching other people's children: Literacy and learning in a bilingual classroom.* New York: Teachers College Press.

In her autobiographical account of learning to see the strengths that Haitian American children bring to their education, and actually changing her pedagogical practice as a result, Ballenger uses Lisa Delpit's work (see below) in framing her own growing awareness of what it means to educate "other people's children."

Delpit, Lisa (1988). The silenced dialogue: Power and pedagogy in educating other people's children. *Harvard Educational Review, 58*(3), 280–298.

In this classic article, Delpit argues that as a first step toward a more just society, teachers need to teach all students, but particularly Black and poor children, the explicit and implicit rules of power.

Ladson-Billings, Gloria (1994). *The dreamkeepers: Successful teachers of African American children*. San Francisco, CA: Jossey-Bass, 1994.

This highly readable book documents the characteristics and teaching practices of teachers who are especially effective with African American students. The last chapter, "Making Dreams into Reality," describes the Paul Robeson Elementary School, the author's vision of a culturally responsive learning environment.

Mahiri, Jabari (1998). *Shooting for excellence: African American and youth culture in new century schools*. Champaign, IL & New York: National Council of Teachers of English and Teachers College Press.

Drawing from findings of four research projects, Mahiri suggests how teachers can change classroom discourse, curriculum, and culture to build on students' authentic experiences and enhance the possibility that they will learn.

What Does It Mean
to Affirm Diversity
in Our Nation's Schools?

INTRODUCTION

Affirming diversity, as you know from the readings you have encountered
in this book, is not simply a question of having a special assembly about
Chinese New Year or making a few curricular changes. It is, instead, a
transformative project that concerns our *society's* commitment to social justice; our *schools'* responsibility to fulfill its pledge of equal opportunity for
all students; and the knowledge, attitudes, values, and beliefs of *teachers*
concerning their students' identities and abilities. If this is the case, then
the question that is the title of this short chapter you are about to read
needs to be answered in a more broad-based way than might be evident at
first glance. That is, affirming diversity needs to be approached as *personal, collective,* and *institutional* change.

In this chapter, I propose five realities that educators need to understand to create schools that are effective for all students. As you read it,
think about the journey you have taken until now in your effort to affirm
diversity.

About 15 years ago, I was interviewing a young woman for admission to
our multicultural teacher education program and I asked her why she had
chosen to apply for this particular program. (At the time, we had a number of undergraduate teacher preparation programs from which students
could choose.)

The young woman, let's call her Nancy, mentioned that she was doing a
prepracticum at Marks Meadow School, the laboratory school of our

School of Education at the University of Massachusetts. Marks Meadow is an extraordinarily diverse place with children from every corner of the globe representing multiple languages and various social and economic backgrounds.

When the children in her 1st-grade classroom were doing self-portraits, one of them asked Nancy for a brown crayon. She was momentarily confounded by his request, thinking *Why brown?* It never before had occurred to her that children would make their faces anything other than the color of the white paper they used. "I decided then and there that I needed this program," she confessed.

As naive as her reaction was, it was the beginning of Nancy's awakening to diversity. It was also a courageous disclosure of her own ignorance.

ILL-PREPARED FOR DIVERSITY

It is by now a truism that our country's public schools are undergoing a dramatic shift that reflects the growing diversity of our population. Yet many educators and the schools in which they work seem no better prepared for this change than was Nancy a decade and a half ago. Most educators nationwide are very much like Nancy: White, middle-class, monolingual English-speaking women and men who have had little direct experience with cultural, ethnic, linguistic or other kinds of diversity, but they are teaching students who are phenomenally diverse in every way.

Given this scenario, what do educators—teachers, aides, curriculum developers, principals, superintendents and school board members—need to know to create effective schools for students of all backgrounds, and how can they learn it? Let me suggest five realities that educators need to appreciate and understand if this is to happen:

Affirming diversity is above all about social justice.

Contrary to what the pundits who oppose multicultural education might say, multicultural education is *not* about political correctness, sensitivity training or ethnic cheerleading. It is primarily about social justice. Given the vastly unequal educational outcomes among students of different backgrounds, equalizing conditions for student learning needs to be at the core of a concern for diversity.

If this is the case, "celebrating diversity" through special assembly programs, multicultural dinners or ethnic celebrations are hollow activities if they do not also confront the structural inequalities that exist in schools.

A concern for social justice means looking critically at why and how our schools are unjust for some students. It means that we need to analyze school policies and practices that devalue the identities of some students while overvaluing others: the curriculum, testing, textbooks and materials, instructional strategies, tracking, the recruitment and hiring of staff and parent involvement strategies. All of these need to be viewed with an eye toward making them more equitable for all students, not just those students who happen to be White, middle class and English speaking.

Students of color and poor students bear the brunt of structural inequality.

Schools inevitably reflect society, and the evidence that our society is becoming more unequal is growing every day. We have all read the headlines: The United States now has one of the highest income disparities in the world, and the combined wealth of the top 1 percent of U.S. families is about the same as the entire bottom 80 percent.

Growing societal inequities are mirrored in numerous ways in schools, from highly disparate financing of schools in rich and poor communities, to academic tracking that favors White above Black and Brown students, to SAT scores that correlate perfectly with income rather than with intelligence or ability. Although it is a worthy goal, equality is far from a reality in most of our schools, and those who bear the burden of inequality are our children, particularly poor children of all backgrounds and many children of Latino, Native American, Asian American and African American backgrounds. The result is schools that are racist and classist, if not by intention, at least by result.

Inequality is a fact of life, but many educators refuse to believe or accept it, and they persist in blaming children, their families, their cultural and linguistic backgrounds, laziness or genetic inferiority as the culprits. Once educators accept the fact that inequality is alive and thriving in our schools, they can proceed to do something about it. Until they do, little will change.

POSITIVE ACCULTURATION

Diversity is a valuable resource.

I went to elementary school in Brooklyn, N.Y., during the 1950s. My classmates were enormously diverse in ethnicity, race, language, social class and family structure.

But even then, we were taught as if we were all cut from the same cloth. Our mothers were urged to speak to us in English at home (fortunately, my mother never paid attention, and it is because of this that I am fluent in Spanish today), and we were given the clear message that anything having to do with our home cultures was not welcome in school. To succeed in school, we needed to learn English, forget our native language and behave like the kids we read about in our basal readers.

Of course, learning English and learning it well is absolutely essential for academic and future life success, but the assumption that one must discard one's identity along the way needs to be challenged. There is nothing shameful in knowing a language other than English. In fact, becoming bilingual can benefit individuals and our country in general.

As educators, we no longer can afford to behave as if diversity were a dirty word. Every day, more research underscores the positive influence that cultural and linguistic diversity has on student learning. Immigrant students who maintain a positive ethnic identity as they acculturate and who become fluent bilinguals are more likely to have better mental health, do well academically and graduate from high school than those who completely assimilate. Yet we insist on erasing cultural and linguistic differences as if they were a burden rather than an asset.

Effectively teaching students of all backgrounds means respecting and affirming who they are.

To become effective teachers of all students, educators must undergo a profound shift in their beliefs, attitudes and values about difference.

In many U.S. classrooms, cultural, linguistic and other differences are commonly viewed as temporary, if troublesome, barriers to learning. Consequently, students of diverse backgrounds are treated as walking sets of deficiencies, as if they had nothing to bring to the educational enterprise.

Anybody who has worked in a classroom knows that teaching and learning are above all about relationships, and these relationships can have a profound impact on students' futures. But significant relationships with students are difficult to develop when teachers have little understanding of the students' families and communities. The identities of nonmainstream students frequently are dismissed by schools and teachers as immaterial to academic achievement.

When this is the case, it is unlikely that students will form positive relationships with their teachers or, as a result, with learning. It is only when educators and schools accept and respect who their students are and what they know that they can begin to build positive connections with them.

Affirming diversity means becoming a multicultural person.

Over the years, I have found that educators believe they are affirming diversity simply because they *say* they are. But mouthing the words is not enough. Children sense instantly when support for diversity is superficial.

Because most educators in the United States have not had the benefit of firsthand experiences with diversity, it is a frightening concept for many of them. If we think of teaching as a lifelong journey of personal transformation, becoming a multicultural person is part of the journey. It is different for each person.

For Nancy, it began with recognition of her own ignorance. For others, it means learning a second language or working collaboratively with colleagues to design more effective strategies of reaching all students. However we begin the journey, until we take those tentative first steps, what we say about diversity is severely limited by our actions.

COMFORT WITH DIFFERENCES

Taking these realities to heart means we no longer can think of some students as void of any dignity and worth simply because they do not confirm to our conventional image. All students of all backgrounds bring talents and strengths to their learning and as educators we need to find ways to build on these.

Acknowledging and affirming diversity is to everyone's interest, including middle-class White students. Understanding people of other backgrounds, speaking languages other than English and learning to respect and appreciate differences are skills that benefit all students and our nation as a whole. We do all our students a disservice when we prepare them to live in a society that no longer exists.

Given the tremendous diversity in our society, it makes eminent good sense to educate all our students to be comfortable with differences.

CRITICAL QUESTIONS

1. Do you agree with the five realities I've suggested that educators need to know in order to be effective with their students? Why or why not?

2. Develop your own list of essential understandings that educators need in order to affirm diversity.

3. How might your school be different if the principal, other administrators, teachers, and all school staff knew and believed the five realities that are proposed? Give some concrete examples.

CLASSROOM ACTIVITY

How far have you progressed in learning to affirm diversity? Do a fishbowl exercise in which you and several other course participants discuss some of the changes in attitudes and beliefs you've experienced in the past few months. Describe some of the changes you've made in your classroom, and evaluate how effective those changes have been. Discuss as well some of the projects you have in mind for the future.

COMMUNITY-BASED ACTIVITIES AND ADVOCACY

1. Join the PTO or PTA of your school and present some ideas that you think can lead to a more effective school climate for more students. Suggest some of the changes that you believe are needed and present them to your School Committee (or local board of education).

2. Think about some of the ways that your school, school system, or state discredits or disadvantages some students. For example, is there an "English-Only" policy in your school? are the Special Education classrooms in the basement? who's on the hiring committees at the district level? are textbooks representative of the U.S. population? has there been a recent effort to do away with state-mandated bilingual education? How can you be involved in making change at each of these levels? Take on one of these issues and write about the results of your involvement.

SUPPLEMENTARY RESOURCES FOR FURTHER REFLECTION AND STUDY

Bigelow, Bill, Christensen, Linda, Karp, Stanley, Miner, Barbara, & Peterson, Bob (Eds.) (1994). *Rethinking our classrooms: Teaching for equity and justice* (Milwaukee: Rethinking Schools, 1994).

   Classroom-tested ideas written by classroom teachers and based on a social justice conception of multicultural education.

Hanssen, Evelyn (1998). A White teacher reflects on institutional racism. *Phi Delta Kappan,* 79(9), 694–698.

   The author, a university professor who returned to public school teaching, discusses what she found out about racism. Includes many anecdotes that can be of help to teachers and future teachers about their own classrooms.

Howard, Gary R. (1999). *We can't teach what we don't know: White teachers, multiracial schools.* New York: Teachers College Press.

Using his personal and professional transformation based on 25 years of experience as an educator, Howard analyzes what it means to be a culturally competent White teacher working with a culturally and racially diverse student population.

Lee, Enid, Menkart, Deborah, Okazawa-Rey, Margo (1998). *Beyond heroes and holidays: A practical guide to K–12 anti-racist, multicultural education and staff development*. Washington, DC: Network of Educators on the Americas [NECA], 1998.

After developing a conceptual basis for anti-racist multicultural education, this book tackles the difficult job of actual implementation in classrooms. Written for and by teachers for classrooms and professional development activities.

Levine, David, Lowe, Robert, Peterson, Bob, & Tenorio, Rita (1995). *Rethinking schools: An agenda for change*. New York: The New Press.

A compilation of some of the best articles to come out of the Milwaukee-based newspaper *Rethinking Schools*, this volume includes a mix of philosophical pieces and practical classroom suggestions for developing anti-bias classrooms. The essays are written by teachers, researchers, and community activists.

Author Index

Subject Index

A

Ability grouping
  student views on, 138–139
  teacher education and, 194–196
Acceptance, 264–266
Achievement
  bilingual education and, 90–93
  cultural capital and, 59–62, 121
  cultural maintenance and, 70,
    147–151
  cultural motifs and, 62–65
  effect of racism and discrimination
    on, 143–144
  expectations of, 139–140, 145, 167,
    169, 188–190
  family motifs and, 62–65
  hardship and, 120–121, 155
  learning context and, 57–59
  native languages and, 61–62, 70,
    84–87, 91, 147–151
  one-size-fits-all approach and, 59
  school policies and practices and, 122
Affirmation
  in model school, 269–273
  as social justice, 278–279
Agency, learning as, 5–8
American identity
  conflict over, 104–111, 113–115
  redefining, 111–113
Anti-Bias Curriculum Task Force, 47
Antiracism and antidiscrimination
  in multicultural education, 30–35
  in professional development, 67–68
Arrogance reduction, 147
Assessment, 196–197, *see also* Testing
Assimilation
  challenging, 148, 150–151
  deficit theories and, 215–216
  reform and, 69–71
  vs. cultural maintenance, 105–111,
    279–280

B

Backgrounds. *see* Cultural capital
Banking education, 5–8
Basic education, 35–37
Biased education, 37–38
Biculturalism, identity and, 105
Bicultural pedagogy, 62
Bilingual education
  achievement and, 90–93
  cultural capital in, 61–62, 91
  defined, 89
  as example of positionality, 14–16
  inequality and, 88–89
  political nature of, 209–211
  raising status of, 212–214
  segregation of, 91–93, 207–208
  success of, 90–93
  teacher education in, 209
  types of, 88–89
  vs. ESL, 88–90